RETAIL STRUCTURE

Edited by
GARY AKEHURST
and
NICHOLAS ALEXANDER

FRANK CASS • LONDON

First published in Great Britain by
FRANK CASS & CO LTD
Newbury House, 900 Eastern Avenue
London IG2 7HH, England

and in the United States by
FRANK CASS
c/o ISBS
5804 N.E. Hassalo Street, Portland, Oregon 97213-3644

Copyright © 1995 Frank Cass & Co. Ltd.

Library of Congress Cataloging-in-Publication Data
Applied for.

British Library Cataloguing in Publication Data
Applied for.

ISBN 0-7146-4176-6

This group of studies first appeared in *The Services Industries Journal*, 1984–95,
published by Frank Cass & Co. Ltd.

Printed in Great Britain by
Antony Rowe Ltd., Chippenham, Wilts

Contents

Introduction

Structure can be defined in a number of ways. In one way, it can be defined as the different characteristics of firms and the relationships between them [Needham, 1970; Devine, Jones, Lee, Tyson, 1976: 55]. A further definition takes as a starting point the economic theory of the firm, where the structure of the market in which a firm operates influences business behaviour. In this latter sense, structure refers to the height of entry barriers, the degree of seller and buyer concentration and product differentiation. Industrial organisation theory suggests that there will be links between different types and forms of market structure, business behaviour and performance. In turn, behaviour will influence structure and performance. Some of the classic work, for example, that concerning barriers to entry into a market, is associated with writers such as Bain [1956].

In the retail distribution context we shall define retail structure *as a snapshot of the state of play in the competitive struggle between retail companies and businesses*, each of which is seeking to not only survive but to grow. Growth is important because the capital markets expect this, shareholders expect growth and managerial rewards are dependent to some extent on it. Growth may also generate the profits which, when reinvested (whether in capital investment or acquisitions of other companies), will further generate growth. This struggle for dominance of markets is continuing and never ending. Companies manoeuvre to gain what they perceive to be a competitive advantage over rivals, and where this advantage can lead to greater control of markets, greater growth may be the just reward. As a consequence, retail companies and businesses experiment with different retail formats in different (and perhaps increasingly marginal) locations, informed by continual marketing research which attempts to understand the needs and wishes of customers. Often, as national markets are perceived to offer less growth opportunities, so retail companies seek new operations in other countries, and so the process of internationalisation continues.

We are defining structure here in terms of *competition* between retail businesses, and this process of competition is ongoing on several levels: locally, regionally, nationally and gradually internationally. Retail-based companies start up, expand, merge, are taken over and some die. In reviewing theories of locational change in retailing Brown [1984 and 1987a] summarises these in three categories of environmental, cyclical and conflict. Environmental theories attempt to explain retail structure in terms of a life cycle of retail businesses (birth, development, maturity and decline) in response to social and economic changes. Cyclical theories explain change in terms of short and long waves of innovation rippling throughout economic history in both a predictable and random fashion. In this way, different retail formats emerge. Conflict theories emphasise the result of 'inter-institutional strife', with established businesses responding to innovators of new retail formats [Clarke, Bennison and Guy, 1994: 11-12].

We see these three broad categories of change theories encapsulated within the term 'competitive struggle'. Just as humans go through life attempting to survive and perhaps prospering through a competitive struggle with other humans who threaten to or actually do invade or stray into their space, so also do companies. Both humans and the human agents of companies (that is, managers and directors) have the capacity to make decisions; inevitably both have to live with the consequences of their decisions, which can have a cumulative and knock-on effect on those people and organisations around them. Survival and prosperity in these conditions hinge on the ability to anticipate and precipitate change before rivals do, and having the resources to so. It may also hinge on the ability to deliver a none-too-subtle knock-out blow before a rival does so to you (or indeed make subtle less visible moves, and in so doing gain valuable time). Such forces have both destructive and constructive effects, and so the capitalist market system evolves.

Other writers have rightly tried to bring together these different strands of explanation for retail development, such as Jones and Simmons [1990] and Wrigley [1993], but almost inevitably each brings an explanation based on their particular discipline base. So we have geographers explaining the spatial dimensions to portfolio investment decisions and location of stores while economists have been conspicuous by their virtual absence in recent years from this analysis of retail development, despite the fact that their theories of competition are some of the most powerful explanators and predictors of corporate retail behaviour yet devised.

Roth and Klein [1993], on the other hand, bring together considerations of organisational resources, environmental change, competition at various levels (but notably at local level) and the influence of human behaviour, as manifested primarily in managerial and consumer decisions. The interaction of these factors are crucial to understanding the dynamics of retail development and give what must surely be a more rounded and balanced view of the whole process.

Tordjman [1994], using a different viewpoint, identifies four stages of development in European retailing:

Traditional retailing, as found in Greece and Portugal. Concentration is low, segmentation non-existent, with new technology take-up and integration yet to be exploited. Retail businesses are often small-scale, family run, with low turnover and employing few people;

Intermediary retailing, as found in Italy and Spain. Retailing shows transformation, being a mix of traditional and modern. Although most businesses are independent, concentration, particularly in food retailing, is increasing. The importance of wholesalers and voluntary chains is still strong. Retail development can, however, be hindered by restrictive and indeed protectionist legislation.

Structured retailing, as found in the Netherlands, France, Denmark and Luxembourg. Retail businesses are larger and concentration is higher. New technology and new retail formats have been widely introduced. These features reflect in part the stage of economic development reached by the country concerned.

Advanced retailing, as found in the UK and Germany. Features include high concentration, well-developed segmentation of the market, high new technology implementation, integration and capitalisation. While UK companies have the largest profit margins, German companies are the largest in size.

While such a classification system is useful in giving us a snapshot of European retailing at a moment in time, at the beginning of the 1990s it does not necessarily explain the dynamic processes at work which have led to these relative states of play in the competitive struggle. We must remember, however, that respected writers such as Hollander have argued that cyclical models of retail development are at best descriptive rather than explanatory [Hollander, 1980].

At local level, Grundy [1991] developed a model to explain the processes and effects of expansion of food superstores. Grundy advances a four phase model of the food store market share cycle. Again in the competitive struggle companies strive to increase market share. In the *introductory* phase the first superstore develops and in so doing captures market share. In the secondary *expansionary* phase, additional superstores (mostly operated by competitors) enter the market and attempt to capture market share. If the market is growing there may well be room for new competitors, as each secures a share of the market. If the market is static, rivalry may be intense, and as a consequence, where there are winners there will inevitably be losers. The third phase, of *characterisation*, where the market may now be saturated, sees most groups adapting their superstores to perceived market segments within their catchment areas, establishing or refurbishing smaller stores in town centres and acquiring local retail operators. During this phase there is a process of consolidation. The fourth phase involves *rationalisation* of original stores, with possible repositioning or closure.

Brown [1987b] brought together three well-known models of institutional change – *the retail accordian* (evolution in terms of the number of lines of merchandise stocked by retail stores [Hollander, 1966]; *the wheel of retailing* (novel retail trading formats enter markets as low-cost, cut-price and low-margin operations but over time trade up; as these original stores mature as high-cost high-margin establishments the way is open to a new low-cost inno-vator [McNair, 1958]); and *the polarisation principle* (the trend towards fewer and larger retail stores is offset by a complementary renaissance of the small shop sector [Dreesman, 1968 and Kirby, 1976]). Brown proposed a 'multi-polarisation' model which brings together institutional types (super-store, hypermarket, convenience store, department store, retail warehouse, limited discount and specialist), merchandise assortment (broad to narrow), sales policy (price-based to service-based) and establishment size. Brown argued that 'retailing polarises simultaneously along each of the price, assort-ment and size dimensions' [Brown, 1987b: 158]. This model suggests that 'inventory diversification inspires specialisation, large outlets beget small and a high level of service gives rise to no-frills retail operations. Each of these dimensions, furthermore, is interdependent with the emergence of hypermar-ket-style operations selling a wide range of discounted goods from large establishments paving the way for limited line discount stores, specialists in gourmet foods and modern convenience stores' [Brown, 1987b: 160].

Whatever the debate about the process of retail development we must not fall into the trap of viewing retail companies as mono competitive enterpris-es, located in one particular sector or market or competing in one activity such as retailing. Increasingly we should view companies as active manipulators of portfolios of investments made on behalf of shareholders and other stake-holders such as the capital markets. Management of these companies seek to maximise the rate of return on these investments, managing the trade-off between risk and rate of return. Retail activities may form part of these cor-porate portfolios but on the other hand they may not.

The human decision-making dimension must also be considered in the retail development process. In the past there have been notable retail families or dynasties, some of which, such as the Sainsbury family, are clearly in evi-dence today. These families passed down knowledge and ultimately control of the retail businesses they had founded to succeeding generations. It can be supposed that some of the members of these families had at least a passing interest in retailing. In the modern corporation there is no room for sentiment. Just as retail activities can be built so they can be shut down or disposed of in the quest for market expected rates of return on investments. We need, how-ever, to make sense of this complex picture of competition at the micro and macro levels influenced by and interwoven as it is with complex societal and economic changes. What we need is a conceptual and theoretical framework within which we can assess the overall picture as far as retailing development is concerned. One discipline alone cannot provide the full answer. The search for such a theoretical framework, like the quest for the Holy Grail, continues.

Since 1945 the changes in retail structure have been profound but then so have the changes in society and economy. These changes, in population, home ownership, credit expansion, technology adoption and increased leisure (to name but a few), have influenced the development of retail distribution in all kinds of ways, sometimes positively and sometimes in a way which has posed significant challenges as retail businesses seek to adapt to changing market conditions. Alexander reminds us that these social and economic factors 'have been numerous, interactive and cumulative' [Alexander, 1988: 78].

Immediately after the Second World War manufacturing industry was faced with a huge pent-up demand for its products which was difficult to satisfy given productive capacity. The first concern was production rather than distribution, selling and marketing [Walters, 1989:1]. During the 1950s and early 1960s companies such as Tesco and Sainsbury were essentially regional businesses while co-operative societies were in their prime.

Resale Price Maintenance (RPM) may well have dampened competition, and its removal in 1964 may have been important in that it enabled retail companies to improve their profitability, and thereby invest in capital intensive supermarkets. Larger shop units enabled economies of scale to be achieved and purchasing power enhanced [Alexander, 1988:85; Yamey, 1966; O'Reilly, 1972]. Abolition of RPM was but one factor in the dynamic development of multiple store groups and the consequent decline in the number of independent retailers, and indeed, total number of shops.

Retail multiples grew out from their regional bases into national businesses. This growth was sometimes organic and sometimes by acquisition. Growth was particularly rapid in groceries, as consumer disposable incomes began to grow and the discretionary element of incomes grew accordingly. Spending on food accounted for one-third of household spending in 1970 but this proportion had fallen to a quarter in 1990 [Tordjman, 1994: 9]. This phenomenon is, however, more pronounced in Northern Europe than the South.

Growth of retail businesses was powered by the search for market share – to dominate the market both in physical presence and in an ability to attract customers to larger and larger stores, increasingly on the outskirts of towns, where the prospects of one-stop shopping were particularly appealing to the consumer. As a consequence, retail concentration grew markedly [Akehurst, 1983]. Concentration continues to flourish; for instance, the top five food retail groups in Britain control over 45 per cent of the market, while in the Netherlands it is 44 per cent, with 43 per cent in Belgium and 41 per cent in Germany [Tordjman, 1994: 5]. Concentration also continues to grow in non-food retailing.

In food retailing the number of grocery stores has fallen by 400,000 while the sales space for food has increased.

This trend towards larger stores has raised important questions about market saturation. Saturation presupposes that there is a maximum number of stores which can trade profitably in any given local market. If a market is static (as food sales were in the 1970s) then in order to grow companies must increase their market share. This inevitably brings conflict. Entry to such a market becomes progressively more difficult [Guy, 1994; Alexander and Morlock, 1992; Duke, 1991; Treadgold and Reynolds, 1989]. Saturation as defined here will almost inevitably lead to one or more consequences: first, acceptance of lower profitability and loss of market share for the laggards; second, diversification in terms of retail format, products and activities (not all of which may be in retailing); and third, internationalisation.

As the 1970s gave way to the 1980s, retailing businesses continued to specialise, not just in food products but also in clothes and durables. Do-it-yourself (DIY) rapidly grew; this was partly in response to the increasing costs of hiring specialised labour and increased leisure time but also due to the diversification activities of several groups and the continued development of new tools and materials. Retail formats have changed and will continue to change. We have witnessed the emergence of not only huge food retail groups but also large non-food specialist stores in electricals, DIY, clothing and discount stores, while department and variety stores have lost market share. We have seen variations of format including 'wide choice', 'limited choice', price-oriented stores and service-oriented stores. The permutations of price, service and size seem endless.

Technological developments have been, and continue to be, profound – the processing and accessibility of information, the microwave, the freezer and television, to name but some; all have had considerable impact upon not only what is purchased and consumed but also when and in what context. New information systems, the development of laser scanning at checkouts and other electronic point of sale equipment, electronic information transfer and the optimisation of stocks and selling space have all transformed management control and decision-making. These developments have given managements vastly improved marketing information.

Linked to increasing expectations and aspirations of consumers, backed by rising real disposable incomes, we can see that powerful forces are at work. No industry or sector could hope to be isolated from such changes. The consumer of the 1990s expects quality, choice, reasonable prices (or value for money), convenience, service, reliability, extended store opening hours, information on product use and often entertainment.

These profound societal changes have altered the way retail companies communicate with their customers and how they attempt to secure customer loyalty (often in the form of brand allegiance and one-stop shopping). Closer attention is paid to market segmentation, customer 'lifestyles' and an increasing emphasis on the brand. In fact, we can see greater attention is being given to *positioning* within the market, while varying the elements of the retail marketing mix (notably place, price and promotion). Companies are striving to understand the 'needs, desires and behavioural characteristics of [their] target customer profile' [Walters, 1989: 16].

So arising out of the competitive struggle, and the desire to grow and dominate particular markets, there has come a whole new range of essentially marketing (and therefore competitive) decisions far beyond the traditional location, buying and selling activities. Such decisions include trading format (location, outlet size and design), marketing research, product range, product development, packaging design, promotions, advertising and customer services.

In the pursuit of growth some companies have diversified (such as Auchan, Kingfisher and Boulanger), some have specialised, and some have opened international operations. Diversification aims to exploit market opportunities in specialised niche markets. It develops risk-spreading portfolios across national boundaries and transfers knowledge and experience between retail (and other) sectors. Not all companies have diversified, however, and there are those (such as Marks & Spencer, Tesco, Toys 'R' Us) who have chosen to concentrate on core activities. This concentration on core activities or 'the principal format' has been called 'intensification' [Tordjman, 1994: 15].

Internationalisation offers further growth. In 1960 there were 35 international retail operations in the European Community, growing to 250 in 1980 and 1,321 by 1992 [Tordjman, 1994: 5–6]. These companies are involved in food, non-food retailing, specialist and general retailing, large and small stores, primarily but not exclusively in the 'big five' (France, UK, Germany, Italy and the Netherlands). The internationalisation process may be driven in part by lower transport costs, improved information systems and the lowering of national boundaries. On the other hand, as national markets become saturated, market share becomes progressively more difficult to grow. We must recognise here, of course, that this search for a better growth rate and greater profitability (and hence better rate of return on capital employed) is driven in part by the global capital markets, where national concerns are of minor importance. The work of Dawson and Alexander is especially useful in understanding these processes [Dawson, 1994; Alexander, 1990].

The studies isn this volume were first published in *The Service Industries Journal*. The first was published in 1983. Although each piece must be read in the knowledge that the authors were writing at a particular point in time, nevertheless they represent some of the most significant articles written on aspects of retail structure in recent years. Taken as a whole they serve two purposes: first, they introduce the concept and process of retail structure taken from the viewpoint of a continuing competitive struggle for market supremacy; and second, they serve as an introduction to the wider study of retail development.

The first study, by Nicholas Alexander, sets the scene by evaluating the key determinants of change which have led to contemporary conditions.

The second, by Stephen Brown, introduces a brave attempt to move forward the theoretical and conceptual debate concerning retail structure by bringing together three well-known models of retail change (the retail accordian, the wheel of retailing and the polarisation principle) into a multi-polarisation model. Such a model can help us to analyse the changing retail scene.

The third essay, by Gary Akehurst, was a pioneering assessment and measurement of concentration in retail distribution, which for the first time systematically measured the extent of control and consequent significance of the top 185 companies in British retailing. Thereafter, concentration was and is a major issue in retail studies.

Alan McKinnon examines the decisions which led to supermarket groups setting up their own distribution systems. Differences in distribution strategies appear to be closely related to growth histories, management investment preferences and size of business.

Alan Thomas's study is another pioneering work on the changes in leadership of some of the largest retail businesses and the important part these changes have played in the post-war development of British retailing.

In Chapter 6, Nicholas Alexander examines the attitudes of leading UK retail companies to the establishment of the European Community's internal market, providing a useful analysis of international expansion decisions and intentions.

John Dawson and Toshio Sato discuss Japanese public policy aimed at controlling large store development. This issue of public control is as pertinent now as when the authors wrote this paper.

In Chapter 8, Gary Akehurst examines a period of intense competition in the food retailing market following the launch by Tesco of its 'Operation Checkout' in 1977. Coming as it did during a period of static food sales growth over many years, this analysis is a useful reminder of what further work needs to be carried out where markets (whether national, regional or local) are static, and companies, driven by the need to secure continual growth of sales and profits, make price and non-price decisions in order to secure competitive advantage.

J. Dennis Lord examines the introduction of a new retail format in the United States – the factory outlet/off-price shopping centre. The question Dennis Lord asked was whether these outlet centres were a creature of recession or whether they represented a significant trend in retailing.

The final essay, by Leigh Sparks, is a comprehensive account of the growth and development of the Kwik Save Group, concentrating on both spatial and structural dimensions of development. Again, in a pioneering way he combines the concepts and ideas of spatial analysis, entrepreneurship, competitive strategy and innovation diffusion.

REFERENCES

Akehurst, G.P., 1983, 'Concentration in Retail Distribution: Measurement and Significance', *Service Industries Journal*, Vol.3, No.2.

Alexander, N, 1988, 'Contemporary Perspectives in Retail Development', *Service Industries Journal*, Vol.8, No.1 .

Alexander, N., 1990, 'Retailers and International Markets: Motives for Expansion', *International Marketing Review*, Vol.7, No.4.

Alexander, N. and W. Morlock, 1992, 'Saturation and Internationalization: the Future of Grocery Retailing in the UK', *International Journal of Retail and Distribution Management*, Vol.20, No.3.

Bain, J.S., 1956, *Barriers to New Competition*, Cambridge, MA: Harvard University Press.

Brown, S., 1984, 'Retail Location and Retail Change in Belfast City Centre', unpublished Ph.D. thesis, Queen's University, Belfast.

Brown, S., 1987a, 'Institutional Change in Retailing: a Geographical Interpretation', *Progress in Human Geography*, Vol.11.

Brown, S., 1987b, 'An Integrated Approach to Retail Change: the Multi-Polarisation Model', *Service Industries Journal*, Vol.7, No.1.

Clarke, I., Bennison, D. And C. Guy, 1994, 'The Dynamics of UK Grocery Retailing at the Local Scale', *International Journal of Retail and Distribution Management*, Vol.22, No.6.

Dawson, J.A., 1994, 'Internationalization of Retailing Operations', *Journal of Marketing Management*, Vol.10.

Devine, P.J., R.M. Jones, N. Lee and W.J. Tyson, 1976, *An Introduction to Industrial Economics*, London: George Allen and Unwin.

Dreesman, A.C.R., 1968, 'Patterns of Evolution in Retailing', *Journal of Retailing*, Vol.44.

Duke, R., 1991, 'Post-saturation Competition in UK Grocery Retailing', *Journal of Marketing Management*, Vol.7, No.1.

Grundy, C., 1991, *Foodstores: a Taste of the Future*, London: Chestertons.

Guy, C.M., 1994, 'Grocery Store Saturation. Has It Arrived Yet?', *International Journal of Retail and Distribution Management*, Vol.22, No.1.

Hollander, S.C., 1966, 'Notes on the Retail Accordian', *Journal of Retailing*, Vol.42.

Hollander, S.C., 1980, 'Oddities, Nostalgia, Wheels and Other Patterns in Retail Evolution' in R.W. Stampfl and E.C. Hirschman (eds.), *Competitive Structure in Retail Marketing: The Department Store Perspective*, Chicago: American Marketing Association.

Jones, K. and J. Simmons, 1990, *The Retail Environment*, London: Routledge.

Kirby, D.A., 1976, 'The North American Convenience Store: Implications for Britain', in P. Jones, and R. Oliphant (eds.), *Local Shops: Problems and Prospects*, Reading: Unit for Retail Planning Information.

McNair, M.P., 1958, 'Significant Trends and Developments in the Post-war Period', in A.B. Smith (ed.), *Competitive Distribution in a Free High-level Economy and its Implications for the University*, Pittsburgh: University of Pittsburgh Press.

Needham, D., 1970, *Economic Analysis and Industrial Structure*, New York: Holt, Reinhart and Winston.

O'Reilly, A.J.F., 1972, 'The Conservative Consumer', *Management Decisions*, Vol.10, Summer.

Roth, V.J. and S. Klein, 1993, 'A Theory of Retail Change', *The International Review of Retail Distribution and Consumer Research*, Vol.3, No.2.

Tordjman, A., 1994, 'European Retailing: Convergences, Differences and Perspectives', *International Journal of Retail and Distribution Management*, Vol.22, No.5.

Treadgold, A.D. and J. Reynolds, 1989, *Retail Saturation: Examining the Evidence*, London: Longman.

Walters, D.W., 1989, *Strategic Retailing Management*, New York: Prentice Hall.

Wrigley, N., 1993, 'The Internationalisation of British Grocery Retailing', in R.D.F. Bromley and C.J Thomas (eds.), *Retail Change: Contemporary Issues*, London: UCL Press.

Yamey, B.S., 1966, 'United Kingdom' in B.S. Yamey (ed.), *Resale Price Maintenance*, London.

1

Contemporary Perspectives in Retail Development

by

Nicholas Alexander

This article suggests that a fundamental shift in retailing has occurred in the last 40 years, and that developments have, to a considerable extent, invalidated certain orthodoxies of retail interpretation. The economic and social pressures of recent decades, coupled with evolutionary changes within the industry, demand a reorientation of certain ground rules, which have been, but are no longer, sufficient to explain the structure of, and trends within, British retailing. In order to indicate this reorientation of perspective, the article plots and evaluates the key determinants of change which have led to contemporary conditions.

Certain trends, such as the expansion of multiple store numbers, which have been identified as important factors in the evolution of retail structures in the late nineteenth and early twentieth centuries, clearly continued to have an effect into the mid-twentieth century. However, a metamorphosis was taking place and the developments pertinent to pre-1950 British retailing, which have been accepted to such an extent that they have become enshrined as the orthodoxy of retail change, are interpretative forms which no longer easily fit the patterns of late twentieth-century retailing in Britain. This article aims to identify key environmental and internal factors which have resulted in a realignment of retailing, and thereby indicate the emerging retailing structures that have replaced the mid-century or traditional structure.

The retailing structures which Jefferys [1954] reviewed in the early fifties, and the patterns of development which he identified as pertinent to the preceding century, described evolutionary pressures which were, in the following decades, to be replaced as the determinants of change, by factors peculiar to post-war Britain. Jefferys' seminal work provides the student of the subject with an unparalleled research work on the subject of retailing, both in terms of trade characteristics, and the forces for change within retailing, consequential to the economic and social upheavals of mid-nineteenth century Britain. The work, however, describes a system that was soon to be challenged by the new environmental forces of the following decades. Jefferys' work, dominated as it was by the institutional pressures of multiple store retailing, provides a system of analysis of retail structures which, as changes have occurred, does not take account of new perspectives in the industry. Undoubtedly this approach has noticeably influenced thinking in terms of retail movements since the 1950s, not least because of the importance ascribed to the relative decline in numbers of independent retailers. Multiple chain expansion has continued to be seen as a crucial factor in the retail environment. The growth of multiple organisations and their increasingly dominant position within retailing is certainly of importance but their dominant position has been achieved not simply through the organic expansionist pressures enshrined in Jefferys' analysis but because of a miscellany of factors which have lent a new bias to the growth and expansion of firms within retailing. The multiple store 'numbers game' is no longer of signal importance.

Those social and economic factors, which have revolutionised the retailing environment have been numerous, interactive and cumulative. Essentially, the retail units, their competitive stances, and the relationship between the retailer and the consumer which existed before these environmental changes were very different from those of the late-1980s. The unit of retailing itself has undergone crucial changes, and if individual retail units have not, they have been met with competition from units which have substantially shifted the ground upon which the 'traditional' retail unit operates. Not only have consumer demands had their effect, but also internal pressures have forced the retailer to redefine spatial and service orientations.

The changes in the structure of retailing since the 1940s have occurred within a market which has experienced the consumer boom of the 1950s and 1960s, and where real personal disposable income has risen from £70.1m in 1950 to £164.8m in 1984 (at 1980 prices) [*Economic Trends* 1987]. The period from the end of the 1940s to the economic crises of the mid-1970s brought about a considerable change in the markets within which the retail trade operated. In Doyle and Cook's [1979] words: 'It was an era of optimism in which retailers benefitted from rising living standards and adapted to freer life-styles and changing spending patterns'.

In 1950, the market for durable goods, an area of considerable expansion, was £2.5bn at 1980 prices; by 1985 the figure had reached £17.8bn [*Economic Trends* 1987]. The significance of these changes may be compared with the socio-economic pressures inherent in the context of industrialisation and urbanisation which sparked off the nineteenth-century revolution in retail development. The economic challenges of the late 1970s and early 1980s have not resulted in a halt to the rapid changes and adaptations prevalent within the retail trade; if anything, the pace of change has increased as competition has become even more acute.

The last few decades have seen the rise of new forms of retailing, a process not unrelated to rising costs, both in terms of wages and overheads. The growth of the self-service system and its revolutionary impact on the food trades in a clear case in point [Mathias, 1967]. The growth of out-of-town, 'one-stop' shopping centres providing ease of access to a population in which 62 per cent of households have access to one car and 17 per cent have access to more than one (1985), compared with 41 per cent and 5 per cent only 20 years earlier (1965), epitomises the factors which have led to a shift in the public's perception of retailing needs and consequently the service provided by the retailer [*Transport Statistics*].

The 1960s saw the emergence of many retail forms and attitudes derived from North American models, including the pace of change of retail life cycles, the expansion of mail order, the emergence of vertical marketing systems, and the growth of a newly enshrined force labelled 'consumerism' [Dawson, Kirby, 1977]. Coupled with such particular developments as the gradual erosion of Retail Price Maintenance (RPM), and finally the 1964 Act covering price maintenance, there has been an increase in competition within the retail sector which has in turn encouraged the adoption of new retail techniques and strategies [Dawson, 1979].

These changes in the social and economic climate, together with the technological developments within retailing provide the backdrop to the fundamental shift in the nature of retail development and, as a consequence, the competitive environment of the late 1980s.

The changes in the structure of the retail trade over the last 40 years have been considerable and have resulted in large-scale changes, in the ownership of retail outlets, their numbers, their size, and the nature of the employment structure within them. In the first Census of Distribution taken in 1950 there were around 400,000 retail businesses, administering over half a million outlets and employing nearly 2.4m individuals [Census of Distribution, 1950]. By the early 1980s there were only 230,000 businesses administering a third of a million outlets and employing 2.25m individuals [*Retail Inquiry*, 1982].

The decline in the number of retail outlets and the ascendency of the multiple store at the expense of the small trader need almost no introduction. Academic articles and trade journal reports have commented for decades on the declining fortunes of the small shopkeeper. Official figures for the amount of trade now in the hands of the single unit operations clearly show their limited degree of influence in the market place. In the 1984 Retail Inquiry, sales through single unit organisations were only 16.2 per cent in the area of grocery sales, and 18.2 per cent in sales of footwear. The scale of concentration of retail sales in the hands of multiple stores in 1950s, although notable at the time, does not resemble the high degree of concentration that has been noted and commented upon in recent years [Jefferys, 1950; Akehurst, 1983]. Akehurst [1983] through the use of published company information, has calculated that the ten largest retail companies increased their share of total retail sales from 16.54 per cent in 1970 to 21.65 per cent in 1978; while the share of the top 100 companies rose from 30.67 per cent to 45.51 per cent. In the Retail Inquiry of 1982, the ten largest enterprise groups in the footwear market controlled 52.8 per cent of sales, while the equivalent groups in the grocery trade controlled 47.5 per cent [Retail Inquiry]. By the end of 1983, Asda, Sainsbury and Tesco controlled two-fifths of the market for packaged groceries.

The Co-operative movement administered 4 per cent of retail outlets in 1950: by 1984 that figure had fallen to less than 2 per cent. Like the independent sector, the Co-operative Societies have fallen prey to the successes of the multiple store chains. Initially the multiples' share of the market was achieved by a rapid expansion in the numbers of outlets administered: from the late 1960s even the multiples have seen a fall in absolute numbers, despite their increasing domination within the market [Census of Distribution, Retail Inquiries]. Considerable changes have, therefore, occurred in the volume of goods sold through retail outlets and the volume handled by the staff employed [Office of Fair Trading].

PRODUCTIVITY AND EMPLOYMENT

The issue of productivity and the changing pressures on employment within retailing have greatly contributed to the reorientation of the industry. These changes have been fuelled by factors both external to retailing and also by operational changes which were in part stimulated by wider socio-economic developments.

It has been calculated that the volume of sales made through retail outlets increased at a significant rate throughout the decades of the 1950s, and 1960s. For the 20 years taken as a whole, the increase in sales amounted to an annual average of 2.5 per cent [Ward]. More specifically, this figure has been broken down to show that between 1954 and 1960, there was an annual increase of 3.4 per cent, slowing to 2.6 per cent between 1960 and 1965 and again slowing to 1.2 per cent in the period 1965–70. Although sales volume increases did not rise as quickly in the late 1960s as they had done ten years earlier, Reddaway argues that productivity saw an upwardly moving trend in these years. In the period 1954–60, he maintains, productivity per annum rose by 2.2 per cent to be followed by 2.7 per cent in 1960–65, and 3.5 per cent in 1965–70. The connotations here are that productivity was bought at the expense of employment in the retail trade. Employment on the basis of the figures saw a 1.2 per cent per annum increase in the late 1950s, followed by a 0.04 per cent and 2.3 per cent per annum fall in the early and late 1960s.

The measurement of productivity within the retail trade is beset with problems. Although calculations may easily be based on considerations of sales per employee or indeed sales per square foot or metre, the service content of sales is less easily quantified. George [1966] and Ward [1973] both used the measure of sales per employee for assessing productivity, while Hall [1963] was prepared to describe it as 'the most relevant measure of productivty'. Since productivity is often measured in this way, the changing retail systems and economic pressures are of vital importance to understanding the apparent increase in the productivity of the sector.

The need for greater productivity on the basis of employee economy was fuelled by rises in real wages. Allied Suppliers had in 1950 the same number of outlets as it had seven years later: its wage bill, however, doubled in those years from £7m to £14m. [Mathias]. Therefore, while productivity may be said to have increased markedly in these years, it may also be said that it did so as a result of the retailing sector's reaction to a major change in the general economic climate of the post-war world, not unconnected with the introduction of the inherently labour-saving device of the self-service system. As McClelland noted in 1963, the move towards labour-saving systems, and the self-service system, was related to the fact that retail organisations were competing with industry for its work-force, in a market where unemployment rates often stood at less than 2 per cent [McClelland].

Dawson and Kirby [1977] in their assessment of shop size and productivity in the 1960s stated that, in the relationship of sales per employee against shop size, the grocery sector showed 'a log-linear relationship with sales per employee increasing arithmatically while shop size increased geometrically'. This trend, they noted, was contrary to the situation in the household goods sector where they found that the size of shops and sales per employee were not 'systematically' related. This sector they described as being as that time 'a more traditional retail sector', where, in contrast to the grocery sector, 'radical technical, operational and managerial changes have been less in evidence during the 1960s'. The emerging retail form, epitomised by elements within the grocery sector, was achieving a substantial lead over the traditional retail system.

While wage pressures were building up within the industry as a consequence of general economic prosperity, a fiscal pressure appeared in the mid-1960s with the introduction of SET (Selective Employment Tax). The tax was introduced in 1966 to cover male employees in the service sector. Initially levied at a rate of 25/-, it was increased by 50 per cent in 1968, and a further 28 per cent in the following year. The aim of the tax, as the White Paper clearly points out, was to encourage the use of labour in the service sector on an economically efficient basis [S.E.T 1966]. Estimates of the effect of the tax suggest an increase of 7–9 per cent of costs in the retail sector [Henley 1982]. If the productivity of the retail sector was rising anyway the effects of the tax are difficult to assess. An increase in costs of 7–9 per cent must have affected the thinking of retail organisations but whether it affected smaller marginal business which soaked up elements within the labour market, but which operate on the basis of non-economic considerations, and do not calculate on the same basis 'as growth minded businessmen', is another matter [Hollander 1966]. However, as Reddaway [1970] noted, since SET did not cover the self-employed, the small shop was effectively exempt from the tax anyway. The tax was undoubtedly an encouragement toward rationalisation. In the larger shops part-time labour did become more of a feature, and proved a disincentive to an increase in the number of staff employed on a full-time basis [Dawson, Kirby, 1977]. The part-time employee had, however, become a viable alternative to the thoroughly trained 'shop assistant' as retail innovations such as self-service allowed part-time employees with a knowledge only of their set and restricted tasks to perform these functions free of a particular service and information content [McClelland 1963].

The effects of SET therefore, may be seen as part of an overall move toward a retail sector aware of the restrictions imposed upon it by the labour market and eager to take advantage of systems which did not depend on the staffing arrangements which had been satisfactory in an economy where labour costs were not at a premium. The system introduced into this context in the 1950s and 1960s, the supermarket, is a prime example of the changing conditions in the retail trade.

PHYSICAL PARAMETERS

The inevitable result of the pressures on employment was the utilisation of a retail operation that would allow for the use of part-time, and consequently less expert staff, unsuited to a retailing operation where a high degree of service was expected, as well as a system which facilitated the cost-efficient use of a relatively expensive full-time labour force. These demands were met by the self-service approach epitomised by the supermarket.

The physical parameters of retail outlets have changed dramatically in the last 40 years. The physical constraints of pre-war retailing, and the shop assistant imbued with a service-orientated approach have been superseded by an emphasis on fast moving goods, an impersonal customer-staff interface, large operating units, and electronic point of sale systems designed to facilitate swift service, efficient distribution as well as generate marketing information. The High Street has seen the emergence of a potent competitive form, the out-of-town, one-stop shopping option, where the motorised shopper is given comparatively easy access to the retail items on offer. The physical changes in the nature of retailing should be clearly noted, for it has in many ways been a common and still developing thread in the changes that have occurred and are occurring.

Self-service in this country has been clearly linked from the start with the food and more precisely the grocery trade and hence the super-market concept. Although the 1966 Census of Distribution contains elaborate details on the spread of self-service, it reported that: 'Although the number of shops in other kinds of business operating on a self-service basis has increased slightly since 1961 the number is still insufficient for full details of them to be shown' [Census, 1966].

The number of self-service grocery operations grew dramatically at the end of the 1950s and in the early 1960s. Co-operative Societies operated 28 self-service grocery shops of over 2,000 sq ft in 1957, the 2,000 sq ft point being considered the minimum necessary for a supermarket operation. In 1961 this figure had reached 308 stores and in 1966, 642. The multiples had also become interested in this retail form, expanding from 52 stores in 1957 to 424 in 1961 to 1,819 by 1966. The independent retailer was, as Dawson has commented, at a disadvantage when adopting this retail system, dependent as the development was on extensive site reorganisation or new site acquisition [Dawson, 1973]. In 1957, therefore, the independent sector was operating 38 grocery stores of 2,000 sq ft and more on a self-service basis and 208 in 1966 [Census, 1966].

The self-service system, introduced into an environment where employment efficiency was of vital importance, began a dramatic phase of self-perpetuating development as the supermarket concept exhibited its appropriateness to contemporary needs. Early innovation of the self-service and supermarket concept had its own drawbacks. The problem of early conversions and their declining competitive position in the light of subsequent innovations and developments had been experienced in the United States in the 1950s as those supermarkets introduced in the 1930s became outmoded in the face of competition offered by new stores. [Mathias, 1967]. This problem was identified by Dawson in his study of the experience of the city of Nottingham at the time of the introduction of self-service [Dawson, 1973]. There the Co-operative Society had proved itself to be the innovatory force which in the 1950s had done much toward the introduction of the sytsem in the area: however, by the 1960s their earlier conversions were proving inadequate as later self-service developments by multiple retailers began to have their effect.

The supermarket development, revolutionary as it was in the 1950s and 1960s in redefining the physical bounds of retail operations, was only the precursor of the superstore and hypermarket, where the supermarket definition of 2,000 sq ft pales when compared with the 2,500–4,999 sq m definition of the superstore and the 5,000+ sq m definition of the hypermarket. Britain's first hypermarket was opened in 1966 and the first superstore in 1967 [URPI 1985]. Although up to the end of 1984 there were 40 hypermarkets operating in Britain, this store type has not seen the dramatic rise in store numbers visible within the superstore definition. From a total of 8 superstores opened by the end of 1969, there were 138 by the end of 1979 and 257 by the end of 1984. The 1970s, therefore, saw, on average, over 13 stores opened each year, and in the first four years of the 1980s an average of 24 stores opened per year. The result of developments within the definition of the superstore and hypermarket has been a dramatic increase in the floor space encompassed under the roofs of these retail forms. From 58,100 sq m in 1969 the figure had risen to 663,800 sq m in 1979 and 1,135,000 sq m by 1984. An addition of over 60,000 sq m per annum in the 1970s and over 94,000 sq m in the early 1980s.

The problem of large supermarkets superseding smaller super-. markets introduced at an earlier stage in the development of the system was soon to appear again with the appearance of the superstore and hypermarket. Thorpe and McGoldrick [1973] discovered that the opening of the Carrefour hypermarket at Caerphilly affected the small and medium-sized supermarket outlets more seriously than any other stores. Thorpe [1977] went on to find that other surveys showed that the small independent trader survived by providing a retailing operation more distinct from the supermarkets in their location and service orientation. This polarisation is supported by Kirby [1982] who suggested that it was the medium-sized shop that had most to fear from the emerging giants of retailing and that the efficiently managed small stores in fact complemented the larger establishments.

The consequences of this situation are, of course, far-reaching. As pressures push the size of units up into the superstore bracket, the large retail firms not only continue to wield a long-standing competitive advantage over the independent shopkeeper, but also significantly outpace the medium-sized multiple operations. The medium-sized firm, although capable of organisational growth, if each new branch is a feasible step, finds itself unable to expand into the new retail units demanded as a consequence of the scale of the innovations of market leaders. Therefore, as development occurs on the basis of superstore units, the medium-sized firm is left operating supermarket units not distinct enough to survive and not large enough to compete.

The physical constraints of the retail scene in the mid 1980s are a long way from the capacity of the retail outlets of the 1940s and 1950s. The small-scale operations which existed in post-war Britain dominated by the small retail operation has been replaced by employee-efficient and capital-intensive multiples.

COMPETITION

The increase in competition in the retail trade may well in part be attributed to the removal of RPM. Finally removed in 1964, the system of price maintenance has been seen as a suffocating influence on the competitive instincts of retail organisations and consequently to have had a detrimental effect on retail marketing. O'Reilly [1972], in his appraisal of the issue, clearly saw the removal of the system as advantageous to the future of retail development. This would seem a logical conclusion, on the grounds that RPM was by its very existence a factor which removed a competitive weapon from the hands of the retailer. However, voices have been raised in opposition to a belief that the final removal of the regulations was at all revolutionary, when it is borne in mind that only one third of retail turnover was affected by price maintenance at the time of the 1964 Act. It would, however, seem unreasonable to underestimate the effects of removal since even one third of items would be capable of having a considerable influence on the general marketing position within the retail scene. However, Yamey [1966] has noted that while RPM controlled one competitive instinct, it allowed those businesses which would in time be able to take advantage of an unrestricted pricing system to increase profits and hence their financial capacity, which, as has been noted, was a crucial factor in the inherently capital-intensive development of the super-market, and which has also proved valuable in the expansion of multiple units across the country. Likewise, the removal of RPM emphasised the need for retail units of suitable size and profitability. Small and large organisations alike were placed in a position where marginal units came under pressure. They could no longer rely on the buffer RPM provided. Although, as Yamey [1966] noted, RPM gave retailers the opportunity to improve their financial capacity, it had also given them the opportunity to maintain and even expand into essentially marginal sites.

Whatever the degree of qualification placed on the interpretation of the removal of RPM it may certainly be seen, as was the imposition of SET, to have been yet another factor which has contributed to the changes in the retail sector of the economy already in progress.

The prominent position of the large retailer and his relationship with the manufacturer and the consumer has been significantly influenced by the changing position of branded goods. The strong emergence of the branded good, particularly in the inter-war years, may be interpreted as having made the retailer nothing more than the servant of the manufacturer. The consumer may be seen to have benefited from the widespread introduction of brands as the consumer may be said to have benefited from the reduction of their influence with the emergence of own label and generic brands offered by the retailer. It was, however, in post-war Britain that the branded good was at its zenith, in the words of Davies, Gilligan and Sutton [1984]:

> The economy wide brand was probably at its strongest in the mid to late 1960s, a position achieved largely with the aid of very heavy manufacturer's advertising expenditure but also with the help of the advantage built up under the Retail Price Maintenance.

The nationally recognisable brand was certainly given a significant boost by the spread of commercial television reception: advertising in the form of television commercials was opened up as far as the British market was concerned in September 1954. The natural result, however, was ever-increasing concentration on certain brands as advertising became more expensive [O'Reilly 1972]. As a corollary of this, fewer brands could be advertised in that way on a cost-effective basis.

The increasing signficance of price after the economic crises of the early 1970s and the higher rates of inflation which followed emphasised the need for strategies which appeared at least to counter the upward movement of prices. Own brands should not be seen as a product of the 1970s (the St Michael label testifies clearly against such a belief) but without doubt it was a decade which saw the emergence in strength of the retailer's own brand and generic label. This trend was again related to the advertising support of these products. Using 1972 as a base year of 100 the advertising expenditure of grocers and supermarkets had reached 684 by 1981, while the advertising carried out by food manufacturers had risen to 312. This trend was reflected elsewhere in the retail field where retailers as a whole had increased their expenditure on advertising to 580 and all manufacturers to 377 [Mintel 1982].

These trends had one clear effect: the emergence within retailing of the large retail multiple on a scale that has previously not been seen. The trends of the last 40 years, outlined above, have led to a retail structure where the issue of retail marketing strategies have become of increasing significance. The scale of changes within retailing have been of major significance, both inside and outside the trade. The large retailers of the 1980s increasingly cause concern not only to their competitors within their own retail market, and indeed other markets where they see potential rewards, but also among manufacturers with whom the large retailers now deal on more favourable terms.

CUMULATIVE EFFECTS OF CHANGE

It would be a mistake to see the emergence of the superstore and hypermarket as merely the development of a large retail unit selling groceries, furniture or whatever. Rather, the last 40 years has seen a fundamental shift in the perspective of retail distribution, as a consequence of socio-economic and technical factors in post-war Britain. What has emerged is a retail form which has epitomised a reverse in the trends that Jefferys identified in 1950. The developments of the last 40 years have led to the replacement of certain retailing orthodoxies. The fundamental approaches of the retailing stars of the 1970s and 1980s are a long way from the small-scale operations of mid-century Britain.

The emphasis placed upon food retailing and especially the grocery sector in this article, and indeed often in other articles on the development of retail techniques and structures, may at times appear to the reader excessive, but the grocery sector has nurtured the seeds of the developments we see in operation today. 'Groceries based companies are the "engine of change" lying at the heart of, and driving forward, the revolutionary changes now beginning to appear in retailing' [Akehurst 1983].

The grocery trade has nurtured these changes, and as the preceding coverage of changes in the retail environment has shown been particularly subject to, and apparently most redolent of, fundamental change. The grocery trade, in helping to create a new retail form, has used its staple trade to expand into a larger market of food and subsequently non-food retailing.

The grocery store was a trading form which relinquished at a comparatively early date its value-adding function, a function the traditional butcher, for example, has not even relinquished today. Jefferys noted that in the 50 years preceding 1914: 'Specialised skill, training and experience were hardly necessary in the handling of the factory-made products and the advantage the skilled grocer had ... was no longer so all important' [Jefferys, 1954].

The grocery store of the inter-war period was, until the 1960s, significantly dependent on the manufacturer for branded goods of national reputation. The own-brand and generic product has reversed the trend which was a prerequisite of the grocery outlet as it emerged before 1914. Branded goods effectively allowed the comparatively small, powerless retailer the benefit of national conformity, standards and reputation, an unnecessary set of factors when there exist nationally recognisable conformity, standards and reputation vested in retail organisations. Marks and Spencers are a prime example of the process where the latter has long negated the former. However, the grocer or general food retailer, of the size of the large operators such as Asda, Presto, Sainsburys and Tescos have captured the markets from other retailers by acknowledging the fact that the value-adding function can be minimised at the point of sale, provided that it is marketed in a way which the customer finds attractive or even appropriate to that customer's changing social environment, and that the personal service of the value-adding function may be positively countered by the exploitation of high reputation. This is not a new approach in itself: the idea of adding new lines as appropriate is the hallmark of the successful mixed retailer. However, what is particularly noteworthy in the grocery store or large food retailer of today is the technological changes which surround its presentation to the consumer, both in a spatial sense and in the customer sales staff 'interface', and what is most fundamental of all, this change has been achieved on the basis of goods which are necessities. The customer is attracted to the store by the necessity of fulfilling certain needs; the store, made convenient to an identified mobile consumer by suitable locations. Once inside the store the customer is given an anonymity, which by virtue of the products concerned facilitates the exchange of goods.

The staffing issues, overcome by the changes inherent within the self-service system and demanded by the social and economic pressures of the post-war period, were an incentive towards the emergence of a less labour-intensive, and even labour-wasteful, system. The single unit retail trader may exist within an economy of high or low labour

demand, immune as he is from much of the changing market by
personal effort and family labour resources. It is, as in the case of
competition from the large retail store, as Thorpe and McGoldrick
[1973] and Thorpe [1977] identified, the medium-sized trader who was·
most at risk from the changes in progress; the retail unit which might be
seen to represent the finest flowering of pre-war trends.

As with the issue of staffing, the removal of RPM must certainly be
seen as somewhat of an incentive towards the exploitation of economies
of scale on the basis of direct competitive confrontation, which cannot
be considered to be unrelated to the disappearance of trading stamps
from the retailers' competitive strategies. The competition engendered by the removal of RPM, recognised by the Monopolies and Mergers
Commission [1981], affected both competitive stances within the retail
sector and also between the large retailer and the manufacturer.

CONCLUSION

The developments in recent decades, therefore, have in many ways
reversed the trends of a century of retail development. The number of
outlets since the mid-1960s have fallen, including the absolute number
of multiples. Thus the number of consumers per retail outlet has risen.
The relationship, enshrined in folk-lore, of the corner shop and its
geographically connected clientele, wrought by the urbanisation
process of the last century, has been badly damaged at the very least,
and broken at the extreme. The same relationship which dragged the
department stores into the suburbs, out of the High Street, in pursuit of
their middle-class clients between the wars, does not operate today.
The modern site of retail development is not residence-oriented as
much as transport-oriented. The process of urbanisation of the population which continued until the 1950s has over the last few decades gone
into reverse. From only one in five of the population living in areas
designated as rural districts in 1951, the figure had risen to around one
in four of the population living in areas designated as' rural districts in
1981 [Annual Abstract of Statistics 1986].

The orthodox catalyst of retail development, that of multiple chain
expansion, has been replaced. The rationale of retail development has
been redefined both in terms of the retail units themselves but also
geographically. The ground rule which demanded new branches in
retail centres across the country has been replaced by a need for greater
technical and operational suitability. Until the last few decades, retail
units as apparently diverse in nature as the corner shop and the
department store offered the same spatially confined and service-
orientated approach to retailing. The variety stores alone, with their
open display concept, challenged in any way these accepted parameters
of retail operation. Recent developments have redefined the
boundaries and purpose of service-dominated retailing and the
economic relationship within retailing between staff activities and the

selling process. Consequently, the customer to whom sales were made has re-emerged as the consumer to whom choice and ease of access has been facilitated.

In conclusion, therefore, what should be construed from the pattern of development within the retail sector, and especially the development of the grocery-cum-large-food-retailer, is not merely the adoption of trading practices leading to a further development within the retail form that was in the ascendant 40 years ago, but a different retail form, exhibiting the characteristics of a market-place, engendered by the demands placed upon it in recent decades. The use of the etymon 'market' in such terms as supermarket and hypermarket is not inappropriate. The traditional High Street shop, with its emphasis on specialism and its spatial restrictions, has been found wanting, while the market form, with an emphasis on comparatively unfettered inspection, diversity and more to the point, the juxtaposition of diversity, has met with customer approval. Both the social demands placed upon retailing and internal economic rationalisations have steered the retailer capable of exploiting current trends towards the recreation of another retail form. The retail form that has emerged is not a further manifestation of the urban shop, with connotations of service and the leisurely dissemination of information at the point of sale, but literally a market-place with the emphasis on clearly-identified consumer needs, which are offered, in forms, at times and in places suited to the social and economic patterns of the later twentieth century, and which thereby engender the facilitation of exchange.

REFERENCES

Akehurst, G., 1983, 'Concentration in Retail Distribution: Measurement and Significance', *Services Industries Journal*, Vol.3, No.2, July.
Annual Abstract of Statistics, 1986, London: HMSO.
Census of Distribution, 1950, 1957, 1961, 1966, 1971. London: HMSO.
Davies, K., C. Gilligan, and C. Sutton, 1984, 'The Changing Structure of British Grocery Retailing', *The Quarterly Review of Marketing*, Autumn.
Dawson, J.A., 1973, 'The Development of Self Service Retailing in Nottingham', *East Midland Geographer*, Vol.5.
Dawson, J.A., and D.A. Kirby, 1977, 'Shop Size Productivity in British Retailing in the 1960's', *European Journal of Marketing*, Vol.11, No.4.
Dawson, J.A, 1979, *The Marketing Environment*, London.
Doyle, P., and D. Cook, 1979, 'Marketing Strategies, Financial Structure and Innovation in UK Retailing', *Management Decision*, Vol.17, No.2.
Economic Trends Annual Supplement, 1987.
George, K.D., 1966, *Productivity in Distribution*, London, Cambridge University Press.
Henley Centre for Forecasting, 1982, *Manufacturing and Retailing in the '80's. A Zero Sum Game?* London:
Hollander, S.C., 1966, 'Notes on the Retail Accordian', *Journal of Retailing*, Summer.
Jefferys, J.B., 1954, *Retail Trading in Britain, 1850–1950*.
Mathias, P., 1967, *Retailing Revolution*, London: Longmans.
McClelland, W.G., 1963, *Studies in Retailing*, Oxford.

MINTEL, 1982, 'Grocers and Supermarkets', *MINTEL Retail Intelligence Quarterly*, Spring.
Office of Fair Trading, 1985, *Competition in Retailing*, June.
O'Reilly, A.J.F., 1972, 'The Conservative Consumer', *Management Decisions*, Vol.10, Summer.
Reddaway, W.B., 1973, *Effects of the Selective Employment*, London.
Retail Inquiry, 1976, 1977, 1978, 1980, 1981, 1984. London: HMSO.
Selective Employment Tax, CMND 2986 (1966).
Thorpe, D. and P.J. McGoldrick, 1973, *Caerphilly-Consumer Reaction*, Manchester: Manchester Business School.
Thorpe, D.(ed.), 1977, *Co-op Society Superstores*, Manchester: Manchester Business School.
Transport Statistics GB, 1974–84, 1975–85, London: HMSO.
URPI, 1985, *List of Hypermarkets and Superstores*.
Ward, T.S., 1973, *The Distribution of Consumer Goods*, London: Cambridge University Press.
Yamey, B.S., 1966, 'United Kingdom', in Yamey, B.S. (ed.), *Resale Price Maintenance*, London.

This chapter first appeared in *The Service Industries Journal*, Vol.8, No.1 (1988).

2

An Integrated Approach to Retail Change: The Multi-Polarisation Model*

by

Stephen Brown

The study of retailing in the United Kingdom has tended to be empirical rather than conceptual in nature. By bringing together three well known but poorly integrated models of retail institutional change, this exploratory article endeavours to provide a theoretical basis for future discussion. The multi-polarisation model maintains that developments along one or more dimensions of retail activity eventually give rise to counterbalancing actions elsewhere in the commercial system.

INTRODUCTION

Doubtless before, and ever since that proverbial debate on the angelic carrying capacity of the head of a pin, academics have been renowned for their ability to quibble over seemingly irrelevant or cut-and-dried issues. However, few if any would deny that the structure of retailing in the United Kingdom has undergone remarkable changes in the last quarter century [Dawson, 1979, 1982; Dawson and Sparks, 1986]. To cite but a few examples: multiple groups have expanded at the expense of independents and co-operatives; the hegemony of the High Street is under threat from the rapidly growing number of peripheral and out-of-town shopping centres; and a whole new breed of novel trading techniques (or institutions) ranging from the superstore and catalogue showroom to the convenience store and super-specialist have appeared. Indeed, the changes of recent years have been so dramatic that many commentators maintain that a 'retail revolution', comparable with the industrial revolution of the nineteenth century, is under way and will take several decades to run its course [Dawson, 1979; Dawson and Kirby, 1980].

Change, however, is not particularly new to retailing – the 'revolutionary' analogy, for instance, has been used to describe earlier periods of commercial flux in the late nineteenth and early twentieth centuries [Jeffreys, 1954; Briggs, 1956] – and some of the most significant

* The author would like to thank Gary Akehurst, editor of the *Service Industries Journal*, for encouraging him to develop an earlier (July 1984) draft of this paper.

scholarly contributions to the study of retailing have been attempts to model its inherent dynamism. Much of this work is concerned with institutional change and, broadly speaking, three conceptual approaches can be discerned; environmental, conflict-based and cyclical [see Brown, 1984]. The environmental approach to retail institutional evolution contends that changes in the economic, demographic, social, cultural, legal and technological conditions of the marketplace are reflected in the structure of retailing. Thus, the emergence of the department store in the mid-nineteenth century represented a commercial response to the growth of middle-class demand, the development of efficient intra-urban transport facilities and customer willingness to accept a fixed price policy [Jeffreys, 1954; Pasdermadjian, 1954; Ferry, 1960]. Similarly, the suburban shopping centre is largely an outgrowth of population decentralisation, particularly the free spending high-income groups, widespread private car ownership and an apparent liberalisation of Britain's restrictive planning procedures [Dawson, 1983; Davies, 1984].

The conflict-based approach to retail evolution, by contrast, concentrates upon the reaction of the established retail system to the threat posed by new institutional forms. Few significant commercial innovations, remember, have failed to be greeted by a storm of protest from disaffected institutions. Department stores, mail order houses, co-operative societies, chain stores, supermarkets, discount houses and, more recently, hypermarkets and superstores were all, at first, maligned, boycotted, accused of unfair trading practices and subject to attempts to stifle their success [see for instance Nystrom, 1930; Edwards, 1957; Oxenfeldt, 1960; Jones, 1979; McAusland, 1980; Guy, 1980]. The term 'department store', for example, was originally an epithet of opprobrium [Hollander 1960a]; co-operative societies were initially portrayed as 'a communistic and anti-Christian movement which seeks . . . the extinction of the private trader' [Winstanley, 1983:83]; and hypermarkets were once described as 'neon lighted obscenities . . . which sprawl in the depths of the countryside, like great leviathans stranded on a beach' [Wrathall, 1974:10].

Although several important conflict-based conceptualisations exist, most notably the dialectical [Gist, 1968; Maronick and Walker, 1975] and crisis-response [Stern and El-Ansary, 1977; Dawson, 1979] explanations of retail institutional change, these, like the environmental approach to commercial evolution, have attracted relatively little academic attention hitherto (an environmental perspective, admittedly, is implicit in many empirical studies). The bulk of scholarly activity has been devoted to cyclical modes of explanation. Once again a variety of formulations have been forwarded, but in the main they maintain that change takes place in a rhythmic fashion, by the repetition of earlier trends (see below). Despite their popularity, however, cyclical models of retail institutional development have been subject to a considerable amount of criticism. S.C. Hollander, a widely respected contributor to this conceptual genre, has argued that, at best, they are descriptive rather than truly explanatory, lack predictive power, are difficult if not impossible to quantify and the patterns, like cloud formations, 'become vaguer and vaguer as we approach them' [Hollander, 1980:81].

Important as these shortcomings undoubtedly are, the fact remains that cyclical models of retail change have long excited academic imaginations and, moreover, appear to have some empirical, albeit descriptive, validity. It is fair to assume, therefore, that Hollander's timely criticisms are unlikely to staunch the flow of papers that he did so much to initiate. A more useful exercise at this juncture may be to attempt to integrate some of the key cyclical conceptualisations. After all, the formulations posited hitherto have tended to concentrate on a single aspect of institutional change, such as sales policy, shop size or merchandise assortment; yet retailing appears to evolve along several dimensions simultaneously – increased store size has implications for merchandise assortment, sales philosophy and so on.

As a first tentative step in the direction of integration, this article endeavours to bring together three long-standing models of retail institutional change: *the retail accordion* [Hollander, 1966], *the wheel of retailing* [McNair, 1958] and *the polarisation principle* [Kirby, 1976]. It should be noted, first, that these concepts were developed with regard to American retail experience, though the self-same patterns are evident in most advanced nations. Thus, while the discussion to follow concentrates upon the retail milieu in which the theories originated, pertinent British examples will also be cited. Secondly, this paper is qualitative rather than quantitative in nature and as such suffers from the descriptive rather than analytical ethos that characterises most considerations of the models of retail change. But, as Davies and Kirby [1984] rightly point out, a serious weakness of distribution research in the UK is its empirical rather than conceptual orientation. Given the dramatic changes that are under way in British retailing, some form of theoretical perspective, however descriptive or exploratory, is sorely needed.

THE RETAIL ACCORDION

The retail accordion, or general-specific-general cycle, describes the evolution of the modern commercial system in terms of the number of lines of merchandise handled by retail outlets. A rhythmic pattern of development, dominated in turn by establishments selling a wide variety of wares and shops specialising in a narrow range of goods, is clearly discernible. In the United States, for example, the rural general store of the nineteenth century gave way to the specialist single-line businesses of the twentieth; which were themselves superseded by the mass merchandisers of the early post-war era [Brand, 1963; Gist, 1968]. Of late, however, highly specialised outlets, selling ski equipment, computers, ties and socks, fine wines, gourmet foods and so on, have come once more to the fore [Mason and Mayer, 1983]. Similar trends are apparent in the United Kingdom with, broadly speaking, the 'one-stop' bandwagon of the mid 1970s making way for the highly focused formats of today.

This cyclical pattern of institutional evolution was first noted by R.M. Hower [1943] and reiterated by Hall, Knapp and Winstein [1961]; but it was Hollander [1966] who extended the accordion principle to its fullest extent. He argued that in addition to the broad general-specific-general cycle, individual retail outlets widen and narrow their inventories with the passage of time. Most American department stores, for instance, began life as specialist establishments [Nystrom, 1930; Ferry, 1960] but, as the nineteenth century progressed, more and more customer services and lines of merchandise were added until the point of maximum diversification was attained at the start of the present century [Hollander, 1960a]. Since then, a large number of departments have been discarded and many modern emporia are more akin to high-fashion specialists than the 'universal providers' of yore [Pennington, 1980; Rosenbloom, 1981].

By dint of its dynamic perspective, therefore, the retail accordion provides a salutary reminder that 'merchandise, unlike eggs can be unscrambled' [Hollander, 1965: 520]. In fact, at any one time some institutions may be in the throes of widespread inventory diversification while others are rationalising their range of goods. Hollander [1966] compares this state of affairs to an orchestra of accordion players some of whom are compressing their music boxes while the remainder are extending them. The orchestra analogy, though striking, must not be allowed to obscure the essence of Hollander's conceptualisation: that the processes of adding and abandoning lines of goods are closely related. The accordion principle suggests, in effect, that excessive inventory diversification creates opportunities for outlets specialising in the range of products either ignored or inadequately covered by the broad but shallow sales philosophy of the mass merchandisers.

THE WHEEL OF RETAILING

Widely regarded as the single most important model of institutional evolution, the wheel of retailing asserts that novel trading techniques enter the market as low-cost, cut-price, low-margin operations. Over time, however, the institutions trade up. Better locations, improved display, increased advertising and the provision of credit, delivery and various other customer services all serve to drive up expenses, margins and prices. Eventually, they mature as high-cost, high-margin, conservative and top-heavy establishments with a sales policy based upon quality goods and services rather than price appeal. This, in turn, opens the way for the next low-cost innovator; and so the wheel revolves.

The wheel theory is usually ascribed to Malcolm P. McNair's famous 1957 paper, 'Significant trends and developments in the post-war period'. In actual fact McNair had outlined the concept some 26 years earlier [McNair, 1931], though it was W.A. Lewis [1945], a British economist, who first employed the cyclical terminology. Its antecedents notwithstanding, the pattern predicted by the wheel of retailing has been demonstrated by a number of institutional forms, including department stores, discount houses, supermarkets and, more recently, off-price shopping centres [Hollander, 1960b; Regan, 1964; McNair and May, 1976; Lord, 1984]. The hypothesis, however, is by no means universally applicable. Many retail innovations, including boutiques, convenience stores and vending machines, entered the market on a high-cost, high-margin basis. Moreover, Goldman [1975] has made the point that not every department store, supermarket or discount house began life as a low-cost, no-frills operation; there were significant variations on each theme. What is more, the wheel hypothesis only holds good for the most advanced economies; less developed nations tend to import the mature, high-cost versions of innovatory retail techniques [Cundiff, 1965; Wadinambiaratchi, 1972; Hollander, 1981].

In order to account for these deviations, many attempts to rework McNair's original model have been made [see for example, Izraeli, 1973; Tinsley, Brooks and D'Amico, 1978; Deiderick and Dodge, 1983]. So much so, indeed, that D'Amico [1983: 160] was recently moved to call for 'a new theory to replace the wheel concept and put an end to its rebalancing, retreading, realignment and so on'. These reformulations, however, and the continuing debate over the validity of the theory are perhaps less pertinent to the present discussion than the underlying premise of McNair's conceptualisation: that there is a dynamic price-service dimension to retailing. At one extreme there are outlets employing an essentially price-based, low-margin–high-turnover approach to selling and, at the other, institutions relying upon a high-margin–low-turnover, strongly service-oriented trading philosophy. Just as the advent of widespread scrambled merchandising creates opportunities for specialist outlets; so too an environment dominated by high-cost, high-margin retailers paves the way for enterprises operating an off-price, no-frills sales policy.

THE POLARISATION PRINCIPLE

First described by Dreesman [1968] and Agergaard, Olsen and Allpass [1970] – though named and quantified by Kirby [1976] – the polarisation principle contends that the well-documented trend towards fewer but larger retail establishments is counterbalanced by a renaissance of the small shop sector. The former is an outgrowth of the self-service technique of selling and a search for associated economies of sale, whereas the latter is a consequence of the tendency for large retail facilities, depending as they do upon extensive catchment areas, to be geographically dispersed [Dawson, 1979]. In America (and moreover Britain) in recent years the rapid development of hypermarket style operations and the modern convenience store has taken place. Offering a wide range but limited assortment of fast-moving merchandise and situated in easily accessible locations, convenience stores provide essential 'emergency' and topping-up facilities for one-stop shoppers and cater for those unwilling or unable to patronise the larger, bulk order-orientated outlets. Small shops, therefore, complement rather than compete with their larger brethren. Indeed, as noted earlier with regard to inventory diversification and sales policy, the growth of one creates opportunities for the other.

THE MULTI-POLARISATION MODEL

Important as the accordion, wheel and polarisation principles are, each describes but a single facet of the changing retail scene. It is apparent, however, that all three are closely inter-related. Thus, the retail environments of Great Britain and other advanced nations today possess many examples of large outlets specialising in a relatively limited range of goods (discount electrical/carpet warehouses); small outlets handling a surprisingly wide variety of merchandise (modern convenience stores); price-cutting operations occupying sizeable premises (hypermarkets) and small stores with a service-orientated sales philosophy (boutiques, super-specialists).

In fact, it is arguable that retailing polarises simultaneously along each of the price, assortment and size dimensions. This point is illustrated in Figure 1 and examples of institutional forms 'typifying' each pole of the model are set out in Table 1. Limited-line discount stores, for instance, occupy small outlets, sell a narrow range of merchandise and rely upon a high-turnover–low-margin sales policy. Catalogue showrooms, on the other hand, while operating from small premises and attracting custom on the basis of low prices are, thanks to their technique of selling, able to retail a very wide range of goods. Similarly, convenience stores sell a wide variety of wares and occupy small premises, but because of their high service input (late opening hours etc) can impose correspondingly high mark-ups.

At the opposite end of the size spectrum, the broad inventories and high margins of traditional department stores are counterpointed by the extensive range of cut-price goods on sale in hypermarkets and superstores. Specialists too, particularly the discount operators, are occupying larger and larger establishments, though the burgeoning success of the new breed of small service-orientated specialists (e.g. Alexon, Early Learning Centre and Culpeper) serve as a reminder that size is not everything. However, the future will undoubtedly lie with large up-market super-specialist outlets offering a very deep assortment of quality merchandise to carefully targeted market segments (arguably, the advance guard of Ultimate and HMV's record superstore has already arrived).

The picture presented by Figure 1, it must be emphasised, is not static. It depicts, in effect, a balanced set of multi-dimensional conceptual scales with developments at one or more poles eventually setting off counterbalancing actions elsewhere. In Great Britain at present the

FIGURE 1
THE MULTI-POLARISATION MODEL

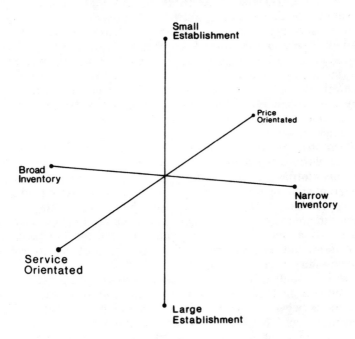

TABLE 1
RETAIL INSTITUTIONAL FORMATS

Merchandise Assortment	Sales Policy	Establishment Size	Institutional Type	Examples
Broad	Price	Large	Superstore, Hypermarket	Asda; Tesco
Broad	Price	Small	Catalogue Showroom	Argos, Littlewoods Catalogue Shop
Broad	Service	Large	Department Store	John Lewis; Debenhams
Broad	Service	Small	Convenience Store	7-11; Cullens
Narrow	Price	Large	Retail Warehouse	Toys R'Us; Texstyle World
Narrow	Price	Small	Limited Line Discount Store	Kwik Save; Victor Value
Narrow	Service	Large	'Super' specialist[1]	Ultimate; Hamleys
Narrow	Service	Small	Specialist	Next; Tie Rack

1. In American parlance, the term 'super' specialist refers to (small) highly specialised retail outlets. Horner (1984), however, uses the label to describe large specialist retailers. The latter usage was utilised on this occasion.

balance appears to be tipping towards the positions occupied by the rapidly growing numbers of small specialists (Next, Benetton, Principles and so on) and convenience stores (Cullens, 7-11, Martins etc) and away from that held by departmental and variety stores and, to some extent, superstores and hypermarkets. The well publicised plight of famous names such as Woolworths and Littlewoods bears witness to the former (even that bastion of the High Street, Marks and Spencer, is known to have suffered at the hands of highly targeted specialist outfitters) whereas the saturation levels faced by superstore operators in certain parts of the country and the general slowing down of large-store openings provides tentative evidence of the latter.

The multi-polarisation model, in short, contends that inventory diversification inspires specialisation, large outlets beget small and a high level of service gives rise to no-frills retail operations. Each of these dimensions, furthermore, is interdependent with the emergence of hypermarket style operations selling a wide range of discounted goods from large establishments paving the way for limited line discount stores, specialists in gourmet foods and modern convenience stores. Thus, the appearance of an innovatory institutional form which combines several pole positions can create opportunities along each of the assortment, sales policy and size dimensions.

Likewise, it is only to be expected that individual institutional types will evolve away from their initial trading stance. Most superstores and hypermarkets began life as cut-price operations but, as today's Tesco typifies, offerings have been considerably upgraded in recent years. Conversely, bouts of severe price-cutting are not unknown among mature, service-orientated, high-margin institutions such as traditional department stores [Cassady, 1957]. Moreover, the recent trend towards sell-everything gigantism in the DIY business brought forth the following astute comment from the manager of a chain of High Street stores: 'The situation is not dissimilar to what happened with the growth of the original food superstores 30 years ago. It has the effect of turning conventional grocers into specialists or delicatessens. It's already beginning to happen in the DIY market' [Davidson, 1986]. Even the highly focused specialist, however, is not immune from change. Victoria Wine, for example, are experimenting at present with late opening hours and a range of convenience store-style 'lifesaver' merchandise (food, toiletries etc). Thus, while a retail organisation may move away from its initial pole position, the very act of doing so creates opportunities for a newcomer offering the attractions of the first generation institution.

If, as the multi-polarisation model argues, developments at one end of the retail spectrum induce activity at another, the mechanisms that stimulate these changes needs must be identified. Clearly, this is a difficult task requiring detailed empirical investigation, but it is not unlikely that the answers will lie in the aforementioned environmental and conflict-based approaches to retail institutional evolution. Changes in the retail environment, whether technological (motor cars, freezers), economic (high inflation, increased consumer expenditure), legislative (planning regulations, shop hours), demographic (household size, age structure) or whatever, create commercial opportunities which are recognised and exploited by perceptive individuals. Retailing, however, is an extremely combative and highly imitative industry and any innovation or competitive 'move' resulting from an entrepreneur's perspicacity will eventually be adopted or matched by other firms serving the market. Thus, a widening of the range of goods held, the adoption of (say) a superstore-based strategy, or the provision of additional customer services often encourages the opposition to opt for a similar trading stance [Alderson, 1957]. In short, any attempt to gain a distinct competitive advantage precipitates a headlong rush to the same strategic position – price wars being perhaps the classic (short-term) example. The net effect is not unlike a seesaw or, as hypothesised above, a set of scales. When all the weight is concentrated at one end, opportunities exist for institutions that will restore the balance; though, given the continually changing retail environment, the original state can never be attained [Agergaard, Olsen and Allpass, 1970]. Retailing, therefore, is in a constant state of flux.

DISCUSSION

Although it represents an interesting conceptual device, the multi-polarisation model refers only to institutional aspects of retail change. But as Dawson [1982] rightly points out, the so-called 'retail revolution' involves dramatic changes in organisation and location, as well as technique. Cyclical trends, however, have long been noted outside the institutional arena; the history of trading stamps, shop hours, brand proliferation, advertising styles, management systems and so on, all exhibit cycle-like tendencies [Hollander, 1965; 1980]. Likewise, the locational pattern of retail activity in the United States – originally focused in the city centre, massive decentralisation and subsequent recovery of the urban core – is broadly compatible with cyclical principles [Hollander, 1980]. Organisationally too, the merger of major British retail organisations, such as Dee and International, Burton and Debenhams, Asda and MFI and BHS and Habitat, indicates a growing polarisation between massive multiple groupings and a hard, albeit diminishing, core of flexible, efficient independents. It may be possible, therefore, to extend the multi-polarisation model to retailing as a whole; certainly Davies and Kirby [1984] appear to be thinking along these conceptual lines.

Such generalisations, however, are beyond the scope of this exploratory article. Indeed, before extensions of the present model are contemplated (business policy and consumer behaviour are other possibilities), it may be prudent to address the shortcomings of the basic concept. As it stands the multi-polarisation model is exceedingly difficult to quantify due to the subjectivity inherent in definitions of large and small retail establishments, wide and narrow ranges of goods, and price- or service-based sales strategies. The real world, moreover, is much more complicated than the conceptualisation intimates. The limited assortment or 'one-stop' superstore philosophies for example, have been adopted by a wide range of trade types (grocers, household goods dealers, outfitters, chemists, etc) and similar techniques, such as the convenience store or specialist, are utilised by multiples, independents, co-operative societies and voluntary groups. Nevertheless, by combining pre-existing theories of institutional change, the multi-polarisation model goes some way towards providing a sorely needed conceptual framework for examining the continually changing structure of retailing.

CONCLUSION

Although the recent period of revolutionary retail change in the UK has aroused considerable academic interest, discussions of the phenomenon to date have tended to be empirical in nature rather than theoretically based. Consequently, the construction of a firm conceptual foundation represents a major challenge for British retail researchers and this exploratory article, by reviewing and bringing together three well known but poorly integrated theories of institutional change, has endeavoured to prepare the model building site. The multi-polarisation model contends that not only does scrambled merchandising, increased store size or additional customer service respectively stimulate specialisation, small stores and cut-price operations, but that any combination thereof gives rise to counterbalancing actions elsewhere in the retail system. In attempting to explain this phenomenon, furthermore, the article drew upon the other principal approaches to retail evolution, thereby providing the basis for a fully integrated model of retail institutional change. Important as recent developments in retail institutions or techniques are, however, the retail revolution also encompasses changes in organisation and location; but here too polarisation tendencies are discernible. It was tentatively hypothesised, therefore, that the multi-polarisation model be extended to the remainder of the retail system, though further research and discussion of the basic concept is necessary before such a step is taken.

REFERENCES

Agergaard, E., P.A. Olsen, and J. Allpass, 1970, 'The Interaction between Retailing and the Urban Centre Structure: A Theory of Spiral Movement', *Environment and Planning*, Vol. 2, pp.55–71.
Alderson, W., 1957, *Marketing Behaviour and Executive Action*, Homewood, Richard D. Irwin.
Brand, E.A., 1963, 'Modern Supermarket Operation', New York, Fairchild Publications, reprinted in R.R. Gist (ed), 1967, *Managerial Perspectives in Retailing*, New York: John Wiley, pp.19–21.

Briggs, A., 1956, *Friends of the People: The Centenary History of Lewis's*, London: Batsford.

Brown, S., 1984, 'Retail Location and Retail Change in Belfast City Centre', unpublished PhD thesis, Queen's University, Belfast.

Cassady, R., 1957, 'The New York Department Store Price War of 1951: A Micro-economic Analysis', *Journal of Marketing*, Vol. 21, pp.2–11.

Cundiff, E.W., 1965, 'Concepts in Comparative Retailing', *Journal of Marketing*, Vol. 29, pp.143–62.

D'Amico, M., 1983, 'Discussants Comments', in J.H. Summey *et al.* (eds), *Marketing: Theories and Concepts for an Era of Change*, Proceedings, Southern Marketing Association, Carbondale, p.160.

Davidson, A., 1986, 'Wickes Expands While Marley Sells Out', *Marketing*, Vol. 24, p.7.

Davies, R.L., 1984, *Retail and Commercial Planning*, London: Croom Helm.

Davies, R.L. and D.A. Kirby, 1984, 'Current Trends in UK Distribution Research', *Management Bibliographies and Reviews*, Vol. 10, pp.68–92.

Dawson, J.A., 1979, *The Marketing Environment*, London: Croom Helm.

Dawson, J.A., 1982, *Commercial Distribution in Europe*, London: Croom Helm.

Dawson, J.A., 1983, *Shopping Centre Development*, London: Longman.

Dawson, J.A. and D.A. Kirby, 1980, 'Urban Retailing and Consumer Behaviour: Some Examples from Western Society' in D.T. Herbert and R.J. Johnston (eds), *Geography and the urban environment: progress in research and applications: volume three*, London: John Wiley, pp.87–132.

Dawson, J.A. and L. Sparks, 1986, 'Issues for the Planning of Retailing in Scotland', *Scottish Planning Law and Practice*, Vol.18, pp.38–40.

Deiderick, T.E., and H.R. Dodge, 1983, 'The Wheel of Retailing Rotates and Moves' in J. Summey *et al.* (eds), *Marketing: Theories and Concepts for an Era of Change*, Proceedings, Southern Marketing Association, Carbondale, pp.149–52.

Dreesman, A.C.R., 1968, 'Patterns of Evolution in Retailing', *Journal of Retailing*, Vol. 44, pp.64–81.

Edwards, C.M., 1958, 'Discussions' in A.B. Smith (ed), *Competitive Distribution in a Free High-level Economy and its Implications for the University*, Pittsburg: University of Pittsburgh, pp.34–40.

Ferry, J.W., 1960, *A History of the Department Store*, New York: Macmillan.

Gist, R.R., 1968, *Retailing: Concepts and Decisions*, New York: Wiley and Sons.

Goldman, A., 1975, 'The Role of Trading up in the Development of the Retailing System', *Journal of Marketing*, Vol. 39, pp.54–62.

Guy, C.M., 1980, *Retail Location and Retail Planning in Britain*, Westmead: Gower.

Hall, M., J. Knapp, and C. Winsten, 1961, *Distribution in Great Britain and North America: A Study in Structure and Productivity*, London: Oxford University Press.

Hollander, S.C., 1960a, 'Competition and Evolution in Retailing', *Stores*, Vol. 42, pp.11–24.

Hollander, S.C., 1960b, 'The Wheel of Retailing', *Journal of Marketing*, Vol. 24, pp.37–42.

Hollander, S.C., 1965, 'Entrepreneurs Test the Environment: A Long-run View of Grocery Pricing', in P.D. Bennett (ed), *Marketing and economic development*, Chicago: American Marketing Association, pp.516–27.

Hollander, S.C., 1966, 'Notes on the Retail Accordion', *Journal of Retailing*, Vol. 42, pp.29–40, 54.

Hollander, S.C., 1980, 'Oddities, Nostalgia, Wheels and Other Patterns in Retail Evolution' in R.W. Stampfl and E.C. Hirschman (eds), *Competitive Structure in Retail Marketing: The Department Store Perspective*, Chicago: American Marketing Association, pp.78–87.

Hollander, S.C., 1981, 'Retailing Theory: Some Criticism and Some Admiration' in R.W. Stampfl and E.C. Hirschman (eds), *Theory in Retailing: Traditional and Non-traditional Sources*, Chicago: American Marketing Association, pp.84–94.

Horner, G., 1984, 'Retail trends – The Search for Diversification', *Retail Britain*, Vol. 1, pp.4–5.

Hower, R.M., 1943, *History of Macy's of New York 1858–1919*, Cambridge: Harvard University Press.

Izraeli, D., 1973, 'The Three Wheels of Retailing: A Theoretical Note', *European Journal of Marketing*, Vol. 7, pp.70–74.

Jeffreys, J.B., 1954, *Retail Trading in Britain: 1850–1950*, Cambridge: Cambridge University Press.

Jones, R., 1979, 'Consumers' Co-operation in Victorian Edinburgh: The Evolution of a Location Pattern', *Transactions, Institute of British Geographers*, New Series, Vol. 4, pp.292–305.

Kirby, D.A., 1976, 'The North American Convenience Store: Implications for Britain', in P. Jones and R. Oliphant (eds), *Local shops: problems and prospects*, Reading: Unit for Retail Planning Information, pp.95–101.

Lewis, W.A., 1945, 'Competition in Retail Trade', *Economica*, Vol. 12, pp.202–34.

Lord, J.D., 1984, 'The Outlet/Off-price Shopping Centre as a Retailing innovation', *The Service Industries Journal*, Vol.4, pp.9–18.

Maronick, T.J. and B.J. Walker, 1975, 'The Dialectic Evolution of Retailing' in B. Greenburg (ed), *Proceedings: Southern Marketing Association*, Atlanta: Georgia State University, pp.147–51.

Mason, J.B. and M.L. Mayer, 1983, *Modern Retailing: Theory and Practice*, Plano: Business Publications Inc, 3rd edn.

McAusland, R., 1980, 'Supermarkets: Fifty Years of Progress', *Progressive Grocer*, Vol. 59, pp.5–155.

McNair, M.P., 1931, 'Trends in Large-scale Retailing', *Harvard Business Review*, Vol. 10, pp.30–39.

McNair, M.P., 1958, 'Significant trends and developments in the post-war period', in A.B. Smith (ed), *Competitive Distribution in a Free High-level Economy and its Implications for the University*, Pittsburg: University of Pittsburg Press, pp.1–25.

McNair, M.P. and E.G. May, 1976, *The Evolution of Retail Institutions in the United States*, Cambridge: Marketing Science Institute.

Nystrom, P.H., 1930, *The Economics of Retailing: The Principles of Retail Store Operation*, New York: The Roland Press, 3rd edn.

Oxenfeldt, A.R., 1960, 'The Retail Revolution: Why and Whither', *Journal of Retailing*, Vol. 36, pp.157–62.

Pasdermadjian, H., 1954, *The Department Store: Its Origins, Evolution and Economics*, London: Newman Books.

Pennington, A.L., 1980, 'The Department Store versus the speciality store', in R.W. Stampfl and E. C. Hirschman (eds), *Competitive Structure in Retail Markets: The Department Store Perspective*, Chicago: American Marketing Association, pp.132–8.

Regan, W.J., 1964, 'The Stages of Retail Development' in R. Cox, W. Alderson and S.J. Shapiro (eds), *Theory in Marketing*, Homewood: Richard D. Irwin, Second Series, pp.139–53.

Rosenbloom, B., 1981, *Retail Marketing*, New York: Random House.

Stern, L.W. and A.I. El-Ansary, 1977, *Marketing Channels*, Englewood Cliffs: Prentice Hall.

Tinsley, D.B., J.R. Brooks, and M. D'Amico, 1978, 'Will the Wheel of Retailing Stop Turning', *Akron Business and Economic Review*, Vol. 9, pp.26–9.

Wadinambiaratchi, G.H., 1972, 'Theories of Retail Development', *Social and Economic Studies*, Vol. 21, pp.391–403.

Winstanley, M.J., 1983, *The Shopkeepers World 1830–1914*, Manchester: Manchester University Press.

Wrathall, J.E., 1974, 'Out of town shopping centres', Huddersfield Polytechnic, Department of Geography and Geology, Occasional Paper No. 1.

This chapter first appeared in *The Service Industries Journal*, Vol.7, No.1 (1987).

3

Concentration in Retail Distribution: Measurement and Significance

by

Gary Akehurst*

Given the lack of economic studies of market structure in retail distribution there is a need to repair some 40 years of neglect. Concentration in UK retailing is here systematically measured for the first time, not using Census of Distribution or other government sources, but based on the identification of the leading 150 or so companies, and the clear identification of turnover and profits derived from UK retailing. The paper discusses the significance of these findings related to the years 1970–78 but the true importance lies in the establishment of a comprehensive, computerised data base, which can be updated, and on which long-term trends can be established in conjunction with behavioural studies of mergers, innovatory activities and pricing behaviour. In this way, a structure-behaviour-structure model may lay the foundations for a theory of competition in retailing, besides various policy implications.

INTRODUCTION

Retailing is generally presumed by economists to be a perfect example of monopolistic competition with the possibility of local oligopolies, entry being so easy and mobility of clientele such that spatial monopolies are but a reasonably transitory phenomenon. Much hinges around the question whether economic theory is justified in assuming falling demand curves for individual goods sold in retailing or aggregate of goods and indeed, whether such demand curves are even identifiable [Akehurst, 1982]. Problems with the traditional methodology – in particular, the traditional theory of the firm; the nature of the products/services being sold giving rise to confusion and needless complexities; and empirical difficulties especially of data collection – have all hindered a thorough and systematic investigation of retailing market structure. There is a distinct

*I wish to acknowledge the kind advice of Julian Edwards of the University College of Wales, Aberstwyth and the particular assistance of Jack Meads and Kieron Lonergan of Manchester Polytechnic in the preparation of the computer programs so important to this study. The usual caveat applies.

need to focus on the elements of structure such as seller concentration, barriers to entry, product differentiation and economies of scale; Tucker [1978] is one of the very few writers to begin this work. Examination of market structure means a change of emphasis away from the individual shop to the firm or organisation of shops (or at very least supplements spatial and operating studies) and in so doing, lays the foundations for the analysis of competition in retailing, a job economics is uniquely able to do.

Back in 1951 Hood and Yamey doubted whether retailer 'private markets' really are private because of customer mobility. Even if a few customers of each retailer are mobile this provides profitable opportunities for any retailer prepared to sell at more attractive prices. Customers do learn about some price differences perhaps of certain non staple goods or key staple goods. Hood and Yamey [1951] suggest shopping habits are not unshakeable but buyer sluggishness does give each retailer time to adjust prices to competitive pressures. Furthermore, even if there were no changes in retail techniques, no changes in consumer tastes, etc., the entry and innovative abilities of new firms would be a constant disturbance; and Hood and Yamey were writing before many consumers had access to private transport, and long before the development of really large retailing groups. If private markets surrounding each retailer are not such a feasible concept, and if the analysis of competition based on single commodities is theoretically unsound (and a troublesome diversion) then in reality retailing should perhaps be viewed as one national market. The concept of overlapping markets is useful in illustration: Shop A is in competition with Shop B for consumer X and Shop B and Shop C are in competition for consumer Y [Aaronovitch and Sawyer, 1975 : 104]. If consumer Y is mobile, and although it appears Shop A and Shop C are indirectly in competition, they are in effect directly in competition. Whilst many studies have examined local areas (for example, Metcalf and Greenhalgh [1968], Naden and Jackson [1953]), giving particular attention to competition within small, well defined market areas, there may also be the need for an overview on which to build which complements these local studies. This is a sentiment Hood and Yamey [1951] would possibly agree with: 'While such analysis serves to isolate certain important considerations, it cannot provide the sole basis for a realistic explanation of situations where markets are not so strictly delimited'. Given overlapping market areas, the growth of large businesses and increasing diversification of retailing companies across conventional retail product boundaries, there is a forceful argument in favour of examining competition in national markets, and hence, national aggregate or overall concentration measures.

It is not the purpose of this paper to examine the major structural changes which have occurred, other writers have covered this more thoroughly, for example, Jeffries [1954]; Stacey and Wilson [1965]; Fulop [1966]; McClelland [1966]; Dawson and Kirby [1979]; Livesey [1979];

Livesey and Hall [1981] and Kirby [1982] to name but a few. But the issues and trends which were considered important at one time may no longer be so; resale price maintenance is a case in point. Many writers have been concerned, not unnaturally, with small retail shops or one establishment businesses because these are the most numerous types of retailing business in terms of numbers of establishments. Much important work has been carried out in this area.

It is really only since the Annual Retailing Inquiries (started in 1976 and replacing the Census of Distribution) that we fully begin to realise the true extent of the growth of large businesses in retailing, especially mixed retailing businesses, that is, businesses which cut across the conventional retail product groupings of groceries, clothing, durables, etc.

By 1978 multiples controlled some 42 per cent of total retail sales [Livesey and Hall, 1981: 33] although on Annual Retailing Inquiry data large multiples (those organisations with over 10 outlets) controlled nearly 54 per cent of retail turnover in 1979 [Livesey and Hall, 1981: 34]. As major multiples extend from original regional bases, like Asda and Sainsbury, so competition intensifies. One-stop shopping, superstore development, greater use of home freezers, etc., all combine to make it difficult for independents and smaller multiples to compete. These developments do not necessarily mean the demise of the small shop:

> Rather, the more likely pattern of development seems to be the polarisation of retailing with the continued decline of medium-sized shops and the growth of efficiently-run large and small stores, complementing each other in the retailing system. [Kirby, 1982 : 13]

Further evidence of the increasing dominance of large businesses can be seen by reference to Table 1. Large companies controlling over 100 outlets had, in 1980, 41 per cent of food sales, 55 per cent of alcohol sales, 38 per cent of clothing and footwear sales, etc. [Livesey and Hall, 1981: 55]. It would be so easy to pass over these statistics without realising the full extent of what is happening. Similarly, Table 2 shows the market shares of large businesses defined by turnover criteria (that is, an index-linked turnover of greater than £5 million at 1976 prices). In 1980 such businesses controlled 68 per cent of total retail sales, 63 per cent of food sales and virtually the entire sales of mixed retail businesses [Livesey and Hall, 1981: 33].

One further development has already been mentioned: the growth of diversification and the emergence of large mixed retail companies. Diversification is a useful growth strategy at times of slow volume growth in certain staples such as food. Particularly since the Annual Retailing Inquiries, new evidence has come to light of the extent of mixed retailing, for example, the 1977 Retailing Inquiry showed that the mixed retailer category increased its share of total retail sales from 22 per cent in 1971 to 28 per cent in 1977, a growth rate of about one and a half times faster than that for the whole multiple sector.

TABLE 1
ESTIMATED SHARE AND FORECAST SHARE OF RETAIL SALES BY LARGE MULTIPLE RETAILERS

| | 10-99 outlets | | over 100 outlets | |
	1980	1985 Estimate	1980	1985 Estimate
Food	19.5	19	41	43.5
Alcohol	18.5	18	55.5	57
Tobacco	14.5	14	29.5	31
Clothing & Footwear	19	19.5	38	38.5
Furniture, etc.	26	28	19	21
Electricals, etc.	14	14	46.5	48.5
Other goods	14	14.5	26.5	28
Total	17.6	17.8	35.7	37.7

Source: Livesey and Hall [1981: 55].

TABLE 2
MARKET SHARE OF LARGE BUSINESSES*

	1976 %	1980 %	1985 Estimate
All Retail Sales	60.6	68.5	77.9
Food Retailers	53.7	62.7	71.5
Clothing & Footwear	49.9	55.2	59.1
Household Goods	49.8	59.0	67.3
Other non-foods	24.2	32.2	37.7
Mixed Retail Businesses	99.3	99.8	99.9

* Large businesses defined as retailers with an index-linked turnover of over £5 million at 1976 prices.

Source: Livesey and Hall [1981: 33] based on Annual Retailing Inquiries.

Whilst many retailing companies are emphasising their differences from competitors, in fact many firms by diversifying and adopting similar modes of operation/retailing techniques are tending to become rather alike. It has been suggested that as companies become increasingly alike, the more prices will become the main area of differentiation [Hedderwick, Sterling, Grumbar, 1980].

As large retailers become more and more alike in terms of product range or mix, store types, etc., the implications for competition are of particular concern. Groups such as Marks and Spencer and Boots have moved well away from their original product bases, even Sainsbury has entered the DIY market, in a joint venture with Grand Bazaar Innovation Bon Marche (Belgium), and Asda, by merging with Allied Retailers, entered the furniture and carpet trade.

Given all these considerations it does seem logical, at least to this writer, to examine overall concentration in retail distribution (as a total economic activity) and in so doing, identify the leading firms. Such a view might have been considered unthinkable, even preposterous, a few years ago when, quite arbitrarily, retailing was classified by economists as being of low concentration. Having been so categorised few have ever thought whether this picture still holds or not. As was mentioned earlier, the issue of local markets or 'private markets' or 'circles of customers' is not proven. The concept is intuitively appealing but with national companies and increasing consumer mobility the question must be asked whether national markets or even regional markets, now take on a greater significance. The first step is to examine and compute national concentration ratios without reference to product groups, and in so doing, lay a foundation for a whole new direction of retailing research.

THE MEASUREMENT OF CONCENTRATION IN RETAIL DISTRIBUTION

The measurement of concentration is far from being a non-controversial area in economics. Why measure concentration if the end result is not some approximation to the market power in the industry and associated policy implications or where on the perfect competition-monopoly continuum a particular industry should be placed (Aaronovitch and Sawyer, 1975: 60] and hence resolve, in part, structural arguments? Advocates of various concentration measures, including Linda indices, Herfindahl, Rosenbluth and entropy measures, are basically arguing over the different weights to place on different features of an industry, for example, the relative importance of small or large firms and the relative size distribution of firms; data availability is an important consideration. Such methodological matters are not the concern of this paper. The concentration ratio is calculated; it is simple to understand, although not without difficulties of interpretation but is readily appreciated by policy makers: 'Concentration ratios relate to only a part of the activities but are a valid measure of the extent to which market conditions are changing at the top end of the size distribution of businesses' [Linda, 1976].

Studies of retail market structure are not common but three studies of concentration in UK retailing, using Census of Distribution data are known: Hall [1971], Aaronovitch and Sawyer [1975] and Tucker [1978]. Further studies examine concentration in the food or grocery sector: Hall [1971], Metcalf [1968] and the EEC [1977]. Several reasons can be advanced for a certain reluctance to systematically measure concentration in retail distribution. The data problem is acute, and if concentration is to be adequately measured, ways have to be devised to overcome it, that is, to extract financial information about the leading firms, and having done so, to prepare computer programs to sort and calculate. The traditional methodology is unequal to the task [Akehurst, 1982 : 67] and yet concentration measurement presupposes a clear definition of the markets and products to be studied. That base has yet to be adequately and rigorously defined, given that the theoretical treatment based on individual commodities is misleading, misconceived and, in this writer's view, has hindered the development of a theory of competition in retailing. Finally, given theoretical limitations and inadequate data, what concentration measure should be taken and what weights to attach to different size distribution features of the retail supply is, at this stage, largely irrelevant.

Aaronovitch and Sawyer [1975: 106] using 1961 and 1966 Census of Distribution turnover data calculate aggregate concentration in retailing whilst omitting the co-operatives and making assumptions to ensure comparability of the two years. Their results were as follows:

	1961	1966
CR	%	%
25	23.1	24.8
50	27.5	30.8
100	30.0	35.5

Aaronovitch and Sawyer do not go further than this, being primarily concerned to provide an overview of concentration in the non-manufacturing sector of the economy, and hence, despite their historical significance, these measures are no longer satisfactory.

Hall [1971] is again subject to certain criticisms one of which is the overwhelming concern with the individual shop and not the organisation or firm. Hall found that for retailing as a whole, shops with a turnover greater than £50,000 in 1966 held 43 per cent of sales. Updating Hall's methodology and utilising 1971 Census of Distribution data, in 1971 these establishments controlled some 55 per cent of total retail sales. The Tucker study [1978], whilst interesting in its own right, and despite an important debate on the merits of absolute versus relative concentration measures, still has a Census of Distribution base hindered by non-disclosure restrictions. What is needed is a new data base from which to work, and this is what this writer sets out to do.

If concentration in retailing was to be adequately measured the Census of Distribution and later Annual Retailing Inquiries would not be acceptable, partly for non-disclosure reasons. Gower has published a listing of the top 100 companies with at least 30 per cent of turnover derived from retailing activities [Gower, 1972; 1974; 1976; 1977]. However, this listing makes the fundamental error of not isolating non-retailing turnover and overseas retail sales particularly in large conglomerates or groups such as British American Tobacco or Sears Holdings. It does seem rather pointless not to attempt to isolate non-retailing sales when producing a list of companies ranked by turnover. There was, therefore, the necessity to carry out entirely new concentration measurements using new data.

METHODOLOGY

Turnover and net profit before tax derived from retailing activities have been extracted for all major companies known to be so involved.[1] Following accepted accounting convention, turnover is taken to be sales to third parties excluding inter-group sales and VAT, and deducting all retail sales outside the UK where known. Turnover and net profit before tax figures have been taken for company accounting periods ending in each year 1970 to 1978. Whilst it is not denied that isolating the retailing part of a group's turnover is difficult, it has not proved impossible.

Bearing in mind that this is the first time that, from a new base not dependent on government data, sales concentration in retail distribution has been thoroughly and systematically measured, two problems needed to be overcome:

(a) to identify all those companies with a significant proportion of their turnover derived from UK retailing activities (not wholesaling and distribution);

(b) to develop appropriate computer programs which would sort and calculate collected data in an efficient and time effective way.

Problem (a) involved a thorough and extensive search of known published financial information on public and private limited companies and those companies with a foreign parent company. It was found possible to isolate the turnover derived from retailing activities in even the largest groups, although the investigations could be time consuming.[2]

Problem (b), the development of appropriate computer programs, was a clear necessity, especially for future work. Computing manually would have been virtually impossible with some 190 companies, nine years, two entries for each company, three calculations and sort routines, and three separate tabulations for each year.[3] Once the computer programs were run three tabulations were produced for each year, 1970–78:

(1) Companies ranked by turnover, and therefore, each companies' market share, together with cumulative turnover (the concentration ratio).

(2) Companies ranked by net profit before tax.

(3) Companies ranked by net profit as a percentage of turnover.

Computer programs have since been developed to update data and add new companies. It is envisaged that a long run series of concentration data from about 1960 to the present time (and of course, future years) can be developed together with associated data on mergers, takeovers and diversificatory/innovatory activities. At present all such material has been analysed for the period 1970–80, but this is the subject of a future paper.

Table 3 summarises the results of the computed sales concentration ratio for each tabulation over the period 1970–78. Clearly in terms of aggregate concentration in retail distribution, that is, taking retailing as a total economic activity, concentration using sales as the size variable is apparently low. In 1978 the largest 100 companies controlled 45.5 per cent of total retail sales; however, it must be remembered that in that year total retail sales amounted to £42,386m, and therefore, 100 firms controlled sales amounting to £19,290m.

TABLE 3

COMPUTED SALES CONCENTRATION RATIOS 1970–78 UP TO CR150

	1970	1971	1972	1973	1974	1975	1976	1977	1978	change 1970-78
	PERCENTAGE OF TOTAL RETAIL SALES									
CR2	4.55	4.55	4.61	4.82	5.78	7.39	7.16	6.52	6.00	1.45
CR4	8.7	8.59	8.71	8.34	10.24	11.86	11.95	11.27	10.41	1.71
CR10	16.54	16.63	16.92	17.26	20.29	21.87	22.74	22.17	21.65	5.11
CR20	21.98	22.3	23.41	25.35	29.28	30.62	31.86	31.65	31.28	9.3
CR30	25.07	25.62	26.86	29.13	33.29	35.22	36.43	36.46	36.17	11.1
CR50	28.0	28.74	30.27	33.04	37.54	39.56	41.19	41.37	41.17	13.7
CR100	30.67	31.84	33.77	37.01	41.63	43.76	45.51	45.67	45.51	14.84
CR150	-	32.88	35.13	38.57	43.19	45.37	47.02	47.17	46.77	13.89*
TOTAL^N	(141)	(158)	(171)	(178)	(183)	(185)	(178)	(174)	(162)	
CRN	31.24	32.91	35.3	38.83	43.51	45.71	47.25	47.35	46.82	
TOTAL RETAIL SALES £m	14829	16296	18251	20680	23906	28420	32608	37155	42386	

*Change 1971–78

TABLE 4

SELECTED FIRMS WHICH SHOWED SUBSTANTIAL GROWTH OF TURNOVER 1970–78

	1978			1970			turnover growth % (current prices)
	turnover £'000	market share %	rank by turnover	turnover £'000	market share %	rank by turnover	
Kwik Save	192890	0.45	28	11076	0.07	59	1641
Assoc. Dairies	536000	1.26	12	48265	0.32	23	1010
Safeway	208975	0.49	25	27297	0.18	35	665
Currys	163137	0.38	30	33327	0.22	31	389
Comet[1]	123937	0.29	36	-	-	-	-
Bejam[2]	90975	0.21	43	-	-	-	-
Wm. Morrison	85669	0.2	44	10221	0.07	62	738
Hillards	80569	0.19	45	7862	0.05	71	925
MFI	55043	0.13	59	3718	0.02	102	1380

NOTES: 1 Comet went public in 1972
          2 established after 1970

Taking arbitrary concentration ratios between CR2 and CR150 all show an increase in the period 1970–78:

CR2 increased from 4.5 to 6 per cent
CR20 increased from 22 to 31 per cent
and CR100 increased from 30.7 to 45.5 per cent.

The greatest changes occur between CR20 to CR150 suggesting that certain middle ranking companies have increased their turnover significantly over the nine years chosen, but that as a group the top 20, 30, 50, 100 or 150 companies have increased their collective share of the total retail market.

Table 4 shows selected companies which have shown considerable growth of turnover during 1970–78 and as a consequence moved up the the listing by turnover. Of the nine companies selected, one is a chain of specialist freezer centres selling frozen food and freezer equipment (Bejam), four are discount chains (Asda, Comet, Kwik Save and MFI). Kwik Save's turnover for instance, grew by over 1,600 per cent; even allowing for inflation this is still impressive growth.

With reference to Table 5 one can identify the top 25 firms, ranked by turnover, in 1978 and the changes in these firms ranking in the period 1970–78. Of the top 25 companies:

(a) 16 had non-retailing activities, usually food manufacturing, finance and property;

(b) two were especially involved in mail order;

(c) 22 were involved in groceries retailing, of which 10 can be considered leading companies in the groceries sector;

TABLE 5

TOP 25 FIRMS IN 1978, AND RANKINGS BY TURNOVER 1970–76

	1978	1976	1974	1972	1970
Cavenham	1	1	2	29	128
Marks and Spencer	2	3	3	1	1
Tesco Stores	3	6	7	5	5
Unigate Foods	4	4	5	4	4
BAT	5	2	1	-	-
Great Universal Stores	6	5	4	2	3
J. Sainsbury	7	10	9	7	8
Boots	8	7	8	6	6
Littlewoods	9	9	10	15	16
F.W. Woolworth	10	8	6	3	2
Assoc. British Foods	11	11	11	8	7
Assoc. Dairies	12	14	19	19	23
Sears Holdings	13	12	13	9	9
Debenhams	14	15	14	13	11
John Lewis	15	16	17	14	13
Grand Metropolitan	16	13	15	12	19
Thorn Electrical	17	17	12	10	10
Linfood Holdings	18	21	-	-	-
Northern Foods	19	19	24	21	28
UDS	20	18	16	11	12
British Home Stores	21	20	20	20	17
House of Fraser	22	22	18	24	22
Gallaher	23	26	35	39	57
Fitch Lovell	24	25	28	25	25
Safeway Food Stores	25	23	26	32	35

(d) 11 were highly diversified companies across the conventional retail product categories whereas only four were narrowly based.

It is not without significance that those companies which decreased their ranking by turnover include several department store groups and less diversified (in retail product terms) operations, whilst those which increased their ranking are, without exception, groceries based. It is this writer's view that groceries based companies are the 'engine of change' lying at the heart of, and driving forward, the revolutionary changes now beginning to appear in retailing.

COMPARISION WITH MANUFACTURING

Having calculated sales concentration ratios for retail distribution without reference to types of commodities sold, how do these compare with manufacturing? Without any shadow of doubt there are more studies of concentration in manufacturing than that of the service industries; this is partly due to data availability and the long and difficult process of extracting data for services. It is possible, however, to broadly compare some results with manufacturing. George [1975] provides details of sales concentration at the CR5 level for different manufacturing sectors for the year 1968. The earliest year sales concentration has been calculated by this writer is 1970, but these results are broadly comparable. Table 6 shows the comparison. Without exception concentration in retailing is lower than that in selected manufacturing sectors, but this comparison needs to be qualified. The manufacturing sectors have been disaggregated whilst that for retail distribution is aggregated. If, say, grocery retailing is taken according to one study CR4 in 1969 was 54.4 per cent and 74.5 per cent at CR8 [EEC, 1977]. Aaronovitch and Sawyer [1975 : 119] provide a further comparison: in 1966 quoted companies obtained 85 per cent of profits in manufacturing, 49 per cent in retail and wholesale

TABLE 6

COMPARISON OF SALES CONCENTRATION AT CR5 LEVEL, SELECTED MANUFACTURING SECTORS AND RETAIL DISTRIBUTION

	CR5, % of sales	
Food, Drink and Tobacco	82	1968
Chemicals and Allied	79	1968
Electrical Engineering	76	1968
Vehicles	93	1968
Textiles	53	1968
Retail Distribution	10.3	1970

Sources:

Manufacturing: George [1975].

Retailing: Computer tabulations, this study concentration data for manufacturing is available for a few years post 1968 but relates to net assets or net output, and hence not directly comparable.

distribution and 36 per cent in construction. Comparison then with manufacturing industries is fraught with difficulties and must be carefully qualified.

In October 1982 the *Financial Times* published a listing of the top publicly quoted European companies ranked by market capitalisation.[4] With reference to Table 7, of the top 300 companies ranked by market capitalisation, 22 had substantial retailing interests; four of these companies (Marks and Spencer, BAT, Grand Metropolitan and Great Universal Stores) appear in the top 25. Only three of these 22 retailing companies were not UK based. Table 8 also gives companies with retailing interests ranked by market capitalisation and turnover in the UK. Again 13 companies appear in the top 100 by market capitalisation and 19 in the top 100 by turnover. Clearly on both European and UK evidence some retailing companies are amongst the largest companies involved in any economic activity.

TABLE 7

COMPANIES WITH RETAILING INTERESTS: RANK BY MARKET CAPITALISATION AND TURNOVER IN FT EUROPEAN 500 LISTING (UP TO RANK 300) 1981/82

COMPANY	U.K. unless stated	Rank by market capitalisation	Rank by turnover	Market capitalisation $m
Marks and Spencer		5	48	3739
BAT		13	5	2853
Grand Metropolitan		19	27	2351
GUS		21	69	2120
J. Sainsbury		29	58	1864
Boots		40	80	1350
Imperial Group		47	22	1238
Sears Holdings		59	76	1030
Assoc. British Foods		71	32	876
Assoc. Dairies		79	94	823
Northern Foods		137	149	527
Carrefour	France	142	50	494
Casino	France	153	99	460
House of Fraser		176	51	402
Tesco		203	52	351
Unigate		215	77	322
F.W. Woolworth		216	111	319
Kwik Save		223	221	314
W.H. Smith		248	145	284
Habitat Mothercare		251	316	281
Burton Group		256	305	273
Gen. Occidentale	France	289	30	232

Source: 'F.T. European 500' *Financial Times*, 21 October 1982.

TABLE 8

COMPANIES WITH RETAILING INTERESTS RANK BY MARKET CAPITALISATION AND TURNOVER IN
FT U.K. 500 LISTING 1981/82

Company	Rank by market capitalisation	Rank by turnover
Marks and Spencer	4	16
BAT	7	2
Grand Metropolitan	8	6
GUS	10	27
J. Sainsbury	14	20
Boots	19	34
Sears Holdings	33	33
Assoc. British Food	38	9
Assoc. Dairies	42	45
British Home Stores	65	109
Northern Foods	69	74
House of Fraser	83	75
Tesco	97	19
Other companies below top 100, by market capitalisation but in top 100 by turnover:		
Unigate	105	32
F.W. Woolworth	106	50
Debenhams	175	92
Booker McConnel	196	58
Linfood Holdings	205	53
Fitch Lovell	273	85

Source: *Financial Times*, 21 October 1982.

TABLE 9

THE TOP N FIRMS RANKED BY NET PROFIT BEFORE TAX, AND THEIR SHARE OF TOTAL RETAIL
SALES 1970-78

Top n firms ranked by profit as a % of turnover	1970	1971	1972	1973	1974	1975	1976	1977	1978	change 1970-78
		% OF TOTAL RETAIL SALES								
2	0.01	0.03	0.05	0.35	0.12	0.02	0.94	0.13	0.14	0.13
4	0.18	0.20	0.50	0.62	0.15	1.10	0.96	1.56	1.49	1.31
10	1.67	1.57	1.78	3.77	0.55	1.50	3.75	4.04	3.94	2.27
20	10.59	7.99	2.31	4.57	8.00	5.23	6.48	8.91	5.59	-5.0
30	13.45	12.79	8.52	9.02	9.16	9.07	9.54	9.67	9.70	-3.75
50	15.31	15.31	14.27	13.45	15.56	12.98	14.32	14.03	14.61	-0.7
100	23.65	21.76	22.54	20.13	22.29	19.46	22.32	25.19	27.25	3.6
150	-	32.49	33.50	33.66	39.64	38.20	45.10	45.46	46.42	13.93*

From computer tabulations

Note: * change 1971-78

TABLE 10

THE TOP N FIRMS RANKED BY PROFIT AS A PERCENTAGE OF TURNOVER, AND THEIR SHARE OF
TOTAL RETAIL SALES 1970-78

Top n firms ranked by net profit before tax	1970	1971	1972	1973	1974	1975	1976	1977	1978	change 1970-78
	% OF TOTAL RETAIL SALES									
2	4.54	4.55	4.61	4.28	4.04	4.18	4.39	4.53	4.53	-
4	8.16	8.10	8.26	7.59	7.43	7.14	7.16	7.12	7.63	0.53
10	15.44	15.38	15.29	13.78	17.03	17.68	17.74	18.11	15.63	0.19
20	21.15	21.74	22.76	23.82	28.07	29.40	30.40	30.77	30.01	8.86
30	23.17	23.99	25.17	27.75	32.04	33.26	24.89	35.03	33.59	10.42
50	26.88	27.47	29.21	31.49	35.86	37.59	39.23	39.92	39.66	12.78
100	30.00	31.12	32.67	36.09	40.99	43.22	44.65	45.29	44.76	14.76
150	-	32.68	34.63	38.02	42.66	44.85	46.54	46.90	46.34	13.66*

From computer tabulations

Note * change 1971-78

Table 9 shows the top n firms ranked by net profit before tax, and their share of total retail sales. This table is not significantly different from Table 3. The top 10 firms by profit controlled 15.6 per cent of total retail sales in 1978, and the top 150 controlled 46.3 per cent of retail sales. Table 10 is, however, somewhat different. The top n firms ranked by profit as a percentage of turnover and their share of total retail sales, produces different results. The top two firms controlled only 0.14 per cent of total retail sales and the top 30 only 9.7 per cent. It is not possible within the confines of this present paper to highlight the extensive statistical tests of significant relationships between concentration and performance, which must be the subject of another paper. One thing, however, is clear: those companies with the largest profit margins on their sales are generally smaller companies, usually selling non-food products or have a wide sales mix. Companies with a food or groceries base, although large in terms of turnover, appear in the middle rankings or towards the end of tabulations.

THE SIGNIFICANCE OF CONCENTRATION IN RETAIL DISTRIBUTION

The term 'retail distribution' covers a wide variety of products, services, locations and organisations; it seems, therefore, that a natural starting point to the economic analysis of retailing is the activity of retailing as the selling of products with associated services to the consumer regardless, in the first instance, of the nature or type of product sold. If one ignores for the moment, segmenting the buyer side of the market for retail goods, and the wide variety of goods, and groupings of those goods, one is left with the organisations of the supply side, that is, firms and possible groupings of firms. A traditional approach would be to group firms selling broad categories of products, for example, groceries, household furnishings, etc. A behaviouralist approach would be to identify groupings of firms based not so much on product categories but rather on behaviour patterns: recognised interdependence and rivalry around certain firms. Such groupings of firms would cut across conventional product groupings. Linda [1976] advocates the industry approach to concentration measurement, that is, an analaysis of the major firms in industries and sub-industry (product) markets. In empirical research such a starting point has distinct advantages; one goes on to identify the major participants in the activity of retailing regardless, in the first instance, of the products each firm actually retails, their geographical location or modes of operation. From this first identification one goes on to examine the size distribution of the major firms and their inter-relationships within groupings which gives structure to the retail trade. Controversy surrounds the structure of retailing [Andrews, 1964; Hall, 1949; Smith, 1948; Hood and Yamey, 1951; Holdren, 1965] but it is nevertheless instructive to examine a dimension of that structure, namely concentration, partly because the knowledge of it is interesting in its own right, but also because having identified the major companies there is an important lead for the research of possible groupings of an oligopolistic nature cutting across established product boundaries. In summary, to understand structure in retailing it proves necessary to examine behaviour and interpret structure in the light of behavioural patterns surrounding key firms, once these key firms have been identified by a process which examines a feature of structure, namely concentration. A modified structure-behaviour-structure model, with a more familiar sub-model system (structure-conduct-performance) is advocated: one measures and identifies certain aspects of structure in order to identify possible behavioural groupings of firms, which in turn, once empirical research has established the existence or not of groupings, throws further light on the structure debate.

One can go on to further consider the significance of concentration in retailing under three headings:

(a) the negotiating strength between retailers and manufacturers; the development of countervailing power?

(b) implications for consumer choice both in terms of range of commodities, brands and points of sale;

(c) the trend towards national mixed retailing groups.

On the extremely rare occasions concentration in retailing has been measured (and then, in all cases using Census of Distribution data) it has been found to be low relative to manufacturing, but it can be considered that the relatively low levels of concentration found do not provide a true reflection of the strength of buying power of large multiple groups. The Monopolies and Mergers Commission (MMC) [1981] found that for certain products examined the three largest retailers took less than ten per cent of the market in 1977, although it was a higher percentage for packaged groceries; but it was felt that concentration was 'an unreliable guide to that part of relative bargaining power which may be ascribed to "muscle"' [MMC, 1981: 31].

The MMC ascribe, in part, the rise of the multiples to the disappearance of resale price maintenance (RPM):

> The progressive disappearance of RPM removed obstacles which had previously hampered the expansion of those retailers who sought to compete on the basis of price, notably the multiple chains geared to the rapid turnover of goods at low prices. [MMC, 1981: 7]

Customers were coming to favour low price retailers rather than receive trading stamps with purchases, and increased mobility led to an increased incident of one-stop shopping. As a result of these, and other developments, manufacturers were finding that the outlets where their products were being sold to the final customer were being transformed, and increasingly owned, by one of a small group of large companies. Manufacturers face, as the MMC [1981] point out, two extremes of buyers: firstly, the very large buyers (multiples, co-operatives, and discounters) and secondly, the small unaffiliated independent traders.

Given increasing concentration of both outlets and turnover, both highly significant, the MMC [1981] considers that the 'retailing threat' is the ability to switch purchases wholly or partially to another supplier, while 'the manufacturers' muscle' is the strength of their product's appeal to the customer. Both the development of increasing rivalry, growing oligopolistic awareness and price campaigns such as Checkout, has meant that few manufacturers (especially food manufacturers) have been able to successfully resist these retailer pressures, especially if their products are ones where there is a surplus production capacity and static volume of sales, as food has been. Price wars, especially that surrounding Checkout, have accentuated these pressures; indeed success in the grocery retailing price wars has depended in part, on success in obtaining large discounts from suppliers [MMC, 1981: 31].

This looks increasingly like Galbraith's concept of 'countervailing power' [Galbraith, 1963], a process whereby the concentration of power in one sector calls forth the development of offsetting concentration of power in another related sector, thus, counteracting or neutralising the effects of the initial concentration. Galbraith emphasises the importance of retailers in this respect, suggesting retailers are required to develop countervailing power on behalf of the consumer, otherwise consumers would have to organise it themselves. In the context of modern retailing this comment now appears a trifle naive.

In part the final price to the consumer will depend on the cost price of the product to the retailer. This will clearly be a function of the negotiating strength between the producer and the retailer. Major retailers can clearly, via bulk purchasing and outlets control, exert great pressure on manufacturers to obtain supplies on highly favourable terms. One cannot underestimate the strength or extent of this power: large multiples can exert dominance over specific branded products. By switching between brands the retailer directly affects the production process, both in the production economies of scale which the producer may reap and the continued existence of the brands. Brands which are not purchased by the large retail groups may well cease production. The producer needs mass sales to reap mass production economies and therefore, the large group superstores and supermarkets are absolutely vital. However, these retail groups hope to achieve economies of scale in marketing by *reducing* the brand range, using simple packaging and own labels. Linda [1976: 90] sums up the process:

> The result is that manufacturers and producers are very highly dependent on the supermarkets and chain-stores and become more and more so as the size and concentration of sales points increase (the multiplier effect).

The problem is self-perpetuating in the sense that, via retailer bargaining strength, producers gradually lose power over consumer demand, which is their reason for existence. The retailer, in standing between manufacturer and final consumer, means in effect that no longer should manufacturers necessarily aim advertising at the final customer, instead they should concentrate on:

(a) establishing and securing numerous retail outlets to ensure sales of their product;
(b) maintaining the goodwill of the owners and managers of these retail outlets;
(c) negotiating suitable sales to prominent retailers

The retailer carries out advertising on his own behalf which may or may not correspond with that which the manufacturer would wish. Over time the brands may become secondary, or be used as pawns to extend the overall 'image' of the retail group. Tucker extends the concept of negotiating power by suggesting that coverage of the national market is important, not just individual products: 'The bargaining strength of retail organisations in relation to manufacturers will depend on the size of their aggregate turnover (i.e., not product markets) in broad kinds of business and their coverage of the national market' [Tucker, 1978: 54]. It looks increasingly likely that if producer industries expand the benefits will be enjoyed not by those industries but by retail groups. As a consequence, producers will either 'engage in a process of concentration, reorganisation and restructuring so as to boost its negotiating strength vis à vis distribution', [Linda, 1976: 92] or producers will attempt to enter retail distribution, and thus acquire their own sales points, thereby ensuring continuity of sales for production economies and long-term profitability.

The implications for consumer choice are equally of concern. The greater mobility of consumers has had profound effects. Many outlets have been located with own transport customers in mind; as consumers shop less frequently but engage in one-stop shopping the large retail group can exert particular power '... by imposing a basket of articles or goods in which the various components – the actual articles and brands – are not determined by the consumer but exclusively by the seller' [Linda, 1976: 89]. This 'market basket' concept is important not only for consumer choice but also for the whole analysis of competition in retailing. Major multiples hope that, over time, consumer preferences will shift from comparing brands between competing stores to choosing brands within one location (and hence establish a spatial monopoly). Certainly as a result of multiple buying power certain brands may disappear altogether. Moreover, availability of retailer own brands at lower prices exerts continuing pressure on the prices of manufacturers' national brands, but particularly, their secondary brands [MMC, 1981: 31]. Although the range of brands may diminish over time, the MMC feels that bargaining by multiples has led to lower retail prices than would have been and that savings have been largely passed on to the consumer [MMC, 1981: 50].

It is not necessary to highlight again the quickening trend towards mixed retailing, but clearly as diversification proceeds it is perhaps inevitable that certain national multiples will come to provide the main outlets for a wide range of commodities, for a majority of consumers. Most groups have central buying and pricing policies. Tucker [1978], amongst others, stresses that non price competition through product, brand and store image differentiation is determined at head office, and that it is nationwide competitive strategies which are fundamentally important. This begs the question whether the study of national companies' behaviour will adequately reflect national and local competition. Tucker believes it does:

> If the nationwide rivalry of firms is equally reflected in local area competitive structures, then it can be expected that national concentration measures will depict adequately the degree of market competitiveness at a regional level. [Tucker, 1978: 54]

If local branches of national multiples have little control over purchasing and pricing, then realistically it is national concentration levels which are important.

CONCLUSION

It will take time to repair to some extent the lack of studies of market structure in retail distribution. Concentration in UK retailing has been measured using non-government sources, and based on the identification of the leading companies, and their turnover and net profits derived solely from UK retailing activities. For the first time there is now a comprehensive, computerised data base, which can be modified and updated as required. This allows long-term trends to be established in conjunction with behavioural studies of mergers, take-overs, innovation and pricing behaviour. In this way a general theory of competition in retailing may be developed.

NOTES

1. Extensive use was made of various sources located in the Manchester Business School Library:

   a. Jordan Dataquest and Financial Analysis reports on private and public limited companies 1970–78;
   b. Extel Statistical Services, London, and company reports;
   c. Financial Times MIRAC service (microfiche of company reports from 1968/69 to date);
   d. Gower Economic Publications 1970 onwards;
   e. McCarthys (photocopy service of major newspaper cuttings of companies);
   f. Miscellaneous sources in London and Manchester.

2. The top 500 private companies per Jordan listings were examined from 1970 onwards, excluding builders merchants, minor garage services, distributors and wholesalers. In 1971/72 this meant all companies with a total turnover threshold greater than £4m, progressively increased to greater than £10m in 1978 to keep pace with inflation. The next 500 private companies were examined in the top 1,000 private companies for significant retailers, i.e., those whose turnover exceeded 75 per cent of total turnover. For public companies, all companies were examined. In addition subsidiaries of other companies were identified to avoid duplication of retailing turnover on consolidation of a group's turnover.

3. A suite of programs was developed: file creation; consolidation from input to output files; sort-calculating and miscellaneous (including an update facility for input files).

4. Market capitalisation is share price x number of shares in company. The average share price over the month of June 1982 was taken, each converted to US $ according to an average exchange rate taken over the month of June. All accounting periods end in 1981 or by March 1982.

REFERENCES

Aaronovitch, S. and Sawyer, M.C., 1975, *Big Business*, London: Macmillan.
Akehurst, G.P., 1982, 'The Economics of Retailing – A Note', *Service Industries Review*, Vol. 2, No. 2.
Andrews, P.W.S., 1964, *On Competition in Economic Theory*, London: Macmillan.
Dawson, J.A. and Kirby, D.A., 1979, *Small Scale Retailing in the UK*, Farnborough: Saxon House.
European Economic Community (EEC), 1977, *A Study of the Evolution of Concentration in the Food Distribution Industry for the United Kingdom*, Brussels – Luxembourg: Commission of the European Communities, Vol. 1, Industry Structure and Concentration.
Financial Times, 1982, 'FT European 500', 21 October.
Fulop, C., 1966, *Competition for Consumers*, London: Allen and Unwin.
Galbraith, J.K., 1963, *American Capitalism*, Harmondsworth: Penguin Books.
George, K.D., 1975, 'A Note on Changes in Industrial Concentration in the United Kingdom', *Economic Journal*, Vol. 85.
Gower Economic Publications (GEP), 1972, *Retail Trade Developments in Great Britain, 1971–72*, Farnborough: Gower Economic.
GEP, 1974, *Retail Trade Developments in Great Britain, 1973–74*, Farnborough: Gower Economic.
GEP, 1976, *Retail Trade Developments in Great Britain, 1975–76*, Farnborough: Gower Economic.
GEP, 1977, *Retail Trade Developments in Great Britain*, Farnborough: Gower Economic.
Hall, M., 1949, *Distributive Trading*, London: Hutchinson's University Library.
Hall, M., 1971, *The Small Unit in the Distributive Trades*, Research Report No. 8, London: HMSO, Committee of Inquiry on Small Firms.

Hedderwick, Sterling and Grumbar, 1980, *Multiple Explosion*, London: Hedderwick, Sterling, Grumbar and Co.

Holdren, B.R., 1965, 'Competition in Food Retailing', *Journal of Farm Economics*, Vol. 47.

Hood, J. and Yamey, B.S., 1951, 'Imperfect Competition in Retail Trades', *Economica*, Vol. 18.

Jeffries, J.B., 1954, *Retail Trading in Britain, 1850–1950*, Cambridge: Cambridge University Press.

Kirby, D.A., 1982, 'Retailing in the Age of the Chip', *Service Industries Review*, Vol. 2, No. 1.

Linda, R., 1976, *Methodology of Concentration Analysis Applied to the Study of Industries and Markets*, Brussels: Commission of the European Communities.

Livesey, F., 1979, *The Distributive Trades*, London: Heinemann.

Livesey, F., and Hall, R.J., 1981, *Retailing: Development and Prospects to 1985*, London: Staniland Hall.

McClelland, W.G., 1966, *Costs and Competition in Retailing*, London: Macmillan.

Metcalf, D., 1968, 'Concentration in the Retail Grocery Industry in Great Britain', *Farm Economist*, Vol. 11.

Metcalf, D., and Greenhalgh, C., 1968, 'Price Behaviour in a Retail Grocery Sub-Market', *British Journal of Marketing*, Vol. 1.

Monopolies and Mergers Commission (MMC), 1981, *Discounts to Retailers*, London: HMSO.

Naden, K.D., and Jackson, G.A., 1953, 'Prices as Indicative of Competition Among Retail Food Stores', *Journal of Farm Economics*, Vol. 35.

Smith, H., 1948, *Retail Distribution*, (2nd Ed.), London: Oxford University Press.

Stacey, N.A.H., and Wilson, A., 1965, *The Changing Pattern of Distribution*, Oxford: Pergamon.

Tucker, K.A., 1978, *Concentration and Costs in Retailing*, Farnborough: Saxon House.

This chapter first appeared in *The Service Industries Journal*, Vol.3, No.2 (1983).

4

The Distribution Systems of Supermarket Chains

by

Alan C. McKinnon

This article considers the benefits supermarket chains may achieve from setting up their own distribution systems and attempts to explain differences in distribution strategies. These differences appear to be closely related to differences in the way chains have grown, management investment preferences and turnover composition, taken in conjunction with total sales, branch size and geographical extent of the business.

The investigation of structural change within the tertiary sector can be seriously constrained by the way in which service activities are classified. This is particularly true of wholesaling and retailing. The traditional distinction between wholesaling and retailing has become blurred as firms have extended their control along the distributive channel to encompass both these activities. In most trades the integration of retail and wholesale functions has been achieved mainly as a result of multiple retailers dealing direct with producers and assuming responsibility for the storage and movement of supplies 'upstream' of the shop. Using statistics currently available, however, it is not possible to measure the extent to which retailers have taken on wholesale functions. Investment and employment data for multiple retailers are presented in highly aggregate form and fail to distinguish between their warehousing and retailing operations.

The nature and location of investment and employment clearly differs between shops and warehouses. Although these two spheres of activity are closely inter-related, their growth potential can also differ significantly. The scale of the retail operation is largely determined by the volume and spatial distribution of consumer expenditure. Even if the level of retail activity remains constant a multiple can vary the demands placed upon its own storage and delivery system by altering the allocation of flows between distributive channels. A multiple retailer can, for example, increase its dependence on its own system of distribution by requiring more manufacturers to deliver supplies in bulk loads to its warehouse(s) rather than in small consignments direct to branch stores (Pettit, 1983). The pressures on multiples to vary their reliance on their own distribution systems are often quite independent of the factors affecting the scale and character of their retail operations.

The failure of the available statistics to distinguish between the 'retailing' and 'warehousing' sides of multiple retail firms would be less serious if these firms divided investment and employment similarly between their shops and their supporting systems of distribution. Sample surveys might then be used to establish a typical division of investment and employment between these activities and monitor how this changed through time. Surveys of this kind (mainly of firms in the grocery trade, for example, Thorpe *et. al.*, 1973; Walters, 1976), have revealed wide differences between multiples in the extent to which they have developed their own systems of distribution. Given the magnitude of these differences, it would be unwise simply to rely on average figures and generalisations based on sample data. There is a need for more detailed investigation of retailers' motives for developing their own storage and delivery systems and the reasons for firms differing so widely in their dependence on such systems. This article assesses the benefits that supermarket chains derive from setting up their own distribution systems and attempts to explain differences in their distribution strategies.

THE GROWING IMPORTANCE OF RETAILERS' WAREHOUSES

Between 1938 and 1982, multiple retailers increased their share of grocery sales from 24 per cent to 65 per cent (Jefferys, 1950; Institute of Grocery Distribution, 1983). In the 1950s and 1960s, while their share of the grocery market was expanding, supermarket chains channelled an increasing proportion of their supplies through their own warehouses (usually referred to as 'central warehouses'). By 1967, grocery multiples were directing, on average, about 60 per cent of their supplies through their own warehouses (Pettit, 1983). This proportion changed little betwen 1967 and 1972 (Thorpe *et. al.*, 1973) but during the 1970s it declined, partly as a result of the development of superstores capable of receiving supplies in bulk loads direct from producers and partly because of the disproportionately large growth of some chains, such as Tesco and Asda, whose dependence on central warehouses was much less than the average for grocery multiples. A survey undertaken in 1978/9 indicated that the proportion of supplies being channelled through central warehouses had declined to 47 per cent (McKinnon, 1984). Between 1972 and 1979, however, the multiples collectively increased their share of the grocery market from 44.5 per cent to 53.6 per cent (Institute of Grocery Distribution, 1982), thereby largely maintaining the volume of flow through their warehouses. All but two of the 23 retailers consulted in the 1978/9 survey anticipated little change in their relative use of central warehouses in the foreseeable future. It has recently been reported, however, that several supermarket chains, including Tesco, now intend to expand their distribution operations (Robson, 1983). At present between 35 and 40 per cent of grocery supplies travel to retail outlets via warehouses operated or contracted by multiple retailers, a higher proportion than flows through any of the alternative channels. In terms of the volume of business handled, the retailer's central warehouse has already become the most important node in the grocery distribution system.

Since 1960, gross capital expenditure by retailers has grown, in real terms, by approximately 170 per cent (Dawson, 1983). Official statistics on retail investment do not distinguish between shops and warehouses. The 1978/9 survey of grocery multiples established, however, that most of these firms' investment in central warehousing had been fairly recent. Roughly 90 per cent of the 66 warehouses they operated had been newly opened or taken over since 1960, over half of them since 1970. To these warehouses must be added those set up over this period by 'third party' distribution contractors partly or wholly for the use of supermarket chains. J. Sainsbury, for example, supplements its own distribution operation with storage and delivery services provided by outside contractors (Barber and Payne, 1976). It is estimated that, overall, supermarket chains possess (or rent) around 850,000 square metres of warehouse floorspace, roughly one square metre for every 3.2 square metres of retail floorspace in their shops.

REASONS FOR MULTIPLE RETAILERS DEVELOPING THEIR OWN DISTRIBUTION SYSTEMS

Multiple retailers have several motives for channelling supplies through their own warehouses. These motives will be considered under eight headings:

1. *Buying Terms:* By receiving goods in bulk loads into their warehouses multiple retailers can qualify for bulk discounts (usually of 1–2 per cent of selling price). These discounts are never large enough, however, to finance multiples' warehouse and transport operations, which are estimated to average around 3–4 per cent of turnover (Thorpe and Shepherd, 1977). To justify incurring the additional distribution costs, the multiple retailer must, therefore, benefit from centralised delivery in other ways. These are listed below.

2. *Minimum order restrictions:* In some cases, distribution via central warehouse is made necessary by a manufacturer's refusal to deliver less than a certain amount direct to the store. Some alternative channel is needed, therefore, to provide small branch stores with supplies in amounts of less than this. (Larger chains often wield sufficient bargaining power, however, to force manufacturers into waiving minimum drop-size restrictions for their smaller branches.)

3. *Product availability:* By holding large central stocks and operating their own store delivery, retailers can reduce the risk of 'stock-outs' (i.e., shops being out of stock in particular products). By offering more frequent deliveries, they can reduce lead times and accelerate the replenishment of fast-moving lines.

4. *Stock control:* The profitability of retailing is critically dependent on the rate of 'stock-turn'. This is defined as the ratio of annual sales to the value of stocks held at the end of the financial year. It is important,

therefore, not only to maximise sales, but also to minimise stock levels. The centralisation of inventory reduces the total volume of stock that must be held to ensure a given level of service (Maister, 1976). In addition to this, stockholding can be more easily monitored and controlled when it is centralised (Millar, 1983). Where delivery is direct from the manufacturer, it is usually the store manager who decides how much to order. This dispersal of responsibility for ordering is particularly inefficient in a trade, such as the grocery trade, where product lines abound and differ greatly in their turnover rates.

5. *Use of shop space:* By relieving shops of the need to hold large amounts of stock, much of the space otherwise used for storage can be used as selling space, thereby raising the productivity of the retail floorspace. It is more cost-effective to concentrate stocks in central warehouses located in peripheral areas where site costs are lower.

6. *Labour costs:* These costs comprise around 50 per cent of average supermarket operating costs (Dawson, 1982). According to one large supermarket chain these labour costs can be disaggregated as follows:

Management 10 per cent
Customer service 10 per cent
Checkout 30 per cent
Goods handling (i.e. unloading vehicles, shelf filling, price marking) 40 per cent
Personnel/miscellaneous 10 per cent

Of these activities, management and goods handling, together representing around half the total labour costs, can benefit most from centralised distribution. In the case of management, less of the manager's time need be spent meeting sales representatives, drawing up orders and processing invoices. Madigan (1980) describes the case of one supermarket at which 79 separate calls were made by salesmen, taking up 26 hours of the manager's time and requiring the processing of 79 invoices. Goods handling can also be rationalised by the arrival of supplies in fewer, larger loads. The scope for rationalisation of this type was indicated by a survey of deliveries to a supermarket in Edgware. Fifty per cent of this supermarket's supplies arrived in the form of large consolidated loads from a central warehouse and took 45 minutes to off-load. The remainder came in 132 small drops directly from suppliers and took in total around 25 hours to unload. The GLC Freight Unit (Greater London Council, 1975) also quotes an example of a supermarket receiving 60 per cent of its throughput from a central warehouse in five consolidated deliveries (average load size = 740 cases). The remaining 40 per cent was received in 95 direct deliveries from suppliers (average load size = 26 cases). The extent of possible cost and time savings from consolidation have been indicated by Kirby (1975). He notes that one order of 500 packs is 31 per cent cheaper and 47 per cent quicker to assemble and unload than five orders of 100 packs.

7. *Security:* It is widely acknowledged that the loss of stock through theft (euphemistically termed 'shrinkage') correlates closely with the number of separate deliveries to the shop and 'number of times the back door is opened'. By greatly reducing the number of deliveries and making it possible to supervise the delivery operation more closely, the centralisation of deliveries can significantly reduce pilferage.
8. *Product range:* Many suppliers are too small to be able to offer direct delivery economically. This is particularly true in the recently developed frozen food industry. By making it possible for the small supplier to deliver in bulk to a central warehouse, the multiple retailer is able to include more specialised goods and lesser brands in his product range.

VARIATIONS IN THE PROPORTION OF CENTRALISED DELIVERIES BETWEEN CHAINS

Despite the numerous advantages of centralised delivery, firms differ widely in the proportion of turnover they channel through their central warehouse(s) (Figure 1). This is a variation that many people within the trade find baffling. Walters (1976) lightheartedly suggests that there are as many views on why this should be so as there are retailers. The variation is sometimes ascribed rather vaguely to differences in 'business philosophy' or 'trading behaviour', expressions that need clarification.

FIGURE 1

VARIATIONS IN THE PROPORTION OF TURNOVER CHANNELLED THROUGH CENTRAL WAREHOUSE BY GROCERY MULTIPLES (1978–9)

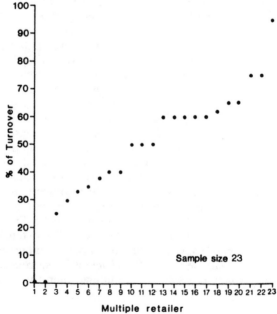

Thorpe *et. al.* (1973) identify eight factors thought to influence the choice of distribution strategy: number, dispersal, size of branch stores, growth history, commodity mix, vertical integration, sales density and site costs. They do not adequately explain the role of these factors, however, and represent the relationships between them and the level of centralised delivery in a series of graphs, several of which show trends that are neither self-evident nor substantiated by empirical evidence. These variables will be considered under five major headings:

1. *Number and size of shops:* There is no significant relationship between the number of shops in a chain and the proportion of centralised deliveries (Figure 2). The number of shops and their sizes (measured in turnover) will together determine the aggregate turnover that will have to exceed a certain threshold level to justify the establishment of a central warehouse. As all the retailers surveyed were large enough to operate at least one central warehouse, it is not possible here to comment on the minimum viable size of a centralised delivery system but above a possible lower size limit, there is no significant relationship between the degree of centralisation and turnover (Figure 3).

FIGURE 2

PROPORTION OF TURNOVER CHANNELLED THROUGH CENTRAL WAREHOUSE
AND NUMBER OF BRANCH STORES (1978–9)

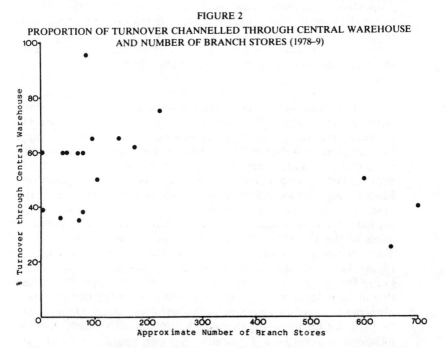

The relationship between the proportion of centralised delivery and the sizes of shop in the chain is complicated by the fact that most chains comprise shops varying widely in size (measured both in floorspace and turnover). Despite this, most chains claim to standardise the

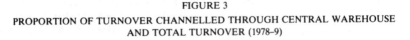

FIGURE 3
PROPORTION OF TURNOVER CHANNELLED THROUGH CENTRAL WAREHOUSE
AND TOTAL TURNOVER (1978–9)

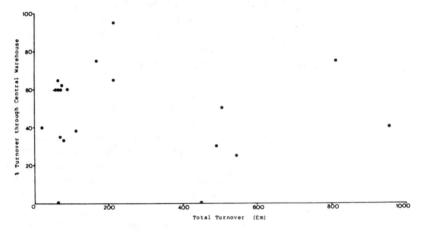

proportion of supplies each store receives from the central warehouse.
While the shop size profile is likely to influence the level at which this
proportion is standardised, in the absence of shop floorspace and
turnover data it is not possible to test this relationship. Nevertheless, it
should be noted that some chains, notably those that include superstores, do vary the proportion of warehouse delivery with shop size.

2. *Spatial distribution of shops: Thorpe et al.* (1973) suggest that the level
of centralised delivery falls with increasing dispersal of branch stores.
Although not made explicit, this suggestion is probably based on the
reasoning that more dispersed chains would be more costly to supply
from a central warehouse (for a given level of service). This would be
particularly so where shops lay beyond the daily range of a delivery
vehicle. Deliveries beyond this range, however, are very exceptional.
Most chains with a centralised grocery delivery system have all their
branches within the daily delivery range. A survey of eight chains by
the author revealed that 94 per cent of their branches were within 100
miles of the central warehouse that supplied them (see Figure 4).
These chains were much more compact than that of Asda (firm 9 in
Figure 4) whose superstores were not dependent on a central warehouse for grocery deliveries. The spread of Asda superstores shows
that its store location policy has not been constrained by the need for
branches to be within easy reach of a central warehouse (Jones, 1981).
In 1978, for example, Asda opened stores in such widely dispersed
locations as Aberdeen, Plymouth, Norwich and Birkenhead (Asda
Annual Report, 1979). The spatial distribution of branch stores is,
therefore, partly related to whether or not the firm operates centralised distribution. There is no evidence to show, however, that in the
case of those multiples that engage in centralised distribution (firms

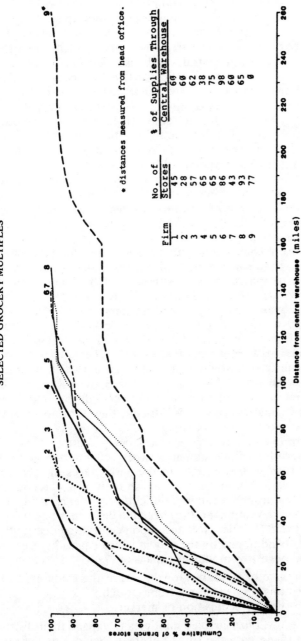

FIGURE 4
DISTANCES FROM CENTRAL WAREHOUSES TO BRANCH STORES:
SELECTED GROCERY MULTIPLES

* distances measured from head office.

Firm	No. of Stores	% of Supplies Through Central Warehouse
1	45	60
2	28	60
3	57	62
4	65	38
5	65	75
6	86	98
7	43	60
8	93	65
9	77	0

Distance from central warehouse (miles)

Cumulative % of branch stores

1–8 Figure 4), there is a significant relationship between the proportion of centralised deliveries and the dispersal of branch stores. Figure 4 shows the cumulative proportion of branch stores over increasing distances from the central warehouses that supply them. In the case of the eight firms sampled there is little relationship between the configuration of these cumulative frequency curves and the proportions of supplies received from central warehouse. A widely dispersed chain such as 7 with stores scattered widely up to a distance of 140 miles from the central warehouse can achieve the same level of centralised delivery (60 per cent) as a very compact chain, such as 1 with all its stores concentrated within a 50-mile radius of the central warehouse. No evidence was found, therefore, to support the contention of Thorpe *et al.* (1973) that the importance of centralised delivery declines gradually with increased dispersal of branch stores.

At a smaller spatial scale, Thorpe *et al.* (1973) claim that shop occupancy costs will affect the relative use of central warehouses. Chains composed of stores located in town centres, where site costs are high, might be likely to make heavier use of central warehouses, reducing the amount of premium space in shops devoted to storage. By comparison, chains of neighbourhood stores, for example, would not be under the same pressure from retail site costs to centralise stocks in a peripheral depot. Although all the chains with highly centralised distribution in the survey (affecting in excess of 75 per cent of their turnover) were 'high street' retailers, it is difficult to confirm this hypothesis, for several reasons. First, several of the chains operated stores in different parts of the urban area. Second, site costs can vary as much between urban areas as within them. To test this hypothesis rigorously, one would require site cost data which most firms are reluctant to provide. Third, the siting of a store is usually closely related to its size, neighbourhood stores generally being smaller than 'high street' supermarkets. It is difficult, therefore, to separate the effects of size from those of siting.

3. *Growth history:* As they have grown, grocery multiples have differed in their allocation of investment between retail outlets and the supporting system of distribution. In the early stages of their growth, those multiples which failed to establish their own warehousing and transport facilities often ran into difficulties (Jefferys, 1954). In later stages of their development, they began to differ in the emphasis they placed on these facilities. Reliance upon centralised distribution has been partly conditioned by the way in which chains have expanded. There have been two modes of expansion.

(a) Organic or 'unitary growth: where the chain expands gradually by setting up new stores from scratch.

(b) Growth by acquisition or merger.

Organic growth has enabled multiples to expand their distribution facilities in phase with the spread of their chains. It is not possible, however, to expand the capacity of these facilities gradually in line with the addition of individual shops, as a central warehouse represents a large indivisible investment. A newly opened central warehouse will have excess capacity to accommodate future growth in turnover and, possibly, plans to centralise the delivery of more products. Bowen and Mundy (1972) have suggested that firms take advantage of this situation to centralise the delivery of a higher proportion of their supplies. As turnover increases, they argue, this proportion is gradually reduced until it reaches the minimum level acceptable to the firm. Warehouse capacity would then be expanded and the same cycle would be repeated. This implies that the proportion of a chain's supplies passing through central warehouse(s) fluctuates through time. Most of the retail chains surveyed by the author claimed that the trend over the previous decade had been towards increasing the proportion of supplies coming through central warehouse and that in many cases this proportion had stabilised (McKinnon, 1984). It is very unusual for suppliers to be asked to revert to direct branch store delivery. The one major instance of this happening was in the aftermath of Tesco's Checkout campaign when the firm's distribution system became seriously overstretched in a very short time (Powell, 1978). If the evolutionary process that Bowen and Mundy describe were widespread, suppliers would be regularly called upon by multiples to switch their deliveries from shops to warehouses and *vice versa*, causing much disruption to their distribution operations. There is little evidence, however, of this occurring in practice (McKinnon, 1984). Bowen and Mundy's idealised model also presupposes that the chain grows gradually and organically, when in fact very few chains have developed entirely in this way: only two, for example, out of a sample of 23 (McKinnon, 1984). The remainder have grown partly and in varying degrees by acquisition.

The scale of an acquisition can vary enormously from the purchase of a single shop to that of a chain of hundreds of shops complete with supporting distribution system. Usually, small numbers of shops can be quite easily integrated into the existing system of distribution. Larger scale take-overs, however, have usually been followed by a process of rationalisation. This often entails the closure of many of the smaller stores in the acquired chain. These need not all be small, unprofitable stores. Where the areas served by the acquiring and acquired chains overlap, it is necessary to eliminate competitive stores. The geography of the chains can, therefore, be radically altered by such a take-over, making it essential to reorganise the system of centralised distribution. This reorganisation can, in many cases, be complicated by the associated acquisition of a central warehouse or warehouses. There have been several instances in the past decade of central warehouses either being sold off separately or being disposed of following the acquisition of a chain. However, roughly a third of the central warehouses operated by a sample of 23 grocery multiples were obtained through the acquisition of chains. The integration of these warehouses into the acquiring firm's existing distribution network has sometimes been further complicated by the fact that the chains they previously supplied provided a significantly different level of central-ised delivery. All this has made it difficult for those chains growing principally by acquisition to plan carefully the long term development of a centralised system of delivery. It is not surprising, therefore, that those large national chains that have expanded mainly by acquisition over the past 20 years channel a significantly smaller proportion of supplies through their central warehouses than chains characterised by a long period of organic growth.

4. *Investment Priorities:* In deciding how to allocate investment between shops and supporting distribution facilities, multiple retailers must exercise their commercial judgment. Clearly firms differ in the amount of importance they attach to central warehousing. The fact that retailers with markedly different distribution policies can co-exist, and indeed compete effectively, in the same trade suggests either that there is no single optimum level of centralised delivery or that profita-bility is not particularly sensitive to the nature of the shop supply system.

5. *Commodity Mix:* The overall proportion of supplies passing through the central warehouse is the net result of the retailer's reception policies for many different classes of product. As some product classes are more suited to centralised handling by the retailer than others, the relative importance of central warehouse deliveries will depend upon the range of goods stocked and their relative contribution to total turnover.

   Some products, such as imported and own-label goods, are typically distributed via central warehouse (Thorpe *et. al.,* 1973). There is a reasonably close correlation between the contribution of own-label sales to total turnover and the proportion of supplies channelled through central warehouse. The decision on which of the remaining products to take through central warehouse is usually based on a consideration of criteria such as value density, rate of turnover, perishability, ease of handling and product compatibility.

CONCLUSION

By acquiring or expanding warehousing facilities and lorry fleets, multi-ple retailers have been able to take on much of the responsibility for localised storage and shop delivery that previously rested with producers and wholesalers. They have had numerous incentives for extending their control back along the distributive channel. Retailers, nevertheless, dif-fer widely in the degree to which they have developed their own systems of distribution. These differences cannot be explained simply in relation to total sales, the sizes and turnover of branch stores or the geographical extent of the chain. They appear to be closely related to differences in the way chains have grown, the investment preferences of their management and the composition of their turnover, all of which are inter-related. As far as the grocery trade is concerned, it is very difficult to generalise about multiple retailers' involvement in distribution 'upstream' of the shop and it is not possible to predict the level of centralised delivery on the basis of retail parameters such as turnover, shop numbers and average shop size. There is no easy way, therefore, of making up for the failure of distribution statistics to differentiate shop-based from warehouse-based activities where these activities are under the control of a single firm. So long as the present system of statistical accounting remains in force, shifts in the responsibility for storage and shop delivery between producers, wholesalers and retailers will remain difficult to monitor and the scale of investment in intermediate distributive facilities between factory and shop will be very hard to assess.

REFERENCES

Barber, N.C.F. and L.S. Payne, 1976, *The Distribution Company's Role in Retailing*, paper presented to the Centre for Physical Distribution Management National Conference, London.

Bowen, D.J. and P.C. Mundy, 1972, *Warehouse and Transport Specialist*, paper presented at Institute of Grocery Distribution Seminar on Distribution Systems, London.

Dawson, J.A., 1982, *Commercial Distribution in Europe*, London: Croom Helm.

Dawson, J.A. 1983, 'Trends in Capital Expenditure in the Distributive Trades – A Note', *Service Industries Journal*, Vol.3, No.1.

Greater London Council, 1975, *A Note on Retail Distribution and Options for Reducing Vehicle Mileage*, London: London Freight Conference Background Paper No.9.

Institute of Grocery Distribution, 1982, *Grocery Distribution 1982*, Letchmore Heath: IGD.

Institute of Grocery Distribution, 1983, *Grocery Distribution 1983*, Letchmore Heath, IGD

Jefferys, J.B., 1950, *Distribution of Consumer Goods*, London: Cambridge University Press.

Jefferys, J.B., 1954, *Retail Trading in Great Britain*, London: Cambridge University Press.

Jones, P., 1981, 'Retail Innovation and Diffusion – The Spread of ASDA Stores', *Area*, Vol.13, No.3.

Kirby, D.A., 1975, 'The Small Shop in Britain', *Town and Country Planning*, Vol.43, No.11

McKinnon, A.C., 1984, *The Spatial Organization of Physical Distribution in the Food Industry*, unpublished Ph.D. thesis, University of London.

Madigan, M., 1980, 'Small Food Firms Fight for Survival', *Retail and Distribution Management*, Sept./Oct.

Maister, D., 1976, 'Centralization of Inventories and the 'Square Root Law', *International Journal of Physical Distribution*, Vol.6, No.3.

Millar, J.L., 1983, 'Distribution in Multiple Food Retailing', in J.F. Malcolm (ed.), *The Changing Distribution and Freight Transport System in Scotland*, Glasgow: Centre for Urban and Regional Research.

Pettit, D., 1983, 'Trends in Distribution/Delivery Operations', in J. Gattorna (ed.), *Handbook of Physical Distribution Management*, 3rd ed., London: Gower.

Powell, J., 1978, 'How Tesco Came Close to Break Down', *Retail and Distribution Management*, July/Aug.

Robson, A., 1983, *Physical Distribution Seminar*, Letchmore Heath: Institute of Grocery Distribution.

Thorpe, D., D.A. Kirby, and P. Thompson, 1973, *Channels and Costs of Grocery Distribution*, Manchester: Retail Outlets Research Unit, Manchester Business School.

Thorpe, D. and P.M. Shepherd, 1977, *Some Aspects of Economies of Scale in Food Retailing, with Special Reference to Two Superstores,* Manchester: Retail Outlets Research Unit, Manchester Business School.
Walters, D., 1976, *Futures for Physical Distribution in the Food Industry,* Farnborough: Saxon House.

This chapter first appeared in *The Service Industries Journal,* Vol.5, No.2 (1985).

5
Leadership and Change in British Retailing 1955–84

ALAN B. THOMAS

From the mid-nineteenth century until the early 1950s the development of the retail sector in Britain was marked by steady evolutionary change centred on the expansion of multiple trading. But since the Second World War, radical changes in the retail environment have led to the emergence of new forms of retail operation which denote a distinct break with the past. This article traces corresponding changes in the leadership of some of the largest firms in the sector, and suggests that these changes have played an important part in the post-war transformation of British retailing.

The structure of the retail industry in Britain has undergone a significant transformation during the post-war period. A complex set of legislative, social and economic changes have occurred since 1945 which have exerted strong pressures on traditional modes of retailing. Consequently, there have been important changes in the numbers and types of retail outlet, in market concentration, in the strategies and structures of large firms, and in the national and international spread of retail businesses, to mention only a few of the more noticeable developments. In addition, the period has seen the creation and diffusion of new retailing forms. Whether seen as a period of steady transformation [Bamfield, 1980] or as one of revolutionary change [Alexander, 1988], there can be little doubt that the retail sector has altered markedly in the last few decades.

Although the significance of environmental changes as initiators of change in retail practices has been widely noted, the means whereby they have been translated into impacts on individual firms have seldom been examined. Yet much of the literature on strategic management suggests that the key mediating factor linking environmental changes to organisational responses is the organisation's leadership [Chandler, 1962; Miles and Snow, 1978; Porter, 1980]. This article therefore aims to examine the contribution of leadership change in the large-firm sector to the more general changes in retailing which have occurred in post-war Britain and so add a further dimension to our understanding of the contemporary retailing revolution.

THE CHANGING CONTEXT

Because of the complex and interrelated nature of the pressures that have been exerted upon British retailing since the Second World War, it is difficult to give a straightforward account of the sequence of developments and their effects. But it seems clear that these pressures have been felt with varying intensity at different times, and that they have tended to accumulate during specific periods. Taking the post-war decades as a whole, it seems that many of the most significant pressures first emerged in the late 1960s and early 1970s.

One of the most important changes in the structure of retailing has been the growth of multiple store groups and the emergence of giant retail concerns which have increasingly come to dominate retail trading [Akehurst, 1983]. These firms rank among the largest of those engaged in any sector of economic activity. By virtue of their enhanced market power and because of their adoption of innovative strategies and structures, giant retail concerns, and especially the grocery retailers, have tended to become the dynamos of change in the retail sector as a whole [Davies et al., 1984].

The growth of large-scale retailing has had a significant impact on both consumers, manufacturers and smaller-scale retailers. From the mid-nineteenth century until the Second World War retail development was essentially evolutionary, centred upon expansion of the multiple shop form [Jefferys, 1954]. But the 1960s saw the growth of the superstore and the hypermarket, pioneered by the large grocery retailers, and the eventual establishment of the out-of-town, one-stop shopping operation. The widespread adoption of these more cost-effective and competitive forms has led to a growing concentration of activity in the hands of giant firms and major changes in retail structure.

The growth of the large multiples has been accompanied by a substantial decline in shop numbers, most noticeably among the independents. This decline was particularly marked during the 1970s. Between 1961 and 1978 the number of retail outlets fell by nearly 30 per cent but 80 per cent of this decline took place between 1971 and 1978 [Bamfield, 1980]. From the mid-1960s there was a considerable expansion in the size of the larger stores operated by the multiples, particularly in the grocery trade. Dawson and Kirby [1977] noted that during the 1960s radical changes in managerial, technical and operating methods were much in evidence in the grocery sector. Self-service, which had begun to be established in the 1950s, spread quickly as did the supermarket form. Supermarket numbers grew from 80 in 1957 to 2,700 in 1966 and 6,200 in 1978 [Bamfield, 1980]. Similarly, following the establishment of the first superstore in 1967, numbers grew rapidly reaching 138 by 1979 [Alexander, 1988]. Thus this period saw the emergence and rapid spread of the root forms of today's out-of-town hypermarket and the sharpening decline of the independent and Co-operative sectors.

Underlying these changes has been a growth in competition and a concern to improve labour productivity. The period from 1945 until the early 1970s seems to have been relatively benign. Rising living standards engendered an 'era of optimism' in retailing [Doyle and Cook, 1979], but as the 1970s progressed the retail sector encountered increasingly hostile conditions. Between 1963 and 1970 retail sales volume grew by 16 per cent but over the next eight years it declined to 9 per cent while costs escalated rapidly. Growing pressure to increase turnover came at a time when the opportunities to do so were declining, partly because of low growth in the economy as a whole. Retail sales were declining as a proportion of consumer expenditure.

The need to control costs and an increase in competitive intensity were fuelled by two legislative developments. The abolition of Resale Price Maintenance in 1964 and the imposition of Selective Employment Tax in 1966 both helped to encourage rationalisation and the adoption of retailing methods which economised on labour. These pressures were intensified by two further developments, the rise of 'consumerism' and the implementation of price-control policies.

The growth of government intervention in economic affairs had an increasingly direct and significant effect on the behaviour of firms in the 1960s and 1970s, but for much of the 1960s the retail sector was insulated to a considerable degree from the impact of government legislation. Trades union legislation, for example, was of marginal significance to retailing because of the low level of unionisation among retail employees. Of greater potential significance was price regulation, but the Prices and Incomes Board, set up by the Labour government in 1965 and subsequently abolished by the Heath administration in 1970, had only advisory powers and was therefore largely ineffective [Lapping, 1970]. However, price control was re-established in 1973 with the formation of the Pay Board and Prices Commission. Unlike the Prices and Incomes Board, this unit had direct power to make rulings on pay and price matters [Livesey, 1979; McKie and Cook, 1974].

The rise of the consumer interest was also one of the significant develop-ments of the 1970s. Consumer protection was covered by the Trades Description Acts (1968, 1972), the Fair Trading Act (1973) and the Consumer Credit Act (1974), all of which placed additional legal con-straints on retailers. These legal changes, together with a move by the Heath government to establish a tripartite system of economic manage-ment which included the CBI and the TUC but which ignored the recently established Retail Consortium, encouraged the retailers to develop their hitherto fragmentary links with government. As Grant and Marsh ob-served [1974, 1977], it was in the early 1970s that the retail sector began to emerge from its position of political obscurity.

These accumulating pressures reached a peak with the onset of the first oil crisis. In the autumn of 1973 the Arab oil-producers announced major fuel-supply restrictions in the wake of the Arab–Israeli War. Fuel prices increased dramatically. Together with the then current domestic difficulties, the oil crisis led to acute problems for British industry. The effects on the retail sector can be gauged from the comments of some of the chairmen of the major retail firms in the Annual Reports of the day. One wrote that 'the introduction of V.A.T. [Value Added Tax], the Government's emergency measures, the three-day working week, rail and coal-mining disputes, the oil crisis and shortages and increased prices of materials all contributed to the problems faced in 1973 and into 1974.' Another chairman summed up the situation by saying that 'there can be few, if any, years since the War when the economy of the country has been faced by so many difficulties. . .'

In response to these hostile conditions, retail stock prices fell heavily. The *Financial Times* Stores Index fell 20 points between November and December 1973 and continued to fall until January 1975 by which time the full effects of the oil crisis had been felt. The movement of the index reflected the falling profits of the retailers which declined precipitously in real terms in the aftermath of the crisis. Following the second oil crisis in late 1979, the Stores Index again fell sharply, losing 36 points between October and November of that year. By the early 1980s there were signs of recovery, but trading conditions remained difficult. As the chairman of one leading retail firm put it in 1980: 'It has been a difficult trading year with high unemployment. Our customers have had to face greatly increased costs of such items as lighting and heating, transport, mort-gages, rent and rates, leaving less money available for high-street shop-ping.'

The period running from late 1960s and early 1970s can therefore be marked out as one in which the retail sector was faced by a series of major, new challenges; inflationary pressures, rising labour costs, growing competition, increasing legislative constraints and the emergence within the grocery sector of the supermarket and superstore forms. Such changes pointed to the need for innovative responses from the leaders of retail firms and a break with the traditional assumptions that had governed retailing during the immediate post-war years.

THE CHANGING LEADERS

One important way in which an organisation adapts to changes in its environment is by changing its leaders. As recent events in Eastern Europe have shown so dramatically, leaders who are committed to the perpetuation of traditional policies and assumptions in spite of their irrelevance to modern conditions may well find themselves deposed or worse. Alternatively, while the leaders may continue to prosper, the institutions they head may not. Leadership change, or lack of it, may therefore have important consequences.

Both anecdotal evidence and systematic research suggest that the appointment of new corporate leaders has often been associated with substantial organisational changes. As in some other industries, retailing has had its roster of 'stars', renowned for their personal impact on their firms, ranging from Sir Charles Clore in the 1950s to George Davies and Sir Ralph Halpern in the 1980s. In addition, Channon's [1978] research showed that the process of organisational change in large service corporations tended to be discontinuous. Periods of gradual, evolutionary development tended to be punctuated by relatively rapid shifts in strategy and structure, and these shifts were almost always preceded by a change in the firm's top leadership.

Of course, a firm's leaders may change for many reasons. Retirements, for example, necessitate the appointment of replacements irrespective of the conditions facing the firm. Turnover among leading personnel is therefore a normal feature of organisational life. But leadership changes may also be induced during periods of crisis or when a firm encounters, or anticipates, adverse conditions. Whether occurring suddenly, as with the oil crisis, or as a consequence of more gradual cumulative shifts in the state of the environment, the onset of threatening conditions tends to increase the likelihood of leader change [Schendel et al., 1976; Mills, 1981]. To what extent, then, has the post-war transformation of the retailing environment been accompanied by changes in the leadership of retail firms, especially those giant companies which have achieved a growing market dominance?

The Leadership Study

To address this question details of the boards of directors of twelve of the largest British retail firms were obtained from the *Stock Exchange Year-book* for each year between 1955 and 1984. Because the aim was to relate changes in the boards of large firms to environmental changes over a 30 year period, the intention was to select only those firms which qualified as very large throughout the period.

Retail firms were selected if they appeared among the first 200 firms listed by turnover in the *Times 1000* listings for both 1975–76 and 1984–85. In all, nineteen retail firms were ranked within the top 200 in each year, but only twelve were listed in both years. Of these, nine were among the largest 200 firms in *The Times* listing for 1964–65 (the earliest available) although there the ranking is by capital employed rather than turnover. A similar listing issued by the Board of Trade in 1957 included eight of the firms. Most of the companies can therefore be taken to have been among the largest firms engaged in retailing throughout the period.[1]

The allocation of firms to industry categories can be problematic, particularly when they are large and diversified. For the purpose of this study a firm was judged to be active in retailing on the basis of the description of its activities given in the *Stock Exchange Yearbook* for 1975–76 and 1984–85 and upon its classification in the *Financial Times International Yearbook* for 1975–76 and the Capel Cure Myers *Retail Data Book* for 1984–85. Foreign-owned firms, such as C&A, were excluded, as were the Co-operative societies and companies engaged principally in leisure services, catering and motor vehicle distribution.

Changes in Board Size

One way of changing the structure of a firm's leadership is by altering the number of seats at the boardroom table. By increasing the board's size new blood can be brought in quickly without having to await the departure of current members although this may be at the cost of creating a larger and hence more unwieldy group. Failure to adopt an appropriate size of board may indeed have serious consequences. In a study of American retailing firms, Chaganti *et al.* [1985] found that those with smaller boards were more prone to bankruptcy.

Figure 1 depicts the trend in the size of the retail boards between 1955 and 1984. This shows a long-term tendency for board size to increase. On average, the boards had grown by 50 per cent over the period with a rise in the total number of directors in post from 101 to 145. Thus by 1984 an additional place in the boardroom had been created for every two places

FIGURE 1

MEAN BOARD SIZE FOR TWELVE LARGE RETAIL FIRMS 1955–84

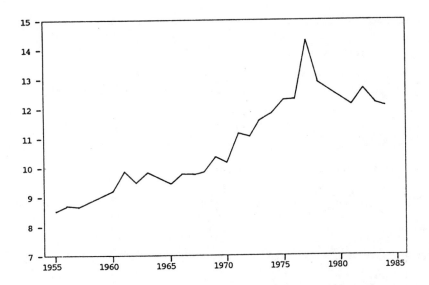

that had been available in 1955. However, there were some noticeable differences among the firms.

The boards of two of the firms (John Lewis and Associated Dairies) hardly changed size at all, two grew steadily over the years (Sainsbury and Tesco) and the remainder generally grew rapidly during a relatively brief period. The latter pattern is exemplified by Marks and Spencer. After an 18-year period during which the board had eleven or twelve members, the board's size nearly doubled. In a single year the membership grew from eleven to 19 and remained much larger than previously for the rest of the period. A similar pattern of rapid growth appeared for the remaining firms, with one exception: Debenham's board decreased in size during the early 1970s, rising again towards the end of the decade only to decline once more in the early 1980s.

In general these boards had grown significantly between 1955 and 1984. One firm's board had tripled in size, two had doubled and a further three had grown by at least 50 per cent. Furthermore, the onset of this growth was concentrated in the 1970s at a time when environmental pressures on the retail sector were intensifying.

FIGURE 2

NUMBER OF APPOINTMENTS AND DEPARTURES OF DIRECTORS OF
TWELVE LARGE RETAIL FIRMS 1955–84

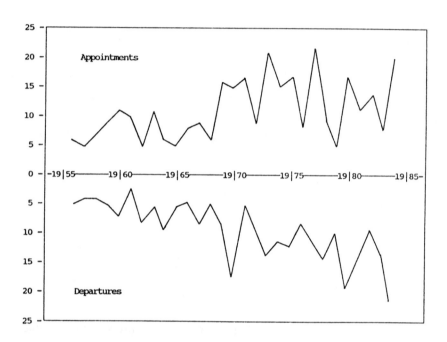

Changes in Membership

Although growth and change in board size gives some indication of the
extent of leadership change in these firms, a more significant indicator is
the degree of change in the boards' membership. Stable board size, for
example, need not imply stable membership just as fluctuations in size
may mask underlying continuities.

Figure 2 shows the patterns of recruitment and departure of directors
across the whole period. In total 322 new directors were appointed to the
boards and 280 directors retired. As can be seen, the volume of appointments and departures increased sharply in the late 1960s and continued
thereafter at a much higher rate than previously. The seven-year period
from 1969 to 1975 saw more appointments than in the previous 13 years
and almost as many departures, and between 1970 and 1974 there were
nearly twice as many appointments and departures as between 1965 and
1969 (Table 1).

TABLE 1

CHANGES IN LEADERSHIP IN TWELVE LARGE RETAIL FIRMS 1955–84

	Time period					
	55–59	60–64	65–69	70–74	75–79	80–84
Board size (mean)	8.6	9.5	9.8	11.1	12.7	12.3
Number or new directors appointed	27	43	44	77	62	69
New directors as % of total appointed	8.4	13.4	13.7	23.9	19.2	21.4
Number of directors retiring	22	36	34	58	54	75
Retirements as % of total retirements	7.9	12.9	12.2	20.8	19.4	26.9
Net membership change	+5	+7	+10	+19	+8	−6
Percentage of board appointed within previous five years (median)	22.5	33.0	32.0	54.0	39.0	35.5
Number of new chairmen appointed	4	4	5	9	3	6
Number of firms appointing new chairmen	4	3	4	8	3	6

The effect of these patterns of recruitment and retirement on the composition of the boards can be gauged from the proportion of 'new' members present at different points of time. In 1969, for example, about one-third of the members of the 'typical' board had been recruited within the previous five years, but by 1974 this had risen to over half (Table 1). By 1979 the proportion had fallen slightly to around 40 per cent and by 1984 to 35 per cent. This again points to the early 1970s as a time of intensified change in leadership.

The Chairmen

As the leading figure on the board, the chairman is of particular interest here particularly because previous work has shown that significant organisational change in service companies has typically been associated with changes of chairman [Channon, 1978].

Thirty-one new chairmen took office during the period, of whom nearly half were appointed between 1965 and 1974 (Table 1). Ten of the firms appointed at least one new chairman during these years; one of these appointed two new chairmen and another appointed three. The peak period, however, was 1970–74 when almost one-third of the total chairman appointments were made. At this time eight of the firms appointed at least one new chairman, twice as many firms doing so as at any time previously. Thus these firms were not only substantially increasing the level of turnover among their directors but also among their chairmen.

Family Representation

One consequence of these changes has been the substantial erosion of the representation of 'founding families' among the firms' leadership. The retail sector has traditionally been closely associated with family owner- ship and has been unusual in that family representation at board level tends to have persisted even when the firms have achieved 'giant' status [Stanworth and Giddens, 1974; Thomas, 1978]. Gradually, however, this family tradition seems to be withering away.

Eight of the companies studied here were headed in 1955 by a chairman who was either the founder or a relative of the founding family. This was still the case in 1969, but by 1984 two of the chairmanships had passed out of family hands (House of Fraser and Marks & Spencer) and a little later a further two firms (Associated Dairies and Tesco) appointed 'outsiders' as chairmen. The proportion of board members drawn from founding families has also declined sharply. In 1955, the median proportion of boardroom seats occupied by family members was about half. By 1969 this had fallen to one-third and by 1984 to one-fifth.

The overall position with regard to family representation has therefore changed substantially for these firms. Whereas three-quarters of the firms had been led by a founding family chairman in 1955, by the mid- 1980s three-quarters were led by 'outsiders'. At the same time, family members have made up a declining proportion of the total board membership. Such changes may well have hastened the questioning of long-standing traditions and assumptions and so contributed to innova- tion. In any event, if these trends continue it seems likely that before long, very few of these companies will have much more than a token represen- tation of their founding families on their boards and most may have none.

CONCLUSION

Taken together, these patterns of change in board size, membership recruitment and retirement, and chairman succession show that while change in the board of directors has not been unusual in the post-war years, the intensity of change grew markedly in the late 1960s and early 1970s. As was suggested earlier, this was also a time of increased environ- mental pressure and innovation in retailing.

The contribution of these leadership changes to developments in the retail sector during the last few decades cannot be assessed with any certainty. Causes and effects are difficult to disentangle. But it seems probable that the post-war 'retailing revolution' has been in part both a cause and consequence of the regeneration of the leadership of the industry's largest firms.

NOTE

1. The selected firms were: Associated Dairies, Boots, British Home Stores, Debenhams, Great Universal Stores, House of Fraser, John Lewis Partnership, Marks and Spencer, Sainsburys, Sears Holdings, Tesco and W. H. Smith.

REFERENCES

Akehurst, G., 1983, 'Concentration in Retail Distribution; Measurement and Significance', *The Service Industries Journal,* Vol.3, No.2.

Alexander, N., 1988, 'Contemporary Perspectives in Retail Development', *The Service Industries Journal,* Vol. 8, No.1.

Bamfield, J.A.N., 1980, 'The Changing Face of British Retailing', *National Westminster Bank Quarterly Review,* May.

Board of Trade, 1957, *Company Assets and Income in 1957,* London: H.M.S.O.

Capel Cure Myers, 1985, *Retail Data Bank,* London: Capel Cure Myers.

Chaganti, R.S., V. Mahajan and S. Sharma, 1985, 'Corporate Board Size, Composition and Corporate Failures in Retailing Industry', *Journal of Management Studies,* Vol. 22, No.4.

Chandler, A.D., 1962, *Strategy and Structure,* Cambridge, MA: M.I.T. Press.

Channon, D.F., 1978, *The Service Industries,* London: Macmillan.

Davies, K., C. Gilligan and C. Sutton, 1984, 'The Changing Competitive Structure of British Grocery Retailing', *Quarterly Review of Marketing,* Autumn.

Dawson, J..A. and D.A. Kirby, 1977, 'Shop Size Productivity in British Retailing in the 1960s', *European Journal of Marketing,* Vol. 11, No.4.

Doyle, P. and D. Cook, 1979, 'Marketing Strategies, Financial Structure and Innovation in UK Retailing', *Management Decision,* Vol. 17, No.2.

Financial Times, 1976, *Financial Times International Yearbook,* London: *Financial Times.*

Grant, W.P. and D. Marsh, 1974, 'The Representation of Retail Interests in Britain', *Political Studies,* Vol.22, No.2.

Grant, W.P. and D. Marsh, 1977, *The Confederation of British Industry,* London: Hodder & Stoughton.

Jefferys, J.B., 1954, *Retail Trading in Britain 1850–1950,* London: Cambridge University Press.

Lapping, B., 1970, *The Labour Government 1964–70,* Harmondsworth: Penguin.

Livesey, F., 1979, *The Distributive Trades,* London: Heinemann.

McKie, D. and C. Cook, 1974, *Election Guide,* London: Quartet.

Miles, R. and C.C. Snow, 1978, *Organisational Strategy, Structure and Process,* New York: McGraw-Hill.

Mills, G., 1981, *On the Board,* London: Gower.

Porter, M.E., 1980, *Competitive Strategy,* New York: Free Press.

Schendel, D., G.R. Patton and J. Riggs, 1976, 'Corporate Turnaround Strategies: A Study of Profit Decline and Recovery', *Journal of General Management,* Vol.3, No.3.

Stanworth, P. and A. Giddens, 1974, 'An Economic Elite: A Demographic Profile of

Company Chairmen', in P. Stanworth and A. Giddens (eds), *Elites and Power in British Society*, London: Cambridge University Press.

Stock Exchange, 1955–1984, *The Stock Exchange Yearbook*, London: Stock Exchange.

Thomas, A. B., 1978, 'The British Business Elite: The Case of the Retail Sector', *Sociological Review*, Vol.26, No.2.

Times Newspapers, 1965, 1976, 1985, *The Times 1000*, London: Times Newspapers.

This chapter first appeared in *The Service Industries Journal*, Vol.11, No.3 (1991).

6

Retailing Post-1992

by

Nicholas Alexander

This article examines the attitudes of the UK's leading retail operations to the establishment of the EC's internal market, planned for 1992, and to expansion within that market. Large UK retailers have shown an interest in markets outside the UK, particularly in North America. In 1992 a market will be created in Europe of over 300 million people. The degree of importance placed on these changes by leading UK retailers, their views on how their operation will be effected, and how they will meet the challenge of 1992, will have a significance both for retailing in the UK and for retailing throughout the EC.

INTRODUCTION

In 1992, the European Community (EC) seeks to establish an internal market free from physical, technical and fiscal barriers, and thereby produce a single market of 322 million people, 1.3 times the size of the US market. If harmonisation is successful UK retailers will find themselves a part of a newly created market over six times the size of their present home market: The opportunities of this enlarged home market, as the internal market must become if it is to be effective, represents a considerable challenge for UK retailers, as indeed does the threat of increased competition.

The considerable and rapid changes which have occurred in UK retailing in recent years bear witness to an industry capable of adapting to changing social and economic trends. The changes planned for 1992 have the potential to give leading UK retailers a better opportunity to exercise their commercial abilities in other EC countries, and also to adapt to the cultural differences the internal market cannot hope to dispel in 1992.

International or multinational retailing, while a feature of most European and, indeed, world markets, cannot yet be considered a dominant facet of retailing. However, as Kacker has noted [1983, 1985], multinational retailing has increased in recent years and has involved retailers in a greater commitment to the environment of host countries. Indeed, it is this commitment to, and appreciation of, the new environment which is crucial to multinational operations. It is important that retailers achieve a close feel for the local retail environment, which is why retailers, as Ball [1980] succinctly put it, 'traditionally stayed on their native soil'. Retailers with a poor understanding of the local environment have little to offer the customer of the host country, and will reap few rewards at best and risk considerable losses at worst.

It is not surprising that White [1984] during a brief survey of multinational retail operations, found that of only 115 companies trading in more than one European country, 66 per cent operated in only two or three countries. Belgium was the most popular market for multinational operations, followed by France and the Netherlands, Germany, Austria and the UK. On the other side of the coin, France with 31, Germany with 19, and the UK with 19 companies were home to the greatest number of multinational organisations.

Although multinational operations do exist in Europe, a situation does not exist where numerous retail operations stretch comprehensively from Norway to Italy and from Portugal to Finland. Indeed, in White's view [1984], geographical proximity has been a general rule of cross-border expansion. Nordic retailers, have, for example, tended to expand into other Nordic countries.

Nevertheless, large European retailers do display an inclination towards international operations, not least if home markets are already saturated. GB-inno-BM, Ahold, Albrecht/Aldi, Vendex International, Makro and Metro have entered other markets for this reason [de Somogyi, 1986]. Companies can also be motivated by the desire to introduce their particular retail concepts into other markets [White, 1984, de Somogyi, 1986]. Carrefour, IKEA, Marks and Spencer, Makro and Metro are operations which fall into this category [White, 1984]. Carrefour has successfully exported the hypermarket to Latin America [Burt, 1986]. Swedish retailer Ingvar Kampered has internationalised furniture retailing with IKEA [Arbose, 1985]. Albert Gubay has taken his discount food store approach to the Republic of Ireland, New Zealand and the US [Lord, Moran, Parker, Sparks, 1988]. European retailers show a propensity to internationalise, yet there remains a lack of uniformity in European retailing.

White [1984] concluded that in Europe genuine multinational operations, as opposed to internationally linked subsidiaries, would develop slowly. However, the changes planned for 1992 have the potential to faciliate business integration. Leading UK retailers, through the process of market concentration, have become powerful entities in home markets both in relation to competitors and suppliers. However, market concentration has not only occurred in the UK [White, 1984]. UK developments have been mirrored to some extent in other EC countries [Kacker, 1986]. Marks and Spencer had a turnover of £4.2

billion in 1987–88, Vendex a turnover of £0.5 billion more, Carrefour had a turnover of £1 billion more [*Times 1000*, 1987–88]. In the context of the EC UK retailers will find they face operations of comparable size. They will therefore need to address the issues raised by 1992, both in terms of EC expansion and the threat to home markets, and perhaps find it necessary to reassess their attitudes.

With the approach of the internal market, it was considered an appropriate moment to look at leading UK retailers' attitudes to the planned changes, to establish whether they consider those changes to be significant, and if those changes will encourage them to expand in the EC post-1992.

METHODOLOGY

The purpose of this survey, carried out in March–May 1988, was to gain an appreciation of major UK retailers' attitudes towards the European Community's Internal Market planned for 1992.

In all, 200 of the UK's largest retail companies were sent a questionnaire. It was not expected that all 200 companies would have operations outside the UK but that the companies canvassed, because of their size, and hence their UK market coverage, were retail companies most likely to have: (a) undertaken retail operations in other countries; (b) considered the strategic implications of operations outside the UK; (c) the potential to consider seriously continental European operations in the light of 1992.

Questionnaires were sent by post to Chief Executives, in most cases addressing the Chief Executive by name. A pilot survey was carried out and results were noted. The main survey followed, followed in turn by a reminder. The questionnaire was timed to coincide with the DTI's 1992 awareness campaign. This timing was used in order to take advantage of the high profile afforded to the issues of 1992. It was also felt that the report, of which participants were asked if they wished to receive a complimentary copy, would be of greater interest in the context of increased awareness, and might, thereby, be of some assistance in strategic planning.

In total 102 replies were received (51 per cent). Of these, 80 included a completed questionnaire (40 per cent). This may be considered an encouraging percentage for a mailed questionnaire, reflecting an interest in the issues raised by 1992. Of the 22 replies which did not contain a completed questionnaire, while most regretted an inability to participate, some replied in letter form and were, as a consequence, most informative. Indeed, some of those who completed the questionnaire also appended an informative letter, again indicating an enthusiastic response.

SIGNIFICANCE OF 1992 TO UK RETAILERS

Asked whether the creation of an internal market would be of importance to retailers, only one in every six respondents was prepared to
deny its importance to their sector of the economy. Although the
criticism may be made that retailers answering yes to such a question
were influenced not be retail factors but an economy-wide recognition
of the internal market's importance, it should be remembered that
retailers in an EC internal market will be influenced by factors not
exclusive to retailing, such as the easier flow of products and employment conditions, which cannot be considered separately. Therefore,
the fact that two-thirds of the leading UK retailers who responded
acknowledged the importance of the internal market is significant in
itself.

TABLE 1

DO YOU CONSIDER THE CREATION OF AN INTERNAL MARKET
OF IMPORTANCE TO RETAILERS?

	(n = 75)
Yes	65.8%
No	15.8%
Don't know	18.4%

TABLE 2

EFFECT OF 1992 ON RETAILERS' OWN COMPANIES

In other EC countries:	(n = 78)
Greater opportunities	53.8%
Limited opportunities	38.5%
Don't know	7.7%
In UK markets:	
Greater pressures	35.9%
Limited pressures	56.4%
Don't know	7.7%

The overall impression suggested that UK retailers did not anticipate
a sudden rush of EC retailer expansion activity in domestic markets,
while envisaging potential benefits outside the UK.

Of those companies which did not consider the internal market to be
of importance, by far the greatest number, two-thirds (66.6 per cent),
believed this was simply because the changes planned would provide
them with limited opportunities outside the UK and would not put
pressure on their home market. Of those who did consider the internal

market to be of importance, more than two-thirds (70.0 per cent) anticipated greater opportunities abroad; of these about half (48.6 per cent), did not consider undue pressure would develop in their home markets, while half (51.4 per cent), expected greater competition.

Essentially, therefore, large British retailers appear to be confident in the face of the changes planned for 1992. The danger, of course, is that confidence can lead to complacency.

UK RETAILING IN THE EC AFTER 1992

Retailers were asked if they were more likely to enter, or expand their presence, in other EC countries as a result of 1992. Nearly half said they would (see Table 3). Of respondents who said that internal market was important to retailers, two-thirds (64 per cent), said that they were more likely to enter, or expand their operation in, the EC; 42.1 per cent of all companies therefore agreed that the internal market was of importance to retailers and that their company, as a result of the planned changes, would be more likely to enter or expand in the EC.

TABLE 3
WOULD YOUR COMPANY BE MORE LIKELY TO ENTER, OR EXPAND ITS
PRESENCE IN, OTHER EUROPEAN COMMUNITY COUNTRIES AS A RESULT OF
THE CHANGES PLANNED FOR 1992?

	(n = 78)
Yes	47.5%
No	38.5%
Don't know	14.1%

The previous question, however, only gave an impression of absolute attitudes toward the EC and did not indicate if 1992 would make the EC the most attractive area of expansion for UK retailers, an important question in the light of UK retailers' past interest in the North American market. Asked whether the EC post-1992 would be the most attractive area for expansion, again half said that it would (see Table 4).

TABLE 4
WITH THE CREATION OF AN INTERNAL MARKET WOULD YOU CONSIDER THE
EUROPEAN COMMUNITY THE MOST ATTRACTIVE AREA OF EXPANSION
OUTSIDE THE UK?

	(n = 78)
Yes	50.0%
No	32.1%
Don't know	17.9%

Of retailers who said the internal market was important to their sector, just over half (54 per cent) said that they would consider the EC the most attractive area for expansion; therefore, a third (35.5 per cent) of all the companies agreed that the internal market was of importance to retailers and their company would, as a result of the planned changes, consider the EC the most attractive area for expansion.

TABLE 5

COMPANIES WITH CURRENT EXPANSION PLANS

	(n = 80)
EC (excl UK) and Non-EC countries	20.0%
EC only (excluding UK)	21.3%
Non-EC countries only	7.5%
No plans	51.3%

These last three questions dealt with attitudes to expansion in the EC and other world markets. Retailers were, therefore, also asked whether their company had any current plans for expansion (see Table 5). More than half (58.8 per cent) did not have plans to expand within the EC. Given the sampling frame, these retailers are a crucial group if the internal market is to have effect. Given that there are certain large retailers who will expand outside the UK regardless, it is this group, of more than half the sample, who, at the time of the survey had no current plans for expansion outside the UK, who will determine the breadth of UK retail penetration in the EC after 1992.

Table 6 shows that although there was little difference in the mean turnover of retailers who intended or did not intend to expand in Europe after 1992 there was a substantial difference between those who planned expansion outside the EC and those who did not.

The implication is that, for some of the largest UK retailers, 1992 will increase the likelihood of their expansion in the EC but the Market will not become their key foreign objective. For retailers who are not among the largest operations, 1992 will increase the likelihood of expansion, while smaller companies are not currently persuaded that expansion within the EC is a realistic objective. This would appear to support the contention that it is medium-sized companies who will benefit most from the internal market; that the largest companies are already active and have a strategy for expansion outside the UK, and that smaller operations will be reluctant or unable to move into Europe. Whereas, those companies who would welcome access to foreign markets, but have been unable to take advantage of them because of restrictive barriers, will be in a position after 1992 to take their operation outside the UK, either for the first time or to a greater number of locations.

TABLE 6
ATTITUDES TO EXPANSION AND MEAN TURNOVER

	Yes £m	No £m
Plans to expand in the EC	556	515
Plans to expand outside the EC	944	378
Will enter EC because of 1992	622	311
EC most attractive area for expansion	434	798

HOW UK RETAILERS WILL EXPAND

It is one thing to consider the attractiveness of EC markets; it is another actively to invest, and to deal with the problems raised. Retailers have to consider strategically how this expansion is to take place, whether through the acquisition of an existing company, joint ventures with local retailers, franchises, or through the opening of new units and the establishment of a new operating structure. These different strategies are not mutually exclusive.

TABLE 7
PROBABLE RESPONSES TO COMPANY OPERATING IN EC COUNTRIES

	All (n=73)	With existing foreign outlets (n=22)	With EC expansion plans (n=30)
Acquire an existing company	46.6%	36.4%	46.7%
Form a joint enterprise with a local retailer	26.0%	18.2%	16.7%
Open new units	45.2%	54.5%	60.0%
Franchise	19.2%	27.3%	23.3%

Asked the most likely form, or forms, expansion would take, companies in the survey indicated that the opening of new units and the acquisition of existing companies were the most likely methods. Table 7 lists the responses made by all companies and compares the results with the responses made by companies with existing outlets outside the UK with those companies currently planning expansion in the EC. Although the acquisition of companies currently operating within the EC was a popular strategy, opening of new units was particularly popular among retailers with definite expansion plans. In contrast, joint enterprises with EC partners was the least favoured option among retailers with definite plans for expansion. Franchising as a means to EC expansion was considered an option by around a fifth to a quarter of retailers, and most popular among retailers with experience abroad.

UK retail development within the EC post-1992 is, therefore, most likely to take the form of company acquisition and organic growth through unit development.

The changes planned for 1992 mean that expansion within this area will not be directly comparable with expansion in non-EC markets: a new environment will have been created. In respect of the method of market penetration there are two basic considerations. First, experience in handling previous cross-border expansion will have to be adapted to the new circumstances, and second, because expansion should be easier, medium-sized companies that would not have contemplated expansion previously, will have a viable proposition before them. Therefore, it is essential that retailers are aware of the advantages and disadvantages of different methods of expansion and the suitability of different options to their kind of business and the environments in which they wish to operate, and not least the changing environment after 1992.

The administrative problems of operating a small group of outlets in a relatively small national market can be too great to justify a direct presence being maintained, as Storehouse discovered in the Netherlands [F.T., 1988]. Although, it is to be hoped the internal market will help to remove many of the administrative problems of small markets within the Community, cultural issues will still involve multinational operations with the minutiae of local circumstance. The nature of retail expansion will undoubtedly have an important impact on success rates. The UK retailers surveyed showed a considerable inclination towards acquisition and organic growth. The convenience of acquisition is of course the provision of an up and running operation with extant distribution facilities. While upgrading, adaptation and reorientation may be necessary a ready-made operation can trade from day one of EC penetration without a period of start-up development. Organic growth may then follow as appropriate geographic and socio-economic targets are identified. Organic development may of course be deemed appropriate as a means of penetration and independent of acquisition activity. The dangers with both acquisition and organic growth is that local knowledge will not be fully utilised as the parent operation establishes a predetermined and possibly unsympathetic operation.

Alternatively, if swift development is desired and capital investment in property is not considered appropriate, then franchising has its attractions, not least if the retailer is in possession of a distinct identify which will attract both franchisees and customers alike, more particularly if the retailer has strong 'own brand' products which further promotes a clear identity. The danger of franchising, of course, is that the retailer loses presence at the point of sale, despite monitoring systems which are and can be employed, while benefits include swift market coverage, reduced capital outlay, and local knowledge and environmental appreciation. Joint ventures go some way to providing the benefits of franchising. Joint ventures provide a pooling of resources and experience in what can be a rewarding exercise. Homebase is a good example of a cross-border venture of this kind, between J. Sainsbury and GB Inno BM of Belgium. The exercise has combined local operational know-how with product experience. The advantages of joint ventures may be considered to be of potential value to retailers who do not have a format and or merchandise which appears particularly relevant to a new market or which may be particularly susceptible to the nuances of a new market.

The choice and ultimate success of different methods will of course depend on the retailers' ability to implement the chosen strategy, and caution over joint ventures and franchising may well reflect a reluctance to introduce operations with which the company is unfamiliar. However, it is certainly possible to conclude that the retailers surveyed were inclined to rely on their own resources.

Inseparable from the issue of how expansion will take place is what operating format and merchandising retailers would consider appropriate to EC expansion. Although strategy may well differ within organisations between EC regions, retailers were asked to indicate their general attitude to format introduction (see Table 8). Overall, while some retailers were prepared to abandon UK format and merchandise, a large proportion were confident of the acceptability of their domestic approach.

TABLE 8

LIKELY LOCAL AND UK INFLUENCES ON FORMAT AND MERCHANDISE

	Store format	Merchandise
UK influence dominant	56.8%	51.4%
Equal UK/local influence	16.2%	14.9%
Local influence dominant	27.0%	33.8%

Neither polarity, undiluted importation nor adoption should be considered the best policy, rather an indicator of how retailers believe their UK format and merchandise is suited to other environments. In some cases, the retailer may well be advised to emphasise UK format and merchandise; in others, radically to revise it.

If retailers are broadly classified according to products sold, it soon becomes evident in which product groups retailers feel most confident about introducing UK operating formats and merchandise (see Table 9).

TABLE 9
DEGREE OF FORMAT ADOPTION

Product Category	5 = high 1 = low	n=74
Food	3.5	(15)
Mixed	2.8	(16)
Other non-food	2.6	(23)
Household and Clothing	2.2	(20)

The results show that while food and mixed retailers are prepared to take account of local practices, household and clothing retailers are prepared to introduce UK practice with only slight modifications. Other non-food retailers would adopt a *via media* bringing together UK and local practice in fairly even proportions.

In terms of merchandise introduction or adoption, the picture is broadly similar (see Table 10). Household and clothing retailers are reluctant to adopt a local input, while food retailers are considerably more likely to adapt to local conditions.

The degree to which UK retailers will be willing, or eager, to adapt their store formats and merchandise will depend to a large extent on how 'saleable' their current image would be within the EC and, as a corollary, whether they have a strong British identity which would in itself serve to differentiate and hence enhance their image.

TABLE 10
DEGREE OF MERCHANDISE ADOPTION

Product Category	5 = high 1 = low	n=26
Food	3.4	(15)
Mixed	3.0	(17)
Other non-food	2.9	(22)
Household and Clothing	1.9	(20)

Overall, 43.6 per cent of the sample considered they had a distinct British identity which could be used as a positive marketing factor in countries outside the UK. However, this figure varied between retailers operating in different product groups, with household and clothing retailers considering they had a high profile in this respect, and food and other non-food retailers considering they had a low profile (see Table 11).

TABLE 11
BRITISH IDENTITY AND PRODUCT CATEGORY

	Yes	n=78
Food	37.5%	n=16
Household & clothing	57.1%	n=21
Other non-food	37.5%	n=24
Mixed	41.2%	n=17

Retailers who said that they would have a British identity that could be used positively when marketing abroad had a mean turnover of more than twice those who said they did not: £785 million as opposed to £295 million.

It may be argued that the larger the retail operation, the higher the profile that organisation has, and, in turn, the greater the association will be with the organisation's home country. That is in itself logical, but it does not automatically follow that the association will work positively in foreign markets, and more to the point, encourage consumer spending in the outlets of that organisation. It is perhaps disturbing to see such a wide gap in mean turnover between those who did not perceive in their organisation a positive British identity and those who did. It is of concern that the rationale which lay behind many answers was not 'Can a British image be projected profitably through our outlets?' but 'We are known abroad and that will stimulate sales'. This is of concern in view of 1992. If the internal market is to benefit medium-sized organisations then it is important that these organisations fully appreciate their potential image in the market place and do not employ false logic.

PROS AND CONS OF EXPANSION

Retailers were asked to rate factors which could be considered to be inducements to EC expansion and problems of expansion. Companies were asked to rate on a scale of 1 to 5 (1=unimportant, 2 = low importance, 3 = moderate importance, 4 = high importance, 5 =

TABLE 12

INDUCEMENTS TO EC EXPANSION

1-unimportant   4-high importance
2-low importance   5-utmost importance
3-moderate importance

		n=
The size of the new market	3.7	72
The level of economic prosperity within the new market	3.7	73
Your company's operating format	3.4	73
Your company's product lines	3.4	73
The under-developed nature of retailing within the new market	3.3	72
Niche opportunities within the new market	3.3	72
Favourable operating environment, eg law, tax in the new market	2.8	72
Favourable exchange rates	2.8	71
Saturation in the home market	2.7	72
Real Estate investment potential in the new market	2.6	72
Favourable labour climate, in the new market	2.4	72
Share prices of companies within the new market	2.3	69

utmost importance) reasons for expansion and the anticipated problems of expansion. The mean score, for each factor was then calculated (see Tables 12 and 13).

The size of the new market and the level of economic prosperity within that new market were considered the most important determinants. Two-thirds of respondents considered these factors of high or utmost importance.

Respondents also rated the level of retail development and niche opportunities with the new market as significant, reflecting the importance retailers placed on their company's operating formats and product lines which were themselves considered major reasons for expansion.

Many factors which have encouraged expansion in North America, highlighted by Kacker [1983; 1985] and Ball [1980] were not stressed by retailers in respect of the EC: that is, those factors which make up the lower half (from favourable operating environment down), of the list in Table 12. This is perhaps inevitable in terms of certain factors such as labour climate, since Kacker [1983] and Ball [1980] dealt with European retailers as a homogeneous group, and in this instance the issue is intra-EC investment. It is, however, significant that other factors stressed in the North American context, such as real estate investment, should be considered relatively unimportant.

TABLE 13

PROBLEMS OF EC EXPANSION

1=unimportant   4=high importance
2=low importance   5=utmost importance
3=moderate importance

		n=
Different consumer tastes	3.7	74
Site acquisition	3.7	73
Recruitment and staffing	3.5	74
Language	3.4	72
Different competitive conditions	3.4	73
Legal and tax regulations	3.2	74
Different retail store environment.	3.1	72
Acquiring marketing information	3.1	74
Different product mixes	3.0	73
Problems associated with suppliers	3.0	74
Different social conditions	3.0	74
Currency exchange	2.8	74
Different economic conditions	2.8	74
Transportation issues	2.7	74

It is noteworthy that, while nearly a half of all respondents (46.6 per cent), considered the acquisition of existing retail operations a likely method of EC expansion, the share prices of companies in the EC were not considered to be a major reason for expansion. One-third of retailers (33.3 per cent), considered share prices to be of no importance.

The issue of a favourable operating environment (brought about by legal and tax regulations) rates a medium score, and is one of the factors highlighted by Kacker [1983; 1985] and Ball [1980]. The claustrophobic atmosphere of European trading was stressed by those writers, and was considered a key determinant of Transatlantic investment. Respondents classified the legal and tax issues in the lower half of the list, thus the European situation was rated more favourably than earlier findings would have suggested. Indeed this suggests the pessimistic picture of European retailing based on the conditions of the 1970s is less relevant than it was.

This further suggests that it will not only be the largest retail operations which will take advantage of other EC national markets after 1992, that is, operations that may be said to have exhausted UK opportunities, rather that medium sized retailers will consider, on the basis of their individual retail offering, operations in non-UK markets.

In terms of the problems of expansion within the EC, site acquisition and different consumer tastes were seen as the most important issues. In the case of site acquisition, 21.9 per cent of respondents considered the issue of the utmost importance, while 21.5 per cent considered different consumer tastes of the utmost importance. Recruitment and staffing also ranked high on the list of problems, with 20.3 per cent considering the issue to be of the utmost importance. Indeed, the problems of fundamental consideration to retailers, location, service provision, and the issues of cultural differences, were highly stressed. The issue of language, for example, ranked high on this list.

The importance assigned to the problems associated with legal and tax regulations underlines the need to remove technical and fiscal barriers within the EC. Transport problems were low on the list, but were nevertheless considered of moderate importance overall. This suggests that the problems targeted by the EC and removed by the internal market are not issues retailers consider the most important when it comes to EC expansion. Admittedly, some retailers did attach some degree of importance to them but they were not on the whole the key decision issues. However, the key issues are not of the kind that legislation would be expected to address; they are culturally and socio-economically based. Of course, as physical, technical and fiscal barriers are removed it may be argued that such barriers will be reduced as a pan-European social homogeneity emerges. However, even this argument would imply that the internal market will only indirectly address the issues large UK retailers consider most important when examining the prospects for expansion in the EC.

CONCLUSIONS

The general impression given by these results is that leading UK retailers welcome the advent of the internal market, and will respond positively to its concomitant challenges. However, this general impression demands qualification.

Leading UK retailers were positively inclined towards an EC free from physical, technical and fiscal constraints but the largest of them were not convinced the EC would necessarily represent the best international option after 1992. Significantly the smaller retailers in the survey were not convinced 1992 had much to offer them in terms of wider markets. These findings emphasise the significance of the medium-large retailer who has not as yet an extensive international operation or indeed does not have any operational units outside the UK. The EC post-1992, it would appear, represents an attractive and geographically convenient theatre for operations. This does not mean that only medium-large retailers will undertake operations in EC after 1992, but that they will be in a position where the easing of regulations will facilitate the greatest change. The largest retail operations may well undertake EC expansion, but may do so not because it represents the best or only feasible option. Some of the largest retailers may indeed feel committed to a strategy which concerns other, notably North American, markets. Expansion in North America and the EC conterminously would not only put pressure on a retailer's administrative abilities but have the potential to inflict a dangerously high gearing.

Therefore, if large retailers consider the EC, even after the establishment of an internal market, to be of secondary concern, UK retailing may well not have as great an impact, at least initially, as might otherwise be expected.

It is also noteworthy that some of the larger retailers who took part in the survey have decided upon EC expansion irrespective of 1992: this supports the belief that international retailing is emerging as a significant force and 1992 is only a benefit along a previously prescribed course.

The methods of expansion favoured by retailers, acquisition and organic developments, indicated a reluctance to devolve or share control of EC operations. Joint enterprises and franchises were not favoured options. This is perhaps surprising given retailers' preparedness to adapt UK store formats and merchandise to the local environment, and retailers' concern over the cultural, economic, and social diversity they expect to find in the EC. This would suggest either an awareness of environmental differences and a policy to counter in-house those differences, or an over-confidence in the face of perceived dangers. Time alone can answer the question and, indeed, that answer will inevitably differ from one organisation to another. Ball [1980] noted in the US context the high success rate among European acquiring organisations that allowed American managers to continue operations along American lines. If acquisition is perceived partly as a learning experience and organic development as a subsequent step, then retailers may well avoid the need for local partnerships. Of course, retailers may see acquisition merely as a means to obtain ready-made distribution facilities. The US experience may not be relevant to post-1992 EC conditions. However, if it is, then White's [1984] contention that genuine multinational operations will develop slowly will hold true despite 1992.

In conclusion, therefore, the removal of physical, technical and fiscal barriers within the EC, according to the UK's largest retailers, is likely to increase UK retailer presence in the Community but it will not remove the important cultural and socio-economic barriers which will remain important determinants of expansion strategy. Indeed, it would not be reasonable to expect 1992 to create an homogeneous market, but it remains clear that the problems uppermost in retailers' minds are based on an appreciation of the issues raised by regional diversity.

REFERENCES

Alexander, N., 1988, 'Marketing the UK's Retail Revolution 1992', *Quarterly Review of Marketing*, October.

Arbose, J., 1985, 'The Folksy Theories that Inspire Lifestyle Merchant IKEA', *International Management* (UK) Vol.40, No.11, November.

Ball, R., 1980, 'Europe's US Shopping Spree', *Fortune*, 1 December.

Burt, S., 1986, 'The Carefour Group – the first 25 years', *International Journal of Retailing*, Vol.1, No.3.
de Somogyi, J., 1986, 'Retail Planning for the Next Ten Years', *Retail & Distribution Management*, Vol.14, No.5.
Financial Times, 2 April 1988.
Kacker, M., 1983, 'Transatlantic Investment in Retailing', *The Conference Board Research Bulletin*, No.138, New York.
Kacker, M., 1985, *Transatlantic Trends in Retailing*, Quorum, CT.
Kacker, M., 1986, 'The Metamorphosis of European Retailing', *European Journal of Retailing*, Vol.20, No.8.
Lord, D., W. Moran, T. Parker, and L. Sparks, 1988, 'Retailing on Three Continents: The Discount Food Operations of Albert Gubay', *International Journal of Retailing*, Vol.3, No.3.
Times 1000, 1987, August.
White, R., 1986, 'Multinational Retailing: A Slow Advance?', *Retail & Distribution Management*, Vol.12, No.2.

This chapter first appeared in *The Service Industries Journal*, Vol.10, No.1 (1990).

7

Controls over the Development of Large Stores in Japan

by

John A. Dawson and Toshio Sato

This paper shows how public policy in Japan has reacted to the location and development of new large stores, and the pressures for large stores. The current policy, introduced in 1979, is attempting to limit the expansion of hypermarkets, large supermarkets, discount stores, etc., and provides a mechanism and procedure for the co-ordination of future growth. The structural changes occurring in Europe are also appearing in Japan. Pre-1979 policy controls are examined, as is the 1979 legislation, together with the growth strategies of large stores in the 1980s. The paper concludes by suggesting that it will be interesting to analyse in the coming years whether Japanese policy aimed at controlling large store development is any more successful than the various, largely unsuccessful, attempts at large store control introduced by European governments.

Public policy to control the location and development of new large stores exists in most European countries. These policies have been the subject of several recent studies both of the policy instruments and of the policy effects [Commission of the European Communities, 1978; Dawson, 1982a; 1982b: 291-6]. The major structural readjustment of retailing which creates the pressures for large stores is not limited to Europe and similarly European countries do not have a monopoly of control measures. The aim of this note is to show how public policy in Japan has reacted to similar problems to those faced in Europe. The current policy, introduced in 1979, is attempting to limit the expansion of large supermarkets, variety stores, discount stores and hypermarket-type operations. A general description of distribution in Japan is provided in Yoshino [1978] and Shimaguchi [1978] whilst Shimaguchi and Lazer [1979: 49-62] and Hayashi [1980: 263-73] provide more recent reviews focusing on changes in the last decade. The publications of JETRO [1978; 1979] and Murata [1973: 4-11] illustrate distribution structures for particular products and a pointer towards the major trends apparent in Japanese marketing as a whole is provided by Nakanishi [1981: 206-8].

These various studies all point to changes in distribution in Japan which are familiar to observers of European distribution. Changes in organisational structure, such as the growth of large firms, diversification, vertical

TABLE 1
SHOP NUMBERS (IN THOUSANDS) IN JAPAN

Number of employees	1970	1972	1974	1976	1979
1 or 2	940.8	927.7	907.2	999.6	1022.1
3 – 9	472.3	505.8	519.0	547.9	577.2
10 – 19	39.1	41.8	41.3	43.4	47.6
20 – 49	14.9	15.9	16.2	17.9	21.1
over 50	4.2	4.3	4.5	4.9	5.7
Total	1471.3	1495.5	1548.2	1613.8	1673.7

Source: MITI Censuses of Commerce.

integration, etc., have taken place alongside changes in sales technique, such as the introduction of self-service, the search for scale economies in establishment operation, adoption of new technology, etc. These changes in organisation and technique have been encouraged by environmental change such as an expanding suburbia, higher levels of car and other durable goods ownership, etc., and consequential conflict has been created between the new retail forms and traditional retailing. Table 1 shows the growth in shop numbers during the 1970s and, although shops of all sizes have increased in number, the increase in large stores is particularly notable because their numbers now mean a wider spatial spread than formerly. Through the 1960s there was rapid growth in supermarket and other large store types but they were heavily concentrated in the four main metropolitan areas. The Tokyo-Yokohama, Kyoto-Osaka-Kobe, Nagoya and Fukuoka-Kitakyushu regions accounted for over 75 per cent of operating supermarkets in 1970. Since 1970 growth has occurred outside these four regions and the suburbs of medium-sized cities now have large store development. Although the proportion of sales accounted for by stores employing over 50 people has remained stable at around 20 per cent of national sales throughout the 1970s, the spatial spread of new large units into expanding suburban areas has meant an increased awareness of large store sales penetration and also an increase in the conflict between new store types and traditional retailers.

PUBLIC POLICY CONTROLS

After World War II attempts to control new large store development through public policy measures began in Japan with the Department Stores Act of 1956. The law was designed to protect small and medium-sized retailers from department store competition. The main provisions of the law were that:

1. new stores had to be authorised by the Minister of International Trade and Industry;
2. the number of closing days and hours for department stores were stipulated; and
3. the provision of free customer transport to and from department stores was prohibited.

Applications for department stores, under the legislation, were considered by the Council on Department Stores which then advised the
Minister. The local business community were consulted regularly by the
Council and so commonly the advice to the Minister suggested a reduction in floorspace of the proposed store. The legislation applied to any
proposed store of over 3,000 m^2 floorspace in the seven major cities and
over 1,500 m^2 floorspace elsewhere. A strategy widely used by supermarket, variety and discount store operators to circumvent the law was to
build stores in which parts were operated by nominal subsidiary companies, such that no single company operated more than the critical
floorspace. Department stores tended not to follow this tactic and so
department store numbers were more severely curtailed by the law.
Department stores, as a consequence, have become more diversified and
have adopted management innovations in order to compete with the
increasing number of mass merchandisers.

THE 1974 LARGE SCALE RETAIL STORES ACT

The problems of the 1956 Act led to the strengthening of controls with the
1974 Large Scale Retail Stores Act. The basic rationale of the legislation
was the same as the Department Stores Act and it was protective legislation for small and medium-sized retailers. Additionally, however, there
were fears for the effect of new suburban units on the trading conditions
in established shopping districts, concern over disruption to the balance
of sales shares amongst cities within metropolitan regions, and also
awareness of the potential adverse environmental and disruptive land-use
effects of some types of new store unit. The 1974 Act introduced specific
time periods for consultation on applications for new stores and required
the Minister of International Trade and Business to collate this advice
within a three-month period. During this period the Minister asked for
advice from the Large Scale Retail Business Council, who in turn asked
for comments from trade organisations. A month was then provided for a
decision to be made. Again all planned stores over 1,500 m^2 were affected
by the legislation with the limit increased to 3,000 m^2 in Tokyo metropolitan area and certain designated cities. The 1974 Act was extended in
1979 to define two classes of large scale store to which the legislation was
applicable:

1. Class 1 stores are units of 1,500 m^2 and over gross floorspace, but
   in the Tokyo metropolitan area and designated cities, with the
   same administrative status as prefectures, this limit remained at
   3,000 m^2;
2. Class 2 stores of over 500 m^2 but less than 1,500 m^2 (500-3,000 m^2
   in the Tokyo metropolitan area and designated cities).

For Class 1 stores the Minister collates advice and makes the decision on
the application, whilst for Class 2 stores decision-making is delegated to

the governors of urban and rural prefectures. The periods available for consultation were increased in the 1979 Act to five months for both Class 1 and Class 2 stores. Despite the strengthening of the legislation, the economic slump of the late 1970s and early 1980s has resulted in even stronger calls from small and medium-sized retailers for protection. By March 1981, 63 cities had declared a freeze on the opening of any new large store. In October 1981 the Ministry of International Trade and Industry (MITI) imposed a three month moratorium on new developments in order to assess the need for either a major revision of the law or clearer guidance on its application.

FIGURE 1

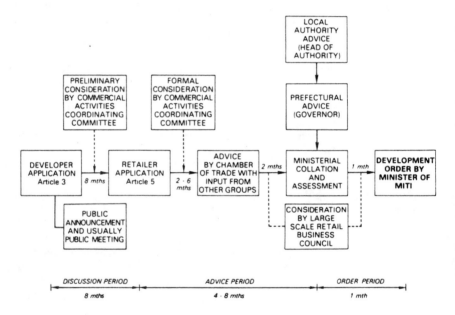

PROCEDURES IN THE 1979 ACT

Figure 1 shows the method of regulation for Class 1 stores under the 1979 legislation. Procedures for Class 2 stores are similar except the functions of MITI are taken by urban and rural prefectural authorities. In the case of Class 1 stores an application is submitted by the developer to MITI via the urban and rural prefectural authorities requesting, in general terms, permission to develop. This application is governed by Article 3 of the Act. There is then a period of up to eight months during which public discussion is encouraged and a local open meeting is convened to discuss the project. The retailer then submits an Article 5 application, which comprises the detailed proposal. In this must be specified the floorspace breakdowns, opening date, plans, etc. Between two and six months are then available for further assessment of the project with formal inputs from the local chambers of trade, consumer groups and retailer groups. A report is submitted to MITI which then has two months to collate assessments and advice from local governments and regional authorities. Sato [1981: 48-59], in a study of Kanagawa prefecture in suburban Yokohama has shown how these local inputs can vary considerably, from being simple applications of MITI guidelines, through the amendment and adaption to local conditions of these guidelines, to, in a few cases, individual local policies being applied to control and direct local retail development. Such local policies tend to have as their aims the advancement of the local economy, the prevention of the decline of local retailing, and the conservation of the existing balance of market shares amongst local areas. They are essentially conservative and protectionist to local retailing. A month is available for final evaluation of these local inputs and the issuing of a development order. The formal advice period on a detailed Article 5 application lasts between four and eight months and overall there is at least 13 months between an initial Article 3 application and the receipt of permission to open the store. In 1981 MITI revised their guidelines for assessment at the final stage of the procedure and have now devised standards of population per square metre of floorspace for four different city size groups. They are also seeking to strengthen the ability of Regional Commercial Activities Coordinating Councils to assess the likely impact of proposed stores. The 1979 Act exhibits a significant strengthening of control policies compared with earlier policies.

GROWTH OF LARGE STORES SINCE 1974

Table 2 shows the growth rates of new large stores during the 1970s and the stiffer controls of the 1979 legislation can be seen reflected in the lower numbers of new stores opened since 1979. The lengthier procedure also results in large numbers of store applications being under consideration. The knowledge of impending tighter legislation and longer decision periods provoked a large number of Article 3 applications in 1979, relatively few of which had obtained development permission by 1981. The over 100 openings in 1980, however, still provoked reaction from the small and medium-sized shopkeeper lobby and the even tighter interpretation of the law in 1981, including total prohibition in some cities, has been mentioned above.

Table 2 shows that under the 1974 legislation almost two-thirds of applications were successful. The percentage success rates are indicative rather than precise, as the percentage figures relate to applications and permissions during the year, whilst applications may be made in one calendar year but permission not given until the following year. Most permissions in 1979, therefore, refer to applications under the 1974 legislation, not to the 1979 Act. Nonetheless, as Table 2 demonstrates, there was considerable growth of large store numbers in the 1970s despite legislation aimed to control their development. Throughout the decade

TABLE 2

GROWTH OF LARGE SCALE STORE NUMBERS IN JAPAN

| | First Class Stores | | | | | Second Class Stores | |
| | Article 3 Applications | | Openings | | | Article 3 Applications | |
	Total	Kanto region	Total	%	Floorspace million m²	Total	Kanto region
Pre 1974	1,815	647	1,714		11.24		
1974	398	148	197	49	1.26		
1975	280	100	176	63	1.09		
1976	265	82	213	80	1.22		
1977	318	104	190	60	1.20		
1978	243	77	188	77	1.31	9,186²	2,986²
1979	576	181	212	37	1.51	1,029	443
1980	371	121	106	29	0.79	426	168
1981¹			7		0.25		
Total to 1981	4,266	1,460	3,003		19.88	10,641	3,597

Notes
1. First three months only.
2. Includes previously registered stores.

Source: MITI.

the Kanto region, including the Tokyo-Yokohama metropolitan region, dominated application patterns with around a third of all applications. Even with the growth that has occurred, however, the number and density of large stores remains relatively low compared with Western Europe.

Table 3 shows the mix of store types within the total of 2,996 large units which had opened or received development permission at the end of 1980. It has been necessary to group together hypermarkets and super-markets in this table because hypermarkets are not separately recognised in Japan. Supermarkets and hypermarkets constitute the single most important group of new stores and any attempt to control the large store sector must control the growth of these stores. Applications for over 500 of these stores were in process of being considered in March 1981; and it is this large number, and their large size, which produced the concern of city authorities and MITI during the summer of 1981. During the period of the 1974 Act, supermarket and hypermarket openings were on average about 120 per year, but in the first year of the 1979 Act the total of permissions fell considerably. There is still considerable demand from retailers and developers, however, for permissions for new supermarkets. The average size of new stores, generally, has risen steadily through the decade. Although fewer units were given permission in 1980 than in any year since 1974, the average size of store was the largest and even larger stores are awaiting permission. Concern, by small and medium-sized retailers, over the operation of the new Act appears justified in this respect, and the almost panic measures of 1981 become understandable. The expansion of the multi-shop department stores (buildings comprising several relocated

TABLE 3

CLASS I LARGE SCALE STORE OPENINGS BY TYPE OF STORE (STORE SIZE IN THOUSAND M²)

	Existing in 1974		Openings 1974–1976		1977–1979		1980		Total to 1981	Applications under consideration, March 1981	
	number	mean size	number	mean size	number	mean size	number	mean size		number	mean size
Full department stores	293	14.8	31	14.0	32	11.4	6	12.9	352	30	16.3
Speciality stores	184	2.8	89	2.9	67	3.8	11	2.7	351	69	3.4
Credit/Instalment department stores	41	4.7	9	7.1	6	9.5	1	7.5	57	4	6.3
Supermarkets and hypermarkets	924	5.5	361	6.9	379	7.4	74	8.3	1,738	509	8.6
Multi-shop department stores	265	4.2	95	3.4	116	4.1	14	4.6	490	50	4.8
Other	7	4.1	1	2.0	0	0	0	0	8	2	8.9
Total	1,714	6.6	585	6.1	590	6.8	106	7.4	2,996	664	8.1

Source: MITI.

TABLE 4

CLASS I LARGE SCALE STORES BY SIZE OF CITY (STORE SIZE IN THOUSAND M²)

City size '000 population	Existing 1974		1974–1976		1977–1979		1980		Total to 1981	Applications under consideration, March 1981	
	number	mean size	number	mean size	number	mean size	number	mean size		number	mean size
10 largest cities	256	13.1	49	8.8	59	11.3	13	8.3	377	54	12.8
over 300	399	6.5	117	6.2	114	7.2	24	16.6	654	92	8.6
200 – 300	286	6.4	91	7.1	68	7.9	12	10.0	457	71	8.3
100 –199	326	5.3	96	6.0	86	8.1	7	9.2	515	69	10.0
50 – 99	272	4.4	113	5.8	107	5.9	24	5.9	516	120	8.5
30 – 49	120	3.4	65	4.9	77	4.8	20	5.7	282	105	7.7
15 – 29	47	2.8	42	4.2	59	3.5	13	5.7	161	116	5.3
less than 15	8	2.7	13	2.5	20	4.0	3	10.2	44	37	4.9

Source: MITI.

small and medium-sized retailers all operating in a joint unit) with a broad product mix has been complemented by an almost doubling, since 1974, in the number of large speciality stores. These store types, however, on preliminary evidence appear to have been subjected to heavy controls in the 1979 Act, but many units are in the permission process. In full-line department stores the trend towards smaller units, suited to medium-sized cities, was already in evidence in the late 1970s, but this trend may not continue under the new Act. Multi-shop department stores and speciality stores are showing interest in middle markets, whilst department store operators are looking towards large suburban tracts around major cities, and are requesting large units in these areas.

The large store units developed in the 1960s and early 1970s were heavily concentrated in the largest cities. Table 4 shows that 38 per cent of large shops accounting for 53 per cent of large shop floorspace, were in the towns of over 300,000 population in 1974. A clear relationship is apparent in 1974 between average size of these large stores and size of city. During the period of the 1974 Act there was notable growth in middle markets: towns of 50-200,000 population accounted for barely a quarter of floorspace in large units in 1974, but over a third of new floorspace between 1974 and 1979 went into these cities. Large stores also were established in small towns of less than 30,000 and, although numbers were not large, there was considerable growth in interest in the market potential of such places, particularly for supermarkets. The size of new store openings in the middle markets increased markedly. In the small places of less than 30,000 population there were a limited but increasing number of developments, but their significance on the economy of the host was considerable. In the smaller places single large units were clearly starting to establish potential monopoly positions. In the largest cities the new units were generally not as large as many of the stores already operating, but the 59 units developed between 1977 and 1979, for example, had an average floorspace of over $11,000 \, \text{m}^2$ and clearly represent a major addition to the stock of large stores.

The introduction of the 1979 Act, however, has strengthened the powers of the retail lobby and local government in the middle markets. Prefectural authorities now have more influence than under the 1974 Act. So, in 1980 and 1981 growth has taken place in the larger places with smaller cities able to limit large store development even to the extent of halting all development, at least in the short term. The relationship between store size and city size is present neither in the figure for developments in 1980 nor in the data for applications under consideration. In these latter figures, the considerable developer and retailer interest in smaller communities is very evident; and a major conflict is likely during the 1980s between large retailers wishing to enter smaller markets, and the traditional retailers' entrenched opposition to the acceptance of the new large units, and the new trading philosophy which such units personify.

DEVELOPMENT IN THE 1980S

The Act of 1979 promises to be more effective than earlier legislation aimed at the control of development of large stores, but new large stores will continue to be built in Japan despite the legislation. Given the pressures for development which are building up, a substantial number of new stores seems likely over the next few years. The aim of the 1979 Act, certainly, is not to halt all new large-store construction but to provide a mechanism and procedure for the co-ordination of future growth. A few areas are close to market saturation of large stores, but these are relatively few; and pressures will be strong for new stores in expanding suburbs and in middle markets where traditional retailers have held the major share for a long time. The new legislation also is likely to encourage adaptive reaction from larger retailers:

(a) Possibly they will seek extensions rather than new developments;
(b) possibly they will move into the retail formats which appear to have greater chance of obtaining development permissions and away from hypermarket type operations;
(c) possibly new store types will evolve;
(d) almost certainly there will be even more scrambled merchandising in existing units;
(e) possibly large stores will be developed as anchors for small shopping centres in which provision is also made for small shops;
(f) it is likely that new stores will be built of a size just below the critical threshold of the Act.

From European experience all these reactions are likely to take place. Large company corporate plans will certainly respond to the tighter controls. This is already apparent amongst some of the largest companies. The Uny Co. Ltd., for example, the tenth largest retail corporation in 1980 is diversifying its trading operations through expanding speciality store retailing in units of about $200 m^2$, operating a range of store formats for mass-merchandising convenience goods and also moving into the allied service sectors of fast foods, travel agencies, and real estate development. Within the convenience goods market Uny is developing large, hypermarket type operations when permissions are forthcoming; it is operating its supermarket chain with stores of around $1,500 m^2$ in anticipation that permissions for Class 2 stores will be more readily available; thirdly, it is operating, via a franchise agreement, a growing chain of convenience stores ranging in size from $75 m^2$ to $140 m^2$ and which fall well outside the critical size threshold of the 1979 Act. Public policy controls are unlikely to halt the restructuring of the retail industry because other large companies are adopting similar growth strategies to that of Uny. Daiei, the largest retailer in Japan, now terms itself a conglo-merchant and similarly is developing speciality stores, discount stores and convenience stores, in addition to diversifying into a variety of consumer services and retail support activities. Capital expenditure in 1981 in Daiei was almost double that of 1980 and similarly large increases in investment are reported for other companies. Investment and structural readjustment in retailing are certainly not being halted by the 1979 legislation.

Policies attempting to control large stores with the aim of protecting small retail firms usually are associated with some more positive policy action taken to promote small business. In Japan, action is being taken to improve small and medium-sized retailer efficiency; but it may simply result in the protection of small and medium-sized firms who become the victims of competition not from large stores but from the small shops operated by large firms. A total ban on large units will encourage large companies to look to chains of small units, both specialist stores and convenience stores. These efficiently operated small units, being part of large vertically integrated and horizontally co-ordinated companies, will be strong competitors to traditional small firm retailers. Furthermore, policies of the Small and Medium Enterprise Agency (1981) do not have a reputation of being effective in promoting rationalization and greater efficiency amongst small and medium-sized retail businesses. It will be interesting to analyse, in the next few years, whether Japanese policy aimed at controlling large store development is any more successful than the various, largely unsuccessful, attempts at large store control introduced by European governments.

REFERENCES

Commission of the European Communities, 1978, 'Aspects of the Establishment, Planning and Control of Urban Retail Outlets in Europe, Studies', *Series in Commerce and Distribution*, No. 4.
Dawson, J.A., 1982a, *Commercial Distribution in Europe*, London: Croom Helm.
Dawson, J.A., 1982b, 'A Note on the Law of 29 June 1978 to Control Large Scale Retail Development in Belgium', *Environment and Planning*, A14.
Hayashi, S., 1980, 'The Japanese Distribution System', *Jounral of Enterprise Management*, Vol. 2, No. 3, 263-273.
JETRO, 1978, *Planning for Distribution in Japan*, London: Author,
JETRO, 1979, *Retailing in the Japanese Consumer Market*, London: Author.
Murata, S., 1973, *Distribution in Japan, The Wheel Extended*, Vol. 3, No. 2.
Nakanisi, M., 1981, 'Marketing Developments in Japan', *Journal of Marketing*, No. 45.
SATO, T., 1981, 'Regional Economy and Retail Policy in Kanagawa Prefecture', *Annals of Association of Economic Geographers*, Vol. 27, Nos. 3-4.
Shimaguchi, M., 1978, *Marketing Channels in Japan*, London: UMI Research Press.
Shimaguchi, M. and Lazer, W., 1979, 'Japanese Distribution Channels', *Business Topics*, 27, 49-62.
Yoshino, M.Y., 1978, *The Japanese Marketing System*. Cambridge, Mass: MIT Press.

This chapter first appeared in *The Service Industries Journal*, Vol.3, No.2 (1983).

8

'Checkout': The Analysis of Oligopolistic Behaviour in the UK Grocery Retail Market

by

Gary Akehurst*

Industrial economics is particularly concerned with the relationships between market concentration, market behaviour, pricing and market performance. When, in June 1977, Tesco launched its 'Operation Checkout' so began one of the most intensely competitive periods of retailing history. Checkout, which was a wide price-cutting campaign backed up by extensive advertising, provides an ideal opportunity to examine the rivalry of leading grocery companies. This paper examines the events leading up to Checkout, during the initial campaign and after; it examines the possible causes of Checkout and whether it was successful. The paper asks whether the behaviour of firms surrounding Tesco can be considered to be oligopolistic and, if so, what this may mean for the future.

INTRODUCTION

Industrial economics has been fundamentally interested in the relationships between market concentration, market behaviour, pricing and market performance, no more so than in the market condition called 'oligopoly', that is, competition between the few. What constitutes 'few' is a matter for theoretical and empirical observation but clearly we are interested in the extent to which an economic activity is dominated by a few large firms and their behaviour. The fewer the businesses in a market the more likely that each firm will be vitally aware of its rivals, and will weigh up the market consequences of its pricing strategies and other competitive devices.

We are interested in the competition existing in the UK grocery market and, in particular, the nature of the competition which occurred when in 1977 Tesco launched its 'Operation Checkout', a wide price-cutting campaign that has continued. The intensity of competition generated, in part, by Checkout, seems to confirm at first glance some very interesting

*I am grateful to Julian Edwards, University College of Wales, Aberystwyth, for his help and advice; any errors remaining are, of course, my responsibility.

behaviour in the period prior to, during and after the initial Checkout moves. We are interested in examining what can now be seen as a quite remarkable period of retailing history, of profound changes and rivalry, of moves and counter moves amongst a group of key firms all with a substantial groceries base. Certainly Checkout led to 'increased competitive pressures in the grocery trade' and, in particular, led to increased pressure by the largest companies on their suppliers for greater discount on the cost price of goods [Monopolies and Mergers Commission, 1981: 8].

To some extent events during the period 1976–80 will appear to be ancient history but their examination serves two purposes: first, the events can now be placed, with the benefit of hindsight and analytical thought, into some perspective within the wider changes now taking place in retailing; second, the examination of certain firms' behaviour may help illuminate, for economists, the market structure and competition of a sector of retailing.

This paper considers:

• an overview of grocery retailing
• concentration in grocery retailing
• identification of a leading group in grocery retailing
• events and behaviour pre-Checkout, 1975–77
• the possible causes of Checkout
• the possibility of an oligopolistic grouping around Tesco
• reactions of rivals to Tesco
• post-Checkout events up to 1980 and the success of Checkout

AN OVERVIEW OF GROCERY RETAILING

In 1978 sales by grocers and supermarkets amounted to some £11,462 million out of total retail sales of £42,378 million [Euromonitor, 1979], and in 1982 grocers' and general food sales amounted to £16,335 million [Economist Intelligence Unit (EIU), 1983]. Obviously the grocery sector is an important part of retailing, and developments within it are likely to have repercussions for retailing as a whole. All writers on retail distribution are agreed that the growth of multiples* has been quite remarkable and is one of the outstanding features of UK retailing since 1945.

Multiple share of grocery sales grew from nearly 27 per cent in 1961 to 55 per cent in 1980, whilst the sales of independent retailers, unaffiliated to any voluntary groups, have steadily declined from nearly 40 per cent to 12 per cent of total grocery sales in the same period [EIU, 1980]. It would be easy to generalise but such developments are a reflection of intense competition, the economies of scale reaped by streamlining multiple operations, buying power and operating efficient large outlets such as superstores.

Over time the multiples have rationalised smaller, uneconomic outlets

---

*In retailing, a multiple is a company operating more than 10 units or shops.

and embarked on ambitious building programmes of superstores. For example, between 1972 and 1980 Tesco increased the number of its superstores from 5 to 53. Asda, a superstore pioneer, now operates some 73 superstores and reckons to be expanding at the rate of six per year. It is, of course, interesting to speculate as to how far the development of superstores is a response to changing consumer preferences and mobility, and how far it is a supplier response to possible economies of operation, leading to greater profitability and market share growth. This consolidates a process which began in the nineteenth century when multiples first emerged in the grocery trade and progressed rapidly by offering price reductions over traditional shops through buying power. Smaller margins, however, means reliance on high sales volume rates to achieve profitability. The growth of superstore trading is, in one sense, a move away from the major features of multiples in the 1960s, namely sites in prominent shopping centres, standardised facias and displays [Fulop, 1966: 71] and a concentration on particular product groupings.

Generally up to the mid-1970s most multiples were clearly identified with certain product groupings but since then many leading grocery-based multiples have diversified into non-food areas, especially DIY, furniture and electrical goods. One study has suggested that such diversification was an attempt to arrest a fall in growth rate caused by the onset of maturity [EIU, 1974: 27] but in the past three years or so there has been a marked move amongst leading multiples towards fresh food and a slowing down of non-food diversification; and whilst investment and modernisation programmes continue, questions are being raised about superstore saturation in some parts of the country, and a concern for the viability of inner-city and high street shopping areas [Jones, 1982].

CONCENTRATION IN GROCERY RETAILING

The number of buying points in the grocery sector has declined substantially from 2,800 in 1950 to 308 in 1977. In 1977, of the 308 major buying points (controlling 77 per cent of total grocery sales), 58 were controlled by multiples, which accounted for 51 per cent of grocery sales [EEC, 1977: Table 9.5, based on A.C. Nielsen data]. Tables 1 and 2 show in more detail the distinction within the multiples category, between major multiples, of which there are generally considered to be six, and other multiples. These six companies in 1978 controlled some 37 per cent of packaged grocery goods sales according to Audits of GB. Other multiples, totalling some 47, controlled 17 per cent of sales, only slightly more than the co-operative societies.

More recent data from the 1980 Retailing Inquiry reveal that concentration has further increased to CR5* 30.9 per cent and CR10 43.6 per cent. Between 1978 and 1983 large businesses' (defined as businesses having a turnover greater than £1 million) share of total grocery retail

*CR = Concentration Ratio. CR5, for example, indicates the top five companies, controlling 30.9 per cent of sales.

TABLE 1

NUMBER OF BUYING POINTS: GROCERIES 1975–78

	1975	1976	1977	1978
Co-operatives	227	215	206	201
Major multiple head offices	6	6	6	6
Other multiple head offices	56	57	52	47
Major symbol wholesalers	55	49	44	43
Total	344	327	308	297
% of grocers' business controlled/influenced	75	75	77	78

Source: The Nielsen Researcher, 1979, No.2.

TABLE 2

SHARE OF 60 PACKAGED GROCERY GOODS SALES

(per cent)

	1976	1977	1978
Co-operatives	14.0	13.8	13.6
Independents	36.6	35.0	33.1
(including major symbol groups)	(12.2)	(11.8)	(11.3)
6 major multiples	31.8	34.3	36.6
Other multiples	17.6	16.9	16.7

Source: The Nielsen Researcher, 1979, No.2.

sales rose from 73 per cent to 81 per cent [EIU, 1983]. The 1980 Inquiry also revealed that in that year 116 large businesses were responsible for 12,218 outlets (out of a total of 56,560), controlling a turnover of £13,205 million (or 76 per cent of total grocery sales). In addition, the Inquiry revealed that large grocery businesses controlled 34.7 per cent of the total retail sales of alcoholic drinks, 33.1 per cent of bakery products, 56.2 per cent of motor parts and accessories sales and 26.3 per cent of meat sales.

IDENTIFICATION OF A LEADING GROUP IN GROCERY RETAILING

Whilst multiples as a group have increased their share of total grocery sales, this growth in effect applies especially to four companies: Sainsbury, Tesco, Asda and Kwik Save; generally most other multiples including Allied Suppliers, Fine Fare, Key Markets and International Stores have seen their share of total UK grocery sales either stay static or decline. The share of Tesco, Sainsbury, Asda and Kwik Save, in total, grew from 18.4 per cent in 1973 to 32.9 per cent in 1978 according to Audits of GB (see Table 3).

TABLE 3

ESTIMATES OF MARKET SHARES OF LEADING
COMPANIES, IN GROCERY MARKET
(per cent)

	1970/71	1973/74	1976/77	end 1978	end 1979
Tesco	7.2	8.6	8.3	12.0	13.6
Sainsbury	6.1	7.0	7.7	11.5	11.9
Asda	1.5	2.5	4.7	5.5	7.3
International	3.2	3.0	3.7	4.0	5.2
Fine Fare	4.8	4.2	4.0	4.2	5.0
Kwik Save	0.3	0.6	1.4	4.0	4.9
Allied Suppliers	7.9	7.0	5.7	5.0	4.8

Sources: For 1978, Economist Intelligence Unit and trade estimates; for 1979, Audits of GB Ltd.

Much of this growth of the leading four grocery retailers, particularly in 1977–80, was achieved not especially via own brands but through traditional manufacturers' brands. It is of some interest to note that Asda and Kwik Save are not primarily own brand merchandisers whereas Tesco, and especially Sainsbury, have successfully marketed own brands. Up to 1977 about two-thirds of Sainsbury's trade, and roughly one-quarter of Tesco's sales, was own label.

Many leading retailing companies have substantial grocery interests. Of the top 25 companies in 1978, 22 were involved in groceries retailing, of which 10 can be considered leading firms in the groceries sector [Akehurst, 1983: 169, Table 5]. From company and concentration data assembled by Akehurst [1983] we can identify:

(a) The Growing Firms

In 1978 seven firms with grocery interests were located in the top ten retailers ranked by turnover [Akehurst, 1983: 169] and the turnover of these firms is considerable. Between 1970 and 1978 Tesco increased its rank in sales concentration from number 5 to number 3, having a turnover in 1978 of £953 million; Sainsbury moved from 8 to 7; Cavenham (Allied Suppliers, Presto, etc.) moved from 128 to 1, whilst the discounters showed remarkable growth. Asda moved from 23 to 12 and Kwik Save from 59 to 28.

(b) Firms which Showed Modest Growth 1970–78

Basically the medium-sized, regionally-based multiples and one freezer centre specialist were the firms which showed modest growth:

Lennons rose from ranking number 60 to number 53.

Safeway rose from 35 to 25.

Amos Hinton rose from 60 to 55.

Wm. Morrison rose from 62 to 44.

Wm. Low rose from 69 (1972) to 54.

Wheatsheaf rose from 89 to 50.

Bejam rose from 101 (1972) to 43.

(c) Firms which Showed a Declined Ranking by Turnover.

Generally variety stores and smaller regional multiples were those which declined between 1970 and 1978:

Associated British Foods fell from 7 to 11.

F.W. Woolworth fell from 2 to 10.

British Home Stores fell from 17 to 21.

Bishops fell from 34 to 38.

Brookton fell from 70 to 82.

Cullens fell from 79 to 111.

Wm. Jackson fell from 39 to 42.

Generally those firms which grew substantially in the 1970s were the discounters and largest multiples, whilst medium-sized regionally-based multiples made modest progress.

The leading firms can be further identified by reference to Table 4, which gives estimates of market share in the grocery sector for 1978 and 1979. Three size groupings can be seen.

(a)   Those organisations with an individual market share greater than 7 per cent in 1979: Tesco, Sainsbury, Asda and Co-operatives.

(b)   Organisations with a market share between 3 and 7 per cent: International Stores, Fine Fare, Kwik Save, Allied Suppliers.

(c)   Organisations below 3 per cent: the rest, including independent retailers.

These data relate to 1978 and 1979 because this paper is primarily concerned with the events surrounding Operation Checkout, which began in June 1977. Since 1979 Asda's share has increased to 9 per cent whilst Sainsbury has emerged with the largest market share at 13.5 per cent. Tesco has fallen somewhat behind Sainsbury.

From all the evidence on concentration in the grocery sector it is clear that a group of leading companies can be identified. We now need to examine the behaviour of these companies, and see whether rivalry and interdependence is recognised.

PRE-CHECKOUT, 1975–77

Operation Checkout was launched by Tesco on 9 June 1977 as an across-the-board price cuts campaign. So began one of the most intense periods of competition in the history of retailing. As such it provides a unique

TABLE 4

ESTIMATES OF MARKET SHARE: GROCERIES

(per cent of value)

	end of 1978	end of 1979
Co-operatives	17.5	17.4
Tesco	12.0	13.6
Sainsbury	11.5	11.9
Asda	5.5	7.3
International	4.0	5.2
Fine Fare	4.2	5.0
Kwik Save	4.0	4.9
Allied Suppliers	5.0	4.8
Spar	4.0	3.2
Marks & Spencer	na	1.9
Key Market	2.0	1.8
VG	1.9	1.6
Mace	1.6	1.5
Waitrose	2.0	1.3
Safeway	2.0	1.2
Boots	na	0.8
Woolworth	na	0.7
Independents	na	15.9

Sources: For 1978, Economist Intelligence Unit and trade estimates; for 1979, Audits of GB Ltd.

opportunity to study the possibility of oligopolistic behaviour surrounding and between the leading grocery retail companies.

The slow awakening of leading grocery groups to the competition of the discounting groups (especially as some of these, such as Asda, were moving southwards away from their northern base), and the need to focus consumer attention onto the aggregate of goods offered for sale – rather than selective price cuts on a very limited range of goods over a period of, say, one or two weeks, led to two developments in 1975 and 1976. The significance of these events is rather over-shadowed by Checkout but they deserve attention. In November 1975 Fine Fare launched a novel kind of discount store called 'Shoppers Paradise' carrying a bare minimum of less than 400 lines compared to the average 2,000–4,000 commodities in a typical supermarket. Furnishings and fittings were kept to a minimum. Fine Fare claimed prices were around 10 per cent lower than the local average in the store locations, and there is indeed evidence that prices were, and are, somewhat lower. Similarly, in the same month Key Markets (then owned by Fitch Lovell) started Key Discount stores with the same cost reducing, limited commodity range. At this point it must be realised that until 1976 grocery and other commodities discounting had been a largely northern phenomenon: Asda had started from a base in West Yorkshire and Kwik Save from a similar location.

Following the Fine Fare example several national groups began experimenting very discreetly with their own discount stores. Tesco's experiment in discounting is especially important although at the time its real significance was not realised. Green Shield trading stamps were dropped in two smaller Tesco stores in Staffordshire. Both stores had a sales area of less then 4000 sq. ft. The experiment was to see whether, in certain areas, cut prices were a better way of increasing turnover than trading stamps. In the Midlands price competition was, and is, intense and stamps apparently did not seem to have the same appeal as elsewhere. Both stores, rather interestingly, used the name 'Adsega', reduced the product range and cut prices by about five per cent. At about the same time, (late 1976/early 1977), Sainsbury also quietly experimented with discounting in selected stores. Clearly several developments were running parallel. The major grocery groups were, in part, reacting to competition from the discounters and, whatever previous economic writers have written about competition in retailing (remembering, of course, that many of these writings were prior to 1966), these events are strongly indicative of a growing awareness of interdependence, of a challenge to traditional retailing selling methods, all at a time of inflation and growing customer sensitivity to price. At the same time companies were promoting a corporate image through very intensive advertising. This advertising message was essentially the same: purchase a wide range of goods at one location, and at the lowest possible prices.

The grocery market, however, was static and at times in decline (see Figure 1 and Table 5). At the time of the initial Fine Fare experiment the volume of food sales actually fell between August and December 1975,

TABLE 5

SALES VALUE AND VOLUME GROWTH 1971–78

(1971 = 100)

	Food Shops			Non-food Shops			All Retail
	£ million	value	volume	£ million	value	volume	volume
1971	6,866	100	100	9,430	100	100	100
1972	7,485	109	101.6	10,770	114.2	107.9	105.3
1973	8,445	125	101.6	12,240	129.8	116.6	110.3
1974	9,950	144.9	102.4	13,960	148.1	113.8	109
1975	12,015	175	100	16,415	174	112.5	106.7
1976	14,060	204.8	98.7	18,550	196.7	112.1	106.5
1977	16,115	234.7	94.8	21,020	223.1	110	103.6
1978	17,975	261.8	98	24,405	258.8	117.4	109.2
1979							
1st quarter		273	96				
2nd quarter		291	100				

*Source:*Department of Industry figures.

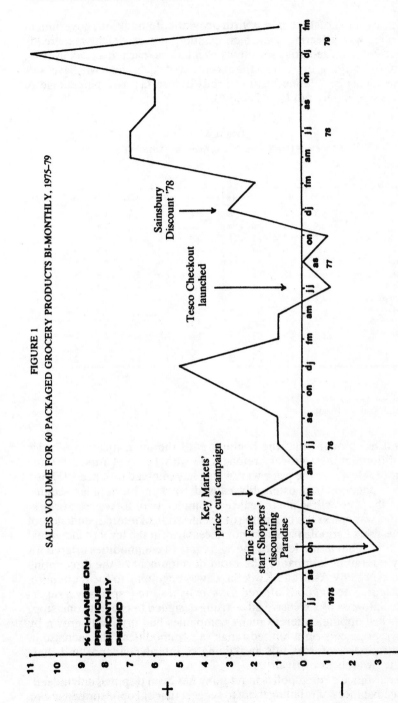

FIGURE 1

SALES VOLUME FOR 60 PACKAGED GROCERY PRODUCTS BI-MONTHLY, 1975–79

Source: The Nielsen Researcher, 1979, No.2.

and during most of 1976 it was virtually static. In addition, government pay policy was affecting consumer spending power which was already affected by increased price sensitivity as inflation reached a peak in 1975. Most of the major groups, with the exception of Asda and Kwik Save, saw their net margins (defined as net profit before tax as a percentage of turnover) gradually fall (see Table 6).

TABLE 6

NET PROFIT AS A PERCENTAGE OF TURNOVER*

	1970	1971	1972	1973	1974	1975	1976	1977	1978	1979
Tesco	5.3	5.4	5.5	6.1	5.8	4.7	4.1	4.3	3.0	3.1
Sainsbury	2.9	3.1	4.0	4.0	4.0	3.6	3.2	4.4	3.5	3.2
Asda	3.8	4.1	4.1	5.1	4.7	4.6	4.8	5.6	4.8	5.2
Safeway	2.9	3.0	3.4	3.3	2.2	2.2	2.3	3.2	3.5	
Kwik Save	5.8	6.8	7.1	8.0	6.8	5.9	5.7	5.7	5.0	4.7
Fine Fare	3.3	1.5	2.1	2.2	2.6	1.0	2.8	2.8	1.5	
International	2.6	2.5	3.5	3.6	1.5	0.4	−0.02	1.1	−1.6	
Allied Suppliers	2.1	—	2.4	3.0	3.2	2.3	1.4	2.4	1.8	1.3
Morrison	4.6	4.3	4.2	4.8	4.9	4.1	3.5	3.1	3.8	
Hillards	1.2	1.6	2.6	4.2	3.5	2.2	2.3	3.7	3.2	
Lennons	2.9	3.6	4.1	4.3	4.2	3.3	2.8	3.0	2.6	
Wm. Low	—	—	4.8	5.1	4.1	3.4	3.1	3.7	2.4	
Hinton	3.9	3.7	3.8	3.3	3.4	3.0	2.0	2.7	2.9	

* Net profit before tax.
Source: See Akehurst [1983].

It is often thought that the beginnings of the intensification of price competition amongst grocery retailers lie with Tesco in June 1977 and Checkout. However the price war, which has rumbled on since 1977, is a complex phenomenon ostensibly caused by a major retailer seeking market share growth while in reality a complexity of forces are at work. The price war marks the beginning of a realisation of interdependence, of recognisable oligopolistic rivalry not necessarily at the level of individual commodities but at the level of the aggregate of commodities offered for sale by a retailing company. The rapid development of the discounting chains, especially Asda and Kwik Save, was beginning to focus attention on the aggregate of goods offered for sale by a store (especially a super-store) reinforced by extensive advertising designed to promote one-stop, low-price shopping, whereas many companies had originally grown by selective price cuts on a limited range of commodities. The increase in concentration reinforces this awakening of interdependence and sharpens the awareness of rivalry.

The existence of oligopolies in retailing has been disputed and indeed, the circumstances of retailing seem to suggest that oligopolistic behaviour is unlikely. Often mentioned in this context is the wide range of commodities sold, the shifting, increasingly mobile clientele and other factors such as ease of entry. The conduct of key companies, the 'market basket' phenomenon (and the oligopolistic awareness this engenders) and the peculiar cirumstances surrounding the Checkout operation are, in fact, closely interrelated. The price war surrounding Checkout is perhaps one indication of a fundamental change occurring apparently in grocery retailing. In fact, rather than being confined to a conventional product grouping, the change is based particularly on companies whose base, and growth to date, has been in groceries and is now extending across a wide range of commodities. The price war in grocery retailing, now partly with the benefit of hindsight, is really but one relatively short-term manifestation of a far wider realignment in retailing. This realignment will inevitably lead to greater concentration, the continued demise of many independent retailers, the merger or take-over of smaller groups, the progressive development and introduction of labour-saving technology and ultimately a significant change in consumer purchasing habits.

Except for Asda and Kwik Save, many of the leading grocery retailers experienced a disappointing growth of turnover and profits between 1974 and 1976 (see Table 7). This was hardly a good base for reinvestment and long-term growth: for example, the 1974–75 financial year for Tesco saw a decrease of 6 per cent in profits at current prices and a decrease of 55 per cent for Fine Fare. Leading multiple groups such as Tesco, Fine Fare and Key Markets were slowly coming to realise that discounting allied to superstores represented a serious threat for two very important reasons. *First*, as mentioned above, Asda and other discounters were extending away from their regional bases and entering the spatial markets of leading multiples. Competition would be direct and obvious: consumers were slowly becoming aware (besides the influence of increased ownership of private transport), and with new discount superstores, the opportunities were being presented of low-cost, one-stop shopping. *Second*, the traditional retailing methods of selected price cuts of items figuring prominently in family shopping requirements (and holding these price cuts for a limited period) were no longer necessarily appropriate in a market of growing awareness of interdependence and rivalry.

The advantage of selective price cuts had been well proven: a low price image could be created on the basis of relatively few price cuts [Livesey, 1979: 52], but this advantage largely disappears if consumer perceptions of price image depend not on large cuts on a few commodities but on information of overall price levels. One source of information became important in the 1970s: the Consumers' Association *Which?* reports on grocery prices together with advertising of across-the-board price cuts by certain retail groups. Given increased information on grocery prices plus rapid inflation, the impact of selective price reductions may be lost, especially since there is no basis with which to compare the reduction. Rapid inflation reduces consumer awareness of the 'normal' price of products [Livesey, 1979: 53]. Discounting was profitable provided manu-

TABLE 7
GROWTH RATES OF TURNOVER AND PROFIT BEFORE TAX:
SELECTED COMPANIES (GROCERIES)

		1969/70	70/71	71/72	72/73	73/74	74/75	75/76	76/77	77/78	78/79
						% change on previous year					
J. Sainsbury	Sales	13	18	18	13	21	24	20	22	22	24
	Profit	16	24	56	13	19	13	7	66	-2	18
Tesco	Sales	25	9	15	20	18	18	23	14	36	26
	Profit	22	10	19	31	13	-6	7	21	-6	32
Fine Fare	Sales	4	12	10	4	10	17	9	14	16	na
	Profit	5	-50	56	12	29	-55	-53	14	-36	na
International	Sales	2	3	13	76*	0†	21	10	35	35	—
	Profit	-8	-1	55	84*	-58†	-68	-106	7247**	-303	—
Asda	Sales	40	51	31	35	23	40	41	37	25	48
	Profit	27	60	31	68	14	36	48	60	7	60
Kwik Save	Sales	—	36	49	24	45	62	40	66	27	34
	Profit	—	60	56	40	22	42	35	67	11	25
Allied Suppliers	Sales	8	(2)	(2)	-9	7	23	13	7	6	9
	Profit	-4	(2)	(2)	12	12	-13	-32	88	-20	-21

Notes: * Results for 1973–74 week accounting period.
 † 1972: 65 week accounting period.
 ** 1976: 60,000 loss; 1977: £4,348,000 profit hence 7247% increase.
 na = not available or not disclosed.

Source: author's computer tabulations.

facturers could be persuaded to grant special discounts and, in particular, it offered an alternative use for small, uneconomic stores which groups wished to dispose of. Given the difficult trading circumstances of the mid to late 1970s, if a grocery group wished to expand, a number of alternative courses of action were open to it (not all of which were mutually exclusive):

(1) Cut prices across the board and, by doing so, risk the possibility of retaliation given the growing awareness of 'market basket' competition. Alternatively, continue with selective price cuts if one was sure of the market. The objective would be increased market shares.
(2) Abandon competitive devices such as trading stamps, redeemable coupons, etc., and instead reduce overall prices. Discounting chains appeared to demonstrate that price seemed to be the dominant strategy for the market circumstances.
(3) Engage in intensive advertising and sales promotion in an effort to stimulate consumer demand, consumer loyalty and goodwill, and a corporate image of one-stop shopping baskets.
(4) Engage in a programme of rationalising retail outlets by closing uneconomic small units, opening superstores or convert small units to limited discounting operations.
(5) Diversify into non-food lines, or speciality foods or fresh foods with the possibility of higher net margins. Growing awareness of interdependence and the intensification of competition which this entails would inevitably lead to smaller net margins on the aggregate of goods offered for sale although variable pricing of individual commodities might yield somewhat higher returns.
(6) Innovate, in an effort to cut operating costs, for example, point-of-sale laser scanning.
(7) Merge to provide a wider locational and product base.

In March 1976 Key Markets, followed by Mac Markets, introduced a price-cutting campaign on a range of 163 high-volume lines. Here was an experiment with a wider price-cuts policy; it was no ordinary weekly promotion and was intended to be long lasting. The reaction of Tesco is interesting. Tesco (or rather Jack Cohen, its founder) had always had the philosophy of 'pile it high and sell it cheap'; indeed in the year ended February 1976 the Tesco directors had scarcely concealed a policy of improving market share by aggressive retailing even though this meant a reduction in trading margins. In addition, Tesco was beginning to see the fruits of its superstore programme which began around 1973/4.

Tesco's first hypermarket was opened in February 1976 at Irlam, Manchester and another was in progress in Pitsea, in Essex. Public statements revealed the Tesco philosophy, at least for publicity purposes, and is also suggestive of the growing awareness of intense rivalry:

> No one worries about price control these days. It's competition that keeps prices down and the only way to survive is to go on building

market share through extra selling space ... if we can carry on we may push some of the smaller fry, like Fine Fare and International Stores, out of business. We could out trade Sainsbury off the face of this Earth if we had to [Mr Ian MacClaurin, Managing Director, Tesco, *Daily Mail,* 31 July 1976].

It is clear, with hindsight, that Tesco felt expansion was being constrained on all sides. By early 1977 there were hopes that local and central government planners were becoming more sympathetic to hypermarkets. These hopes were somewhat premature: for example, in March 1977 both Sainsbury and the Co-op had planning applications for southern superstores rejected at Chichester and Sanford near Oxford, respectively. In April, Tesco's appeal against local authority refusal of a 90,000 sq. ft. store near Newton Abbott, Devon was rejected by the Secretary of State for the Environment. Superstore expansion, especially in the south and greater London, was (and is) seen to be absolutely essential to long-term growth and survival.

Tesco, in fact, gave several weeks' notice that across-the-board price cuts were likely in 1977 (in what was to be called Checkout). In an oligopolistic market a price cut should be introduced unannounced and so gain a short-term advantage over rivals. Its retailing success would depend on broadcasting the price cuts to the consumer (and hence rivals). On 21 April 1977 Tesco announced it was to renegotiate its Green Shield stamps contract. Green Shield stamps were costing about 2½ per cent of turnover. At this time Tesco had six Adsega shops and clearly was monitoring the experiment closely. Green Shield stamps had once been a mainstay of Tesco policies and had been defended vigorously, but the day of the trading stamp was coming to an end. Companies such as Fine Fare which had abandoned stamps back in the 1960s now had a price advantage. The problem was that, if Tesco abandoned stamps, it had to convey to the customer that its prices were really cheaper across the range and that it had not, by retaining stamps, been overcharging in the past. Clearly a major advertising campaign would be needed to reinforce a market basket approach.

Rumour and speculation continued in late April. The *Financial Times* on 26 April reported that Tesco had asked the managers of its larger stores not to take holidays in early June. Publicly Tesco said this was because of the Silver Jubilee!

Meanwhile, on 5 May 1977, the Sainsbury interim results (24 weeks to 2 March) showed a rise in net margins from 2.83 to 3.81 per cent and a 5½ per cent sales volume increase. Part of this increase was due to increased selling space and store closures by rivals International and Fine Fare. In addition, in the first four months of 1977 Tesco's market share fell from 8.4 per cent to 7.9 per cent and Sainsbury's rose from 8.8 to 9 per cent.

Between 21 April and 6 May the Tesco decision must have been made, although it is conceivable that by January 1977 Tesco had formulated rough price-cutting plans. On 9 May Tesco announced that it was dropping trading stamps in all its 700 stores on 8 June and using the money saved to cut prices. Tesco said that research (and it probably meant its Adsega experiments) had shown that the housewife preferred cheaper prices to stamps. Tesco did not announce the size or range of price cuts, and was in effect giving one month's notice.

During this one month's notice competitors speculated as to the size of the price cuts. It was known that Tesco had perhaps about two per cent leeway on overall gross margins by dropping Green Shield stamps; but it would need to decrease prices by more than this amount to compete with, for example, Sainsbury. In many areas there was a tendency for Tesco to be somewhat more expensive overall than its rivals (see Figures 2 and 3 and also the Notes, for an analysis). This may account for the possible 'wait and see' attitude adopted by some competitors. Indeed, we know that many firms believed that even after price cuts Tesco would continue with selective price cuts to maximise the advantage of stopping Green Shield stamps. On 10 May International Stores announced that it would like to increase the number of its shops offering Green Shield stamps, hoping to take up the 100 stamp franchises abandoned by Tesco. This was a curious move, particularly as by August 1978 International was announcing that it was dropping trading stamps from many of its stores. Of course by August 1978 the grocery retail market had been substantially changed but International's 1977 moves could probably be ascribed to the retailing inexperience of the parent company, British American Tobacco.

THE POSSIBLE CAUSES OF CHECKOUT

Before examining the possible causes of Checkout it is worth stating the significant steps Tesco took up to the Checkout campaign.

(a)   Limited discounting experiments.
(b)   21 April 1977: Tesco announced that it was to renegotiate the Green Shield trading stamp contract. This alerted rivals to the possibility that some stamp franchises might be dropped.
(c)   21 May 1977: Tesco announced that it was dropping Green Shield stamps in all stores as from 9 June, with a price-cuts campaign starting from that day. The size of the price cuts was not announced.
(d)   9 June 1977: price cuts announced, the beginning of Checkout. Wide range of goods prices cut by about 10 per cent. Intensive Tesco advertising campaign.

Several causes of Checkout can be suggested, especially in relation to the enhancement of market share.

1. In the financial year ended 26 February 1977 Tesco sales volume had declined about 4½ per cent. During the first half year sales rose 18 per cent but during the second half they rose only 14 per cent. Similarly, although over the year net margins rose slightly from 4.06 per cent

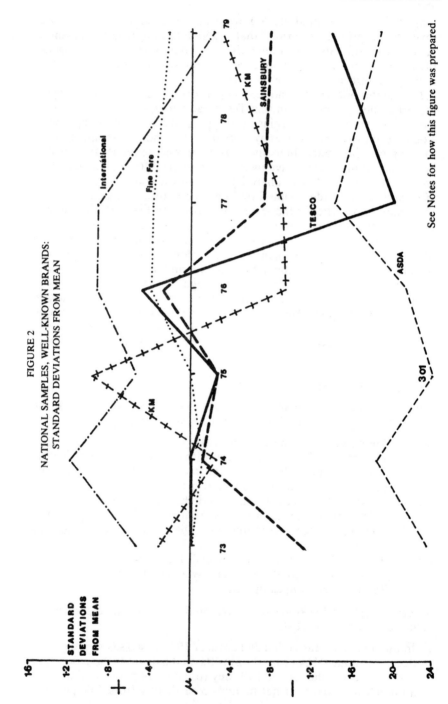

FIGURE 2
NATIONAL SAMPLES, WELL-KNOWN BRANDS:
STANDARD DEVIATIONS FROM MEAN

See Notes for how this figure was prepared.

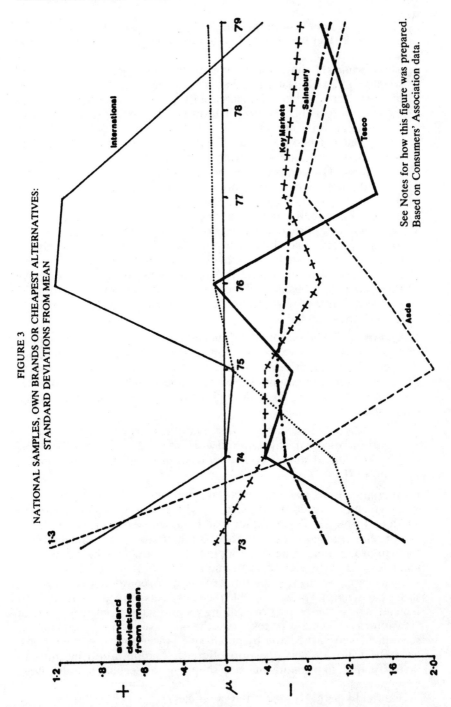

FIGURE 3

NATIONAL SAMPLES, OWN BRANDS OR CHEAPEST ALTERNATIVES:
STANDARD DEVIATIONS FROM MEAN

See Notes for how this figure was prepared.
Based on Consumers' Association data.

(1976) to 4.3 per cent during the first half year, net margins fell to 3.3 per cent on average. The yearly figure was helped by a rise during the second half.

2. Tesco's market share was falling. In the period 1976–77 Tesco had slightly increased its market share but this was due primarily to opening new stores rather than increased volume. During the final three months up to February 1977 market share was falling in a static or declining grocery market.

3. Tesco had reached a period of maturity. Green Shield stamps had been used in the quick-growing years but had now out-lived their usefulness. The company had been used to quick growth and now faced the possibility of stagnation, whilst at the same time selective price cutting, on which the company had partly based its growth, was no longer as effective in the face of competition from the discounters.

4. The possibility of stagnation and slower growth, with a consequent fall in share prices and dividends, was making the company vulnerable to takeover. It was well known at that time that International Stores would have liked to acquire the Tesco management team to revive their stagnating business. Tesco was also coming to terms with the problems caused by second-generation managers taking over from Cohen, the founder.

A study by Euromonitor [1979] suggests that, given the static demand for food and competitive pressures on operating costs and profit margins, the key to profitability lay in achieving a higher volume of sales to compensate for low margins. The way to achieve higher volume, together with cutting operating costs through economies of scale, was to open larger stores:

> It is this urge to achieve large store outlets that laid the basis for the current price war which started with Tesco's decision to withdraw its Green Shield stamps and adopt a cut price image. [Euromonitor, 1979: 7].

Euromonitor have made an important point but it was companies like Asda which pioneered the superstore, with growth based on low prices and high turnover. Tesco, rather than being an innovator, was in fact a late developer responding to the across-the-board price cutting and consequent promotion of one-stop shopping as practised by the discounters, and later in 1976 by Key Markets and Fine Fare. If Tesco had grown by selective price cutting then, at times of inflation, consumers could not be sure what a 'normal price', on which selective cuts were made, really was. Instead, across-the-board price cutting was attractive from every point of view but to achieve low prices across the board substantial economies of scale, achieved particularly by purchasing power and store operations, had to be achieved. The superstore offered a solution, and an incentive to diversify, first, to promote one-stop shopping and second, to utilise large selling areas.

Bamfield [1980: 41] makes the point clear:

The 'price war' started by Tesco in 1977 with substantial across the board price reductions costing £20 million ('Operation Checkout') is really a misnomer. It marks a change in retail techniques, particularly promotional methods, rather than being a temporary phenomenon after which retail prices might revert to normal. The 'price war' is the response of major retailers to a change in consumer buying habits as reflected in the rapid growth of low cost discounters. The period 1977–80 deserves closer attention.

AN OLIGOPOLISTIC GROUPING AROUND AND INCLUDING TESCO?

The circumstances surrounding Checkout and the behaviour of leading companies surrounding Tesco may yield clues as to the possibility of oligopolistic behaviour, and at the same time yield interesting pointers to the nature of competition within a grouping of firms based partly on similarity of product field and partly on perceived interdependence and rivalry. This identification of a move towards a possibly oligopolistic market structure does not rely on counting numbers of firms, as Linda [1976] would have us believe. In addition, it may be possible to extend the statement made by Livesey [1979: 76]:

> It is very difficult to determine whether in practice retailing can adequately be described by this oligopoly 'model'. If we consider pricing policies in the U.K. grocery market in 1977 and 1978, as discussed above, there would seem to be evidence of interdependence, of action initiated by one firm, Tesco, leading to reactions by other firms such as Sainsbury. On the other hand the fact that Tesco delayed this action for several years, despite a steady loss of market share to the discounters, suggests that the level of interdependence was rather weak.

A number of hypotheses can be considered:

1. There is no oligopolistic rivalry/interdependence in either grocery retailing or an identified grouping of leading firms with a base in groceries.
2. Oligopolistic interdependence is only weakly perceived and observed.
3. Interdependence is weakly acknowledged but growing stronger given market conditions.
4. Interdependence is strongly perceived.

Given the increasing concentration in grocery retailing it is inconceivable that some interdependence was not recognised at some point, probably between the emergence and growth of discounting, and either prior to or after Checkout. We can speculate that interdependence was beginning to be fully realised after 1974/75 when clearly by across-the-board price cuts the discounters were gaining market share. Because the volume of sales was generally static in the 1970s, growth would be at the expense of someone. Share of the market would not necessarily be lost equally across the leading companies. Asda's share of the market increased from 1.5 per cent in 1970/71 to 7.3 per cent at the end of 1979, and Kwik Save from 0.37 to 4.9 per cent during the same period. (See Table 3.) Note, however, that this growth has not, with the exception of Allied Suppliers, led to a rapid loss in market share of the leading grocery companies. Now this is interesting: the growth of discounting must have been at the expense of firms *outside* the leading group, in this case the independent retailers.

The discounters posed a threat not directly in terms of taking market share from the leading multiples (although this is a future possibility) but in the rapid nature of their growth founded on superstores, their movement into southern locations and the education of consumers in terms of low price expectations and one-stop shopping. Instead, attention should be focused on Tesco, as the largest grocery retailer by market share, and which, after the Checkout campaign, increased its market share by 50 per cent; not that Tesco or Sainsbury, by increasing their market shares, did so at the expense of their immediate rivals. Again, it was the independents and co-operative societies which lost market share. Does this mean interdependence was not strongly recognised? Those companies in the neighbourhood of discounting chains, especially discounting superstores, are likely to suffer the largest competitive impact and possible loss of market share. However, although many companies appear to be largely regionally based (except Tesco and Fine Fare), markets are generally interlocking and over-lapping. A price reduction in market basket may have an immediate effect on 'near neighbours', that is, the firms located nearest to discounters and other price cutters. The fewer the neighbours, the more their market share is squeezed. Neighbours are likely to retaliate by reducing the price of their market offering or market basket, which, in turn, leads to reactions from the 'near neighbours'. Advertising of market baskets has a cumulative effect over time, concentrating consumer preferences on one-stop shopping and emphasising the disutility of moving between competing stores.

The interesting consequence of market basket or aggregate goods competition is that within a store a firm can diversify and emphasise the heterogeneity of commodities with variable pricing. Within the store commodities take on an identity and compete with each other, whereas, at the market basket level, promotion of a group image of low cost leads not so much to *brand* loyalty outside the shopping environment, but *firm* loyalty, so that in effect there is product differentiation within stores but store differentiation at market level. Advertising builds up a stock of 'store loyalty' or goodwill which is then an element of market structure [Hay and Morris, 1979: 199]. With fewer rivals a firm is more likely to be able to monitor their activities closely and react rapidly, if necessary, to their changing activities.

First we turn to previous theoretical and empirical studies of competition in grocery retailing. The evidence for oligopolistic structures in retailing has been either disputed or confirmed, usually without substantial empirical analysis, and all prior to the rise of discounting groups, new technology and greater consumer mobility [Hood and Yamey, 1951; Holton, 1957; Metcalf, 1968; Metcalf and Greenhalgh, 1968].

Baumol, Quandt and Shapiro [1964] examined oligopoly theory and retail food pricing while Cassidy [1957] examined a retail price war in New York. Baumol *et al.* suggest a stumbling block to the development of a powerful theory of oligopoly has been the vast variety of behavioural patterns. They set out to test empirically a few types of conjectured oligopolistic interdependence. Baumol *et al.* highlight three types of oligopoly:

(a) A reacting oligopoly of the Cournot – Bertrand – Edgeworth type.
(b) Imitating or differentiating oligopolies, that is, seeking to resemble competitors, or one of them. Baumol suggests comparison shopping may lead to this kind of behaviour or alternatively a firm may make decisions distinct from competitors.
(c) Pseudo-independent oligopoly, where it is assumed that firms ignore their competitors when making routine decisions (perhaps the pricing of individual commodities, where a retailing firm may ignore competitors), but closely imitate or differentiate in terms of the contents of 'market baskets'.

Rather interestingly, the authors focus on weekly newspaper advertising run by large retailing chains, which specify their prices for a 'selected set of items' [Baumol *et al.*, 1964: 348]. They go on to state that while these prices may not be completely representative of either in-store prices or the 'competitive' interaction taking place, they are of importance in the 'competitive stance' of a chain.

Baumol *et al.* go on to state [1964: 348]

> These are the prices and the items which are designed to lure the purchaser into the advertiser's stores during the all important week-end shopping trip. Here, we felt, were the prices most likely to be set and the items most likely to be chosen only after careful deliberation and consideration of one's competitive position. Here, if anywhere in super-market behaviour and pricing, response patterns may plausibly be expected to show up. Shelf prices, while important, seem usually to be set by standard policy rules and pricing procedures, quite removed from the arena of gaming or of active oligopolistic interaction.

For the same point, see Holdren [1960: 100].

Baumol *et al.* hypothesised, and later proved, that since price cutting by a firm A is more likely to make inroads into the sales of firm B than does price raising, periods of price cuts tend to bring forth more advertising activity than in other periods. Intense advertising activity may be a recognition of interdependence or random responses to common market circumstances. Oligopoly models often start with firms assuming that all other firms will maintain their price in the time period during which a price cut is being considered, the firm making this naive assumption goes on to cut price, hoping to increase its profits. If all firms act in this way, general price cutting occurs. In grocery retailing we may note that a firm could cut the price of a particular product and, provided this cut is not advertised outside the store, the other firms are unlikely to be aware of it. Profit may be increased if the price cut is brought to the attention of consumers on entering a store, if they buy the product in sufficient numbers, and if this in turn leads to increased purchases of other products. There is no oligopolistic behaviour surrounding the individual product and it has been argued before [Akehurst, 1982] that analysing retail markets in terms of individual products is an inappropriate theoretical and empirical starting point.

What Checkout does is to focus our attention on the emergence of oligopolistic behaviour at the aggregate level of goods, selected in well-defined baskets or ranges. This is a well-known marketing and retailing device: advertise and highlight the low price of regular family purchases (bread, sugar, fresh meat, etc.) and lure shoppers into the store. This is more subtle than 'loss leaders' which as a concept has, in this writer's view, been over exaggerated. That market baskets are a competitive device which should be accorded more attention is a point made by Naden and Jackson [1953: 248]:

> The main significance for marketing research is that since buyers and sellers at retail do not think or operate exclusively in terms of individual commodities but to a large extent in terms of an aggregate of goods and services, it appears that the ordinary concept of a retail market for any *single product* has to be reconsidered.

We can state that if grocery retail companies are operating two pricing policies, one at individual goods level and one at aggregate goods level, two levels or types of competition may be in operation. Although individual good pricing can be flexible, both Naden and Jackson [1953] and McClelland [1966] suggest the total cost of the market basket has to be substantially identical or give an appearance of identity, to that of competing stores. If this is the case, interdependence is undoubtedly recognised, otherwise why go to the trouble of promoting identity? It can be argued that, given differences between companies in terms of buying power, cost price differences, differences in locations, distribution networks and inevitable differences in operating costs, there are no reasons why there should be virtually identical retail prices. If price uniformity is found in practice this should be examined, for it will say much about the intensity of competition in a market and the structure of that market. Uniformity of market basket prices may well be indicative, therefore, of oligopolistic behaviour at aggregate goods level, with monopolistic competition at individual goods level, within the store. As individual commodities may not define the structure or intensity of competition, and given the duality of competition, and since individual prices among stores cannot usually be compared without difficult and expensive surveys, some measure of the price competition of whole groups would be extremely useful. Each year the Consumers' Association publishes a survey of grocery prices, based on the price of a typical family shopping basket of items in shops run by the main grocery chains throughout the UK. If the market basket is the principal competitive device, the Consumers' Association data is most valuable; see the Notes at the end of this paper. To examine oligopolistic behaviour in grocery retailing one perhaps needs to do the following.

1. Analyse the intensity of price competition in the UK regions.
2. Measure the dispersion of prices as a proxy for the intensity of price competition.
3. Compare Tesco prices with those of other leading multiples in the UK regions.
4. Compare monthly advertising expenditure intensities.
5. Undertake behavioural analysis of the major grocery based companies over a specified time period, plotting all major developments, especially in terms of price initiatives, innovation and diversification.

We leave points (1) and (2) to a further paper, and will concentrate, in the first instance, on (3), (4) and (5).

A THEORETICAL AND EMPIRICAL FRAMEWORK

Hay and Morris introduce a useful oligopoly model utilising profit outcomes from certain price strategies [Hay and Morris, 1979: 153–59]. A matrix of profit outcomes for a firm is derived, based on an assumption that firms are aware of alternative outcomes arising from price cutting, raising or maintaining.

Profit change matrix

Other Firms

		Maintain	Cut
Firm I	Maintain	π_0	$\Delta\pi_3$
	Cut	$\Delta\pi_1$	$\Delta\pi_2$

(a) $\pi_1 > \pi_0 > \pi_2 > \pi_3$ (π_3 is negative).

(b) Profit outcomes depend on:

(i) level of concentration; (ii) price elasticity of demand; and (iii) costs of firms.

Examining possibilities, the rational firm will cut price. If other firms cut price, then $\Delta\pi_2$ is preferred to $\Delta\pi_3$. If other firms maintain their price then $\Delta\pi_1$ is preferable to π_0. Thus cut price is the dominant strategy as it gives a greater profit. Therefore, there is every expectation that all firms will cut price and end up with $\Delta\pi_2$. Agreement to maintain price would be the best solution.

In retailing, let us assume 'price' means the price of a 'representative market basket'. An across-the-board price cut will then, if rivalry is recognised, call forth similar cuts *if* it is that by cutting its price the initiating firm is now seen to be lower in price than its competitors. If the initiating firm is believed by *some* firms still to be somewhat higher in price, then no response may be forthcoming because clearly no response is called for. Price cutting for a competitor would, in this case, be clearly of little use in terms of profit outcomes. Instead a logical response would be to intensify advertising and emphasise their overall price. Therefore, following a 'price' cut, three outcomes could occur; as follows.

(1) No reaction, price or non-price, either because the new 'price' of the initiating firm is still higher than that of competitors or interdependence is weakly perceived or non-existent, or competitors decide not to respond.
(2) Advertising is increased by competitors but no 'price' cuts because, again, it is felt that the initiating firm is still higher in 'price'.
(3) 'Prices' of competitors are cut to match or undercut that of the initiator.

We know from Consumer Association grocery prices data (see Figures 2 and 3, and Notes) that just prior to Checkout, (June 1977) Tesco was, in terms of market baskets, selling well-known manufacturers' brands, both nationally and regionally, somewhat more expensive than were Fine Fare, Sainsbury, Asda and Key Markets but cheaper than International Stores. In terms of 'own brands' just prior to Checkout, Fine Fare and International were dearer but Sainsbury, Key Market and Asda were cheaper than Tesco. In the six to twelve months immediately after Checkout (June 1977), in terms of well-known manufacturers' brands, the picture changes somewhat. Tesco became the cheapest, followed by Asda, Sainsbury and Key Markets in that order, with Fine Fare and International much more expensive.

By 1979 the position of cheapest, in terms of well-known brands, passed to Asda again, followed by Tesco, Sainsbury, Key Markets, International and Fine Fare. In terms of own brands, or cheapest alternative brands, in the six to twelve months following Checkout, generally the same picture as that of well-known brands emerges; but by 1979 Asda is cheapest, then Sainsbury, Tesco, Key Markets, International and Fine Fare, in that order. In the regions, the picture sketched above is broadly the same. What can be deduced from this in terms of the three outcomes of a 'price' cut outlined above? Logically we would *expect* the following results.

(a) The period mid-May to Checkout, 9 June 1977, when a Tesco price cut was expected but no details announced:

(I)   No reaction because new 'price' of Tesco is *expected* to be still higher than that of competitors, with the strong possibility that Tesco would continue with selective price cuts: Sainsbury, Fine Fare, Asda and Key Markets, in terms of nationally well-known brands; and Sainsbury, Key Markets and Asda, in terms of own brands or cheapest alternative brands.

(II) Advertising increased by competitors but no price cuts because: (a) undefined threat from Tesco; (b) 'price' of Tesco still *expected* to be higher after cuts; or (c) responding to common market pressures, i.e. static sales volume. This result would be a possibility for all companies mentioned in I or, if alternative (c), for all companies.

(III) 'Prices' of competitors cut: unlikely in this period as the extent of the cuts was not yet known; the threat was undefined.

(b) Checkout, 9 June to 10 January 1978

(I)   No reaction because new 'price' of Tesco is higher that that of competitors. This possibility is *unlikely*, except for those firms not directly in competition with Tesco in terms of location because in this period, Tesco is cheapest in terms of both well-known brands and own brands. Furthermore, increasing concentration must have made firms more aware of rivals, and no firm could have missed the Checkout campaign.

(II) Advertising is increased by competitors but no price cuts because Tesco is still seen to be dearer overall. Advertising could logically be expected to be increased to counter Tesco's increased advertising intensity both during the initial launch of Checkout and later. No price cuts would be *unlikely* as all competitors of Tesco were now much more expensive.

(III) Price cuts would be expected from all competitors as Tesco was now cheapest according to *Which?* data [Consumers' Association] and advertising had made this fact known. The largest price cuts could possibly be expected from those multiples now appearing most expensive, that is, Fine Fare and International, and to a lesser extent Key Markets.

What actually happened can be seen by reference to Figure 4 and Tables 8, 9 and 10.

1. In the period just prior to Checkout, mid-May to 9 June 1977 (Price cuts expected, undefined magnitude):

(a)   No increase in advertising intensity: Asda, Key Markets, Lennons, Lipton, Morrisons.

(b)   Advertising intensity increases: Sainsbury, International, Fine Fare, Hillards, Gateway, Safeway, VG.

FIGURE 4
GROCERY SECTOR: MONTHLY PERCENTAGE CHANGES IN ADVERTISING
EXPENDITURE, COMPARED TO FORECAST, 1977

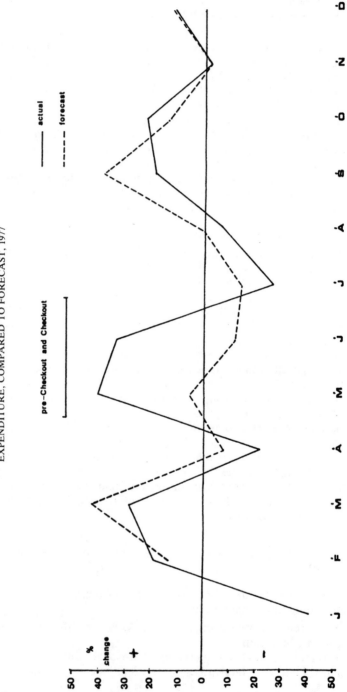

Source: Based on MEAL data.

TABLE 8
YEARLY ADVERTISING EXPENDITURE 1969–79, MAJOR GROCERY-BASED RETAILERS
(£1000s)

	1969	1970	1971	1972	1973	1974	1975	1976	1977	1978
Tesco	438	513	560	939	669	1056	1164	1594	3988	4559
J. Sainsbury	167	122	86	152	185	156	489	585	1186	2071
Asda Stores	–	–	67	192	179.7	306	236.6	589	1499.6	2652
Co-operatives	2415	2288	2174	3000	3323	4066	5348	7186	8827	9315
International	51	94	95	119	111	288	854	1098	2547	1251
Fine Fare	534	774	857	1011	1042	1400	1746	1378	2068	2441
Key Markets	20	41	72	27	55	128	32	558	680	419
Cavenham	102	131	66	175	113	154	227	81	84	428
Morrisons	1	16	3	–	–	87	175	190	218	200
Hillards	–	–	–	16	7	25	71	210	611	293
Bishops Food	34	14	40	9	–	–	7	23	98	176
Gateway	–	4	–	–	–	4	18	24	42	38
Hinton	–	–	–	6	–	24	–	64	85	85
Safeway	62	59	58	126	114	155	143	117	149	498
MacMarkets/ MacFisheries	93	26	24	44	76	85	44	65	294	343
Budgen	–	–	–	11	25	32	45	9	55	33
David Greig	3	17	9	23	66	22	169	–	–	–
Pricerite	24	10	43	54	23	10	5	–	–	–
Lennons	–	–	–	–	3	46	36	68	72	47
Mace	233	176	203	224	217	265	367	443	417	500
Spar Vivo	–	–	–	–	104	357	30	–	4	2
Spar	202	196	299	208	219	93	480	543	906	967
VG	188	175	366	303	382	352	486	526	440	551
Wavyline	–	1	17	7	–	–	65	95	106	112
Vivo	23	25	3	16	8	32	13	–	–	–

Source: MEAL reports 1969–79

TABLE 9
CHANGES IN ADVERTISING EXPENDITURE
(per cent)

	1973–79	1976–77
All grocers	253	51
Tesco	636	106
Asda	1289	161
Sainsbury	900	109
International	809	158
Key Markets	46	34*
Fine Fare	129	48
Co-operatives	149	23

* 212% in 1975/76 when Key Markets' price campaign started.

Source: Calculated from MEAL reports.

(c)   'Price' cut: no known price cut – campaigns.

2. *During June to October 1977* (i.e. Checkout and immediately after):

(a)   No increase in advertising intensity: Lennons.

(b)   Advertising intensity increases: most companies, but particularly: Asda, Co-operatives, Fine Fare, Hillards, International, Key Markets, Lipton, Mace, Sainsbury, Spar, VG, Wavyline.

(c)   'Prices' cut or other moves: International, 25 July, 'Plain and Simple' campaign; Fine Fare introduce medium-sized discounting stores 'Elmos'.

From October 1977 to 10 January 1978, when Sainsbury launched Discount '78, the situation became confused by Christmas price and advertising campaigns. For the moment, post-October 1977 is not examined.

From the hypotheses above, and empirical observation, all outcomes correspond with what could have been expected to occur. This is a first stage which, as far as leading multiples is concerned, *points* towards oligopolistic interdependence and rivalry but not conclusively.

Hay and Morris [1979: 153–54] also extend their oligopoly model to include price raising. In terms of price cutting their model is not consistent with a kinked demand curve model because the kinked demand curve assumes the only tactics open to firms are either to maintain price or all to cut price – that is a choice between a zero change in profits and a negative change $(\Delta \pi_2)$ – hence, no price cuts occur. Hay and Morris' model is consistent with the kinked demand curve analysis in that prices will not be raised.

TABLE 10

ABSOLUTE CHANGES IN MONTHLY ADVERTISING EXPENDITURE, 1977

(£1000s)

	D-J	J-F	F-M	M-A	A-M	M-J	J-J	J-A	A-S	S-O	O-N	N-D
Asda	-14	—	39	-21	12	28	11	160	-49	5	-22	9
Bishop	1	—	-1	-4	3	3	—	1	-1	18	8	-30
Budgen	1	-1	1	-1	—	28	-28	—	6	-24	5	-9
Caters	-36	7	4	2	1	-4	-4	-7	24	—	-2	38
Centra	—	—	1	-1	—	—	—	—	1	1	—	—
Co-op (local)	-268	82	97	-25	8	33	-77	1	52	37	27	24
Co-op (national)	39	-68	158	-37	5	-96	-28	-42	146	-100	-69	179
Fine Fare	4	31	7	-1	153	-41	-108	24	15	312	-174	39
Gateway	2	-1	—	-1	3	2	-3	-1	1	1	-3	—
Hillards	10	23	23	-35	43	-68	20	-24	85	-14	3	-46
Hinton	-1	-2	2	—	1	—	-1	-1	17	1	2	—
International	-62	11	56	-52	177	38	-106	-12	-45	46	47	-20
Key Markets	-69	17	87	-87	-8	70	-79	135	-94	-24	171	-127
Lennons	2	1	8	-3	-16	-1	1	-1	-2	1	11	-6
Lipton	-124	-40	23	-10	4	43	-65	64	-39	-44	57	66
Wm. Low	-2	-2	—	—	—	1	-3	2	2	1	6	10
Mace	1	110	-109	36	-3	-32	-3	1	75	-6	-65	25
Mac Markets	-20	22	-18	—	1	8	-2	—	-8	14	75	-36
Morrisons	-21	3	25	-7	-14	9	-9	2	10	—	19	-22
Safeway	-20	-4	1	2	6	5	-8	-2	-1	-6	—	-3
Sainsbury (local)	43	4	8	-7	3	-4	18	-21	5	8	-2	-105
Sainsbury (national)	—	-10	-30	-14	58	-76	369	-369	70	117	149	64
Tesco (checkout)	—	—	—	—	—	—	1075	-762	292	-78	68	1
Tesco (store)	-198	46	40	-47	73	-168	-29	-4	7	-7	-7	10
VG	-100	23	-10	-16	104	-104	8	6	13	71	-96	8
Wavyline	9	1	-11	6	-7	2	-11	2	-4	2	-3	7
Scottish Co-op	-19	6	7	7	-9	1	-61	6	26	-6	12	18
Spar	90	-31	—	-34	-9	143	-61	-99	20	126	-126	—
Total Grocers	-1123	246	455	-432	633	733	-762	-166	382	542	-27	309

Source: Calculated from MEAL reports.

Profit change matrix

Other Firms

		Raise	Maintain
Firm I	Raise	$\Delta\pi_6$	$\Delta\pi_4$
	Maintain	$\Delta\pi_5$	0

$\Delta\pi_4 < 0 < \Delta\pi_6 < \Delta\pi_5$

The worst position for Firm I is to raise its 'price' when others do not, that is, $\Delta\pi_4$ is negative. Profits are increased $(\Delta\pi_6)$ if all firms raise 'price' but the best position for Firm I is if it maintains a 'price' while the others increase their 'price' $(\Delta\pi_5)$. If other firms increase their 'price' then $\Delta\pi_5 > \Delta\pi_6$, so Firm I should maintain. Again, if other firms maintain, $0 > \Delta\pi_4$; to maintain price is again profitable. The maintain tactic dominates.

One problem with the Hay and Morris model is that it does not reflect time, and over time firms learn of the possibilities of outcomes. They refine the analysis to account for the learning of the experience of the behaviour of rivals over time, so that certain outcomes are expected from a given price initiative. In turn greater probabilities are assigned to some outcomes than others. For example, a firm experiments, with a price cut: if other firms maintain their price the change in profit is positive $(\Delta\pi_1)$ and negative $(\Delta\pi_2)$ if they cut. Over time the firm could attach probability weights to the two alternative responses:

λ: the probability that other firms maintain their price;
$1-\lambda$:   the probability that they cut their price.

The expected gain from a price cut is:

$$E(\Delta\pi) = \lambda\Delta\pi_1 + (1 - \lambda)\Delta\pi_2$$

[Hay and Morris, 1979: 160].

Provided that $E(\Delta\pi)$ is positive, a further price cut will be tried. Over time with experimentation, the probabilities change, so that we would expect λ to diminish until when $E(\Delta\pi)$ is negative price cutting ceases.

As far as the grouping of leading companies we have been examining is concerned, much hinges around the question of whether we are entitled, on the basis of an observation of the facts, to consider the possibility of reactions and reaction lags, that is, how far independence is perceived, and how far firms act *independently*. Again, we come back to the question of what 'price' to take; we can state that the prices of individual commodities can be adjusted easily, and because of the sheer number, range of quality, size of packages, etc. can do so without continuous reference to competitors. To utilise a Hay–Morris model 'price' becomes again 'market basket price'. With this in mind we can proceed.

If it is assumed that the grouping of leading firms based on groceries is vaguely interdependent, then much will depend on how long it takes rivals to be aware of a price initiative by a firm and how long it takes to make a new pricing decision. Once price competition in groceries moves to across-the-board pricing policies, then 'price' is that of an aggregate of goods. Much hinges on the question of how far competitors will be aware of actual changes in this aggregate price or awareness of perceived changes in this composite price. Three possibilities may arise.

(a) A firm's aggregate 'price' could change without competitors being aware for some time, but in this case how will consumers be aware of this fact?

(b) An across-the-board price campaign, such as Tesco's Checkout, could, or should, alert competitors, who will:

    (1) respond immediately on imperfect information, most probably based on the initiating firm's advertised prices of items in a known 'basket' (which is a known marketing and sales promotion device); or

    (2) not respond within a given time period because of a range of considerations: the identification of the initiating firm's new 'price', the need to consider own pricing policies and tactics, etc.; or

    (3) have an independent pricing and non-pricing policy, that is interdependence is perceived as weak or non-existent.

(c) A firm could engage in selective price cutting to which competitors respond or not according to information flows.

There is then, a difficult choice for a firm in grocery retailing.

(a) Cut prices across the board independently; increase advertising to bring this to the attention of consumers but at the same time alert competitors.

(b) Cut prices across the board; maintain usual advertising intensity but rely on the difficulties of identifying prices by competitors. Will consumers be aware?

(c) Selectively price cut, reduce price on selected items by perhaps a large margin and highlight these in advertising and in-store. The problem is that the consumer has now been educated to expect low prices across-the-board.

There are other alternatives, of course, but these do not aid the analysis. Given that many retailing firms, if not all, face a shifting clientele switching between firms, the incentive to introduce a cut-price strategy must increase with increasing mobility of customers. With a large firm the probability of detecting a price cut increases. In some industries the length of time required to establish the identity of a secret price cutter is longer when the market contains many equal-sized sellers. A secret price cutter *in this sense,* is unlikely to occur in retailing. Consumers must be made aware of price promotions and so will rivals. However, difficulties in establishing the aggregate price or market basket price may give great scope for increasing profitability in terms of individual commodities, both well-known brands and especially own brands. If rivals are less sensitive or unaware of individual prices there is much a firm can do without inviting retaliation.

The length of time it takes to make a pricing decision could be important. Individual commodity price changes of a random nature can probably be carried out relatively quickly but an across-the-board price cut is another matter, not only for the initiating firm but also for competitors. Consider the position of Tesco's competitors immediately after Checkout began.

(a)   Are Tesco's prices now significantly cheaper than our own?
(b)   On which products have the prices been cut, and by how much? (Advertised prices will help here.)
(c)   Is it necessary to respond either with advertising or price cuts, selective or across-the-board?
(d)   How much should our prices be cut, if at all; which products, brands, etc.; how will cuts on gross profit margins affect profitability in the short and long run?
(e)   How long to reticket goods if price cuts decided (an enormous labour-intensive task, although future laser scanning of bar coded goods will eliminate this problem)?
(f)   Is advertising necessary to highlight existing or new prices, particularly of a representative 'basket'?

A number of constraints act on grocery advertising, of course. Increasing advertising in response to a rival price initiative is unlikely to be instantaneous. Advertising campaigns need to be carefully prepared; all are lengthy labour-intensive activities and expensive. Furthermore, the results of an advertising campaign will be difficult to measure; increased sales after an advertising campaign may not be solely due to that advertising, for example, seasonal factors may be more important. In addition, advertising requires forward booking of television advertising time and newspaper space. At certain times of the year television advertising time may be at a premium and reliance on cancellations an insecure and undesirable basis for an advertising campaign.

In an industry where there is a limited number of products, where price identification is a relatively easy matter, interdependence may, given the degree of concentration, be easily recognised. In grocery retailing, and in other retailing sectors, interdependence is a more subtle matter, which, on the face of it, appears to be at variance with economic theory, bearing in mind also that retailing markets are not based on single commodities.

All of the above begs the question of whether Checkout was perceived to be a real threat to the markets of other leading multiples. One cannot be sure, without knowing the minds of the decision makers in these leading companies, how far the various price and non-price actions after Checkout do in fact constitute a reaction to the original price-cutting initiative, Checkout, or how far these were independent actions. It is possible that some price cuts which followed Checkout in time were, in fact, being considered in *advance* of Checkout and were responses to common market circumstances and pressures (e.g. static volume of food sales) and not reactions. (I am grateful to Mr J.R. Edwards of the University College of Wales for making this point, which cannot be substantially proved or disproved.) It is possible that the true significance of Checkout was to accelerate price and non-price tactics that would have occurred anyway without the Checkout initiative.

In search for possible clues in this complex market, two steps were taken.

(a) The examination of yearly and monthly advertising expenditure by grocery-based companies in the period 1976–79, data obtained from MEAL (Media Expenditure Analysis Ltd.) reports (see Tables 8, 9 and 10).

(b) The activities of the major grocery-based companies over the period 1975–80 were plotted (see the Notes), to pinpoint over a long time period all major developments, especially in terms of price initiatives, innovation and diversification, etc. This was a lengthy exercise carried out over several months but we can be absolutely sure that all major developments in this period have been identified.

Advertising expenditure can clearly be used for two conceptually distinct but overlapping purposes: (a) to create a favourable 'image' of the firm; and (b) to reply to the competitive challenge posed by other firms' activities [Baumol et al., 1964]. To this can perhaps be added a third purpose: (c) in support of a price promotion campaign.

Examination of advertising intensity will reveal some clues as to possible oligopolistic behaviour. If advertising expenditure increases significantly in a given time period, this must indicate something. Advertising is a potentially competitive act but silence (that is little advertising activity or no price campaigns) is not treated as being significant. In addition, advertising expenditure can be considered in three contexts.

(1) Advertising activities can be essentially random with respect to competitors: an independent policy where interdependence is weak or non-existent or competitors are disregarded.

(2) Imitative behaviour where a firm decides to advertise those products in week t that were advertised by its competitor(s) in week t−1.

(3) Diversificatory behaviour where a firm decides to advertise in the tth week *especially* those products its competitor(s) did not advertise in the t−1 week [Baumol et al., 1964: 354].

Increasing advertising intensity could be indicative of the possibility of awareness of rivalry or interdependence and it is with this in mind that advertising expenditures were examined. Over the period 1969–79 the intensity of advertising expenditure was carefully examined, including:

- yearly advertising expenditure, 1969–79
- monthly expenditure, 1969–79
- absolute changes in monthly advertising expenditure
- above mean advertising expenditure per month, 1976–79
- a forecast, using 12 monthly moving average time series analysis and least squares computation, of what advertising expenditure could have been expected for 1977.

See Tables 8 to 11 and Figures 4, 5 and 6. It is wise, however, to use this wealth of data with caution. Yearly advertising totals will not reflect the profound monthly changes which may occur, especially those supporting price promotions. Furthermore, retail advertising will concentrate in normal times on the main consumer spending periods, occurring twice a year, that is Easter (March–April) and Christmas (October–December). Clearly we can identify abnormal increases in advertising by examining absolute changes in monthly advertising expenditure which may highlight possible reactions, campaigns, attacking and defensive positions, although one cannot be absolutely sure; one needs to examine all other available evidence but even then an element of doubt must remain. Above mean monthly advertising expenditure (the monthly mean being the yearly total divided by the number of months) recognises the different starting points for companies: for example, a company may at the beginning of a time period have a low level of advertising expenditure but, over time, increase that level significantly, or vice versa. Percentage changes on a high starting point are misleading when compared with percentage changes on a low starting point. Together with measures of advertising to sales ratios for leading companies (see Table 12) an accurate picture of advertising intensity can be established over a long time period.

The quite extraordinary changes in advertising expenditure can be seen by examining Table 8 and 11. Companies or organisations which substantially increased advertising expenditure in May 1977, just prior to Checkout, (that is during the period when Tesco announced it was dropping Green Shield stamps, etc.) were:

Fine Fare	Gateway	Safeway	Mace
International	Hillards	Sainsbury	Tesco
VG	Wavyline		

This may have been a possible anticipatory reaction to Checkout but it would be difficult to substantiate this idea, as it can be argued that there was little time between announcing a price campaign by Tesco and the releasing of price details and the start of the Checkout campaign one

TABLE 11

PERCENTAGE CHANGE IN ADVERTISING EXPENDITURE ON PREVIOUS MONTH

	Jan	Feb	Mar	Apr	May	Jun	Jul	Aug	Sep	Oct	Nov	Dec
1976:												
Grocers	—	18	41.1	1.1	-12.5	0.1	-25.6	-2	68.1	11.6	-5	30.2
Other Retail	—	-25.1	53.5	18	-10.8	-8.3	-4.8	-17.6	43.9	34.9	-7	5.7
Mail Order	—	6.2	-1.3	-18.9	14.7	-6	-8.9	-10.1	62.1	32.3	-18.4	-59.1
1977:												
Grocers	-46.2	18.8	29.3	-21.5	40.1	33.2	-25.9	-7.6	18.9	22.6	-0.9	10.6
Other Retail	-34.4	-21.5	80.3	-6.4	-5.1	-0.4	5.2	-20.8	42.3	12.4	6.8	7.2
Mail Order	107.3	5.6	3.4	-12.1	2.8	-12.9	-2.2	-12.3	56.9	20.2	-2	-50.6
1978:												
Grocers	-42.6	-1.3	80.4	-20.0	16.9	-32.5	-29.4	10.3	61.8	30.3	11.1	-14.3
Other Retail	-38.4	-22.1	62.3	3.5	-11.4	6.9	-1.3	-8.1	39.6	9.4	5.4	4.9
Mail Order	87.7	-5.6	-16.7	42.9	-22.2	2.4	-2.2	-12.9	65.5	20.2	-4.7	-56.8

FIGURE 5

OTHER RETAIL SECTORS: MONTHLY PERCENTAGE CHANGES IN ADVERTISING
EXPENDITURE, COMPARED WITH COMPUTED AVERAGE, 1977

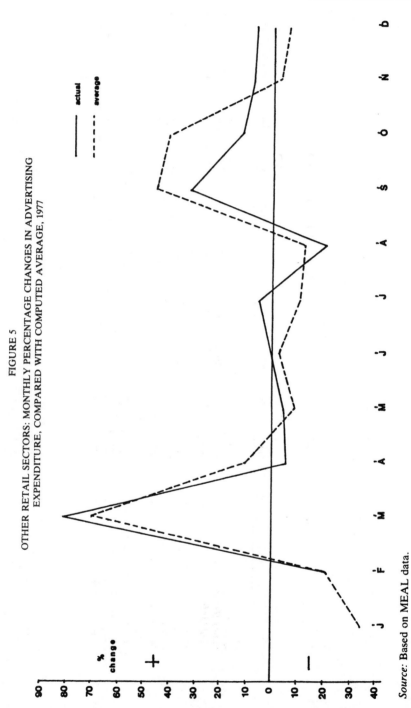

Source: Based on MEAL data.

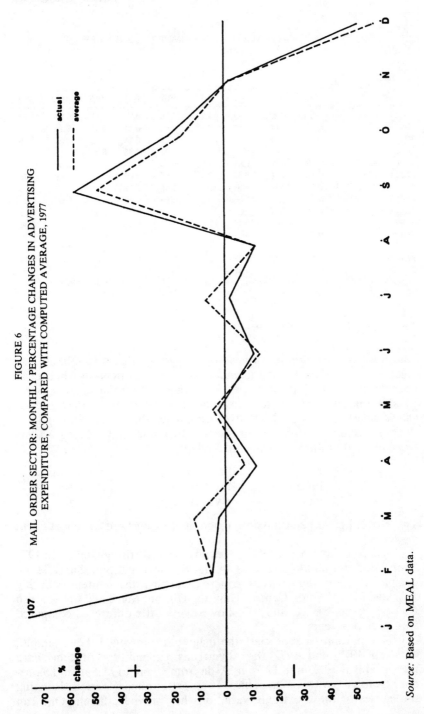

FIGURE 6
MAIL ORDER SECTOR: MONTHLY PERCENTAGE CHANGES IN ADVERTISING
EXPENDITURE, COMPARED WITH COMPUTED AVERAGE, 1977

Source: Based on MEAL data.

TABLE 12

ADVERTISING/SALES RATIO, PRINCIPAL COMPANIES

(per cent)

	1970	1971	1972	1973	1974	1975	1976	1977	1978
Tesco	0.2	0.22	0.31	0.19	0.25	0.23	0.26	0.57	0.48
Sainsbury	0.07	0.04	0.06	0.06	0.04	0.11	0.11	0.18	0.26
Asda	—	0.09	0.2	0.14	0.19	0.11	0.19	0.35	0.49
Co-operatives	—	—	—	0.43	0.43	0.45	0.51	0.55	0.53
International (BAT)	0.09	0.08	0.09	0.05	0.13	0.31	0.37	0.63	0.23
Fine Fare (ABF)	0.50	0.50	0.53	0.53	0.64	0.69	0.49	0.65	0.66
Key Markets (FITCHL)	0.09	0.14	0.04	0.08	0.15	0.02	0.39	0.47	0.23
Cavenham	8.4	0.76	0.3	0.03	0.03	0.02	0.005	0.006	0.03
Morrisons	0.16	0.02	—	—	0.35	0.5	0.39	0.33	0.23
Hillards	—	—	0.14	0.06	0.15	0.21	0.39	0.88	0.36
Bishops Food	0.05	0.12	0.02	—	—	0.02	0.03	1.0	0.16
Hinton	—	—	0.04	—	1.0	—	0.15	0.16	0.14
Safeway	0.22	0.16	0.27	0.18	0.17	0.12	0.08	0.08	0.24
Pricerite	0.03	0.12	0.12	—	—	—	—	—	—
Lennons	—	—	—	0.02	0.21	0.12	0.15	0.12	0.07

Source: Calculated from MEAL reports.

month later. Furthermore, it has been suggested that it is unlikely that companies would respond to an *undefined* threat, particularly when it was believed that Tesco's prices were, on average, higher than many groups. In addition, the four year seasonal index calculated for the 1977 forecast shows clearly a May peak of advertising expenditure (see Figure 4).

Those companies or organisations with intense advertising activity prior to, and around Checkout included:

Co-operatives	International	Morrisons
Fine Fare	Key Markets	Gateway
Lipton	Wavyline	Spar

These could have been possible reactions to Checkout or independent moves.

Those companies where there was intense advertising later on in 1977 after Checkout had begun were: Asda, Safeway and Sainsbury. Those companies where there was little increase in advertising intensity during 1977 included: Caters, Centra, Hillards, Hinton, Mace and the Scottish Co-operatives. Bishop and VG showed very little difference compared with previous years.

It is important to appreciate the magnitudes involved. For example, between 1976 and 1977 the advertising expenditure of Fine Fare increased from £1.3m to £2.06m; Asda from £0.6m to £1.5m; and Sainsbury from £0.6m to £1.2m. This was an extraordinary period. Isolating the causes of these extreme variations has proved difficult. One can speculate but there is, as yet, no way of being completely sure. Later on, it was possible to see whether the advertising patterns in 1977 could have been predicted, that is, what advertising expenditures might have been without Checkout, and whether there were similar variations in other retailing sectors, but first it is necessary to point out what these advertising data do not indicate.

It proved to be a mistake to expect these advertising patterns to fall into four main categories, that is normal Easter and Christmas promotions (which are quite distinct in all the years examined) and three stages of advertising reactions by those companies which possibly constitute an oligopolistic grouping, and around which the across-the-board pricing policy was becoming recognised as a legitimate competitive strategy. The three possible stages which were *not* proved were as follows.

(1) An anticipatory advertising reaction during May 1977, prompted by Tesco's decision to stop Green Shield stamps, and undefined price cuts due in June. This was not substantiated by the evidence and is largely erroneous.
(2) A first reaction to Checkout, during June and July 1977.
(3) A secondary and reinforcing advertising reaction in August–October 1977 or a late first reaction or possible reaction to International Stores' 'Plain and Simple' campaign.

This speculation however, could not be substantiated by the data, partly because one cannot be sure that all peaks of advertising intensity are not due to a reaction to common market stagnation, the growth of discounting, etc.; but there are sufficient signs of mutual recognition of interdependence, otherwise it would be difficult to explain the explosion of advertising expenditure in the second half of 1977. Instead, one can offer a more complex explanation which admits the possibility of parallel advertising policies at the same time, but with the strong possibility that Checkout had a peculiar effect (see Table 13). To consider anything else is to read too much into the data available.

WAS CHECKOUT UNIQUE: AN ANALYSIS OF OTHER RETAIL SECTORS

If Checkout was a response to the changing competitive environment, including lack of sales volume, etc. there should be evidence of parallel reactions in other retail sectors, to what would have been common pressures. After all, in 1977, sales volume growth was poor in all sectors (see Table 5 and Figure 1) and discounting chains were not by any means confined to groceries, and were, if anything, more concentrated in electrical goods. Were there similar developments to Checkout in other sectors? By examining the available evidence one should logically see:

• different advertising patterns and intensities in 1977 compared to previous and following years, in each retail sector;
• the possibility of intense advertising at times of stagnant or declining

TABLE 13

POSSIBLE ADVERTISING REACTIONS TO CHECKOUT, 1977

Options	Jan	April	June	July	Oct	Dec
1		Anticipatory reaction	First reaction (a) imitative (b) diversificatory (c) other	Secondary reinforcing reaction		
2			First reaction	Secondary reaction		
3				First reaction	Secondary reaction	
4		Random advertising				
5		Independent policy / Reactions to various companies				
Normal						
6		Easter advertising			Normal Christmas advertising	
7		Advertising related to own price promotions				
		Reactions to market circumstances				

market growth, assuming increased advertising is the preferred tactic for all firms;

• price cutting to gain market share growth.

The following section briefly examines the evidence for the period 1976–78 for selected non-grocery based retailing companies (or at least where groceries are but part of the business in the cases of Boots, Lewis's, British Home Stores and Littlewoods). The following companies were selected as broadly representative of other retailing product sectors:

Consumer electricals: Comet, Rumbelows, Currys

Consumer furniture,
   carpets, etc: Boardmans, ELS, Kitchen Queen, MFI

Department stores: Debenham, Lewis's, British Home Stores,
                               UDS, Littlewoods

Variety stores: Boots, Woolworths

Books, stationery, etc: W.H. Smith

Children's clothes, etc: Mothercare

With reference to Figures 5 and 6 advertising periods for the chosen companies/product groups can be identified as follows:

Furniture: Autumn–Christmas – January–February

Electricals: September–December,
                               secondary period March–April

Department stores: September–December–January

Children's clothes: Easter, July–August

Much of this corresponds with the well-established pattern of seasonal sales.

Livesey [1979: 59] believes that, as a rule, selective price cuts are likely to be less efficient in retailing sectors outside groceries, the principal reason being that one-stop shopping or the market basket is not as important, at the present time (although this is changing). As a consequence, price competition in consumer durables has concentrated on across-the-board cuts and not as much on selective price cuts. This is interesting because in grocery retailing, across-the-board price cuts are designed to encourage one-stop shopping. The discounting electrical chains, such as Comet and Trident, have increased market share by emphasising low across-the-board prices. In addition, consumer products such as pharmaceuticals and toiletries have considerably less own brands than groceries do. With these products there is a clear consumer identity with well-known manufacturer brands as being indicative of quality. With consumer durables, because purchases are infrequent, it is less likely that brand loyalty will develop to the same extent as more frequently purchased, highly routine purchases. However, the generally higher gross margins obtained by selling consumer durables allows considerable price reductions to be made which firms such as Comet have made full use of. These differences between groceries and other retailing products have, if anything, led to an increase in diversification as companies have sought to obtain a sales mix where the advantages of selling both types of goods, food and non-food, could be exploited to the mutual advantage of both retailer and consumer, one of which is the advantage of one-stop shopping for a wide range of commodities, durable and non-durable.

In the period 1976–78 the majority of non-food retail firms selected showed no significant differences in advertising expenditure patterns or intensities. For Boots, Lewis's, Littlewoods and Rumbelows there are recognisable differences in advertising expenditures during the summer of 1977.

(1) In 1977 the period of increased advertising, which previously took place later in the year, was for Boots brought forward to May–June. Livesey [1979: 56] suggests one of the reasons for the disappointing performance of Boots in 1977 was the diversification of grocery based companies into non-food goods and goods stocked by Boots. Boots, in turn, have diversified away from pharmaceutical goods.

(2) Lewis's, during 1977, increased advertising levels in July.

(3) Similarly, Littlewoods introduced more advertising in the summer months of 1977 and 1978, compared to 1976, as did Rumbelows in June of 1977.

Clearly, except for Rumbelows to some extent, those companies just mentioned overlap the product areas in which Tesco is located – that is, food, toiletries and household materials. Logically one would have expected some reaction amongst this group but one can only speculate whether these increases in advertising expenditures were either some responses to Checkout or responses to the same market conditions or for reasons totally unconnected.

From Table 11 and Figures 4, 5 and 6 the following observations can be made. First, the grocery sector tends to concentrate its heaviest advertising in two periods, March to April and September to December, and occasionally in May. The mail order sector, however, tends to advertise primarily September to October and in January, with sometimes a secondary peak in April. The 'other' retailing sectors, that is department stores, durables and furnishings, have two periods of intense advertising in April and September to October. Second, by calculating an average monthly advertising expenditure, that is average of the months during 1971 to 1976, one can smooth out odd or random fluctuations and provide a standard against which to measure 1977 advertising patterns. Plotting 1977 data in comparison with these average data one can clearly detect any deviations from the norm.

For the grocery sector however, instead of calculating an average for the years 1971–76, a forecast for 1977 was made using time series analysis, a 12 month moving average and least squares computation. The data for 1972, 1973, 1975 and 1976 were used (data for 1974 were not available).

With reference to Figure 6, the mail order sector: 1977 advertising closely follows the average, and we can safely conclude that 1977 was not, for this sector, any different from previous years. There was no Checkout type of advertising intensity.

With reference to Figure 4, the grocery sector: this shows quite clearly the exceptional advertising in the period June to July 1977, that is, the immediate Checkout campaign period, while for the January to April period, advertising levels closely follow previous patterns. May appears to be a month when advertising is generally increased and although May 1977 shows an exceptionally high advertising intensity, it would be difficult to conclude that May 1977 was some kind of anticipatory reaction to the undefined Checkout threat. For the period August to October, advertising levels for 1977 are somewhat below what could reasonably have been expected. One can speculate that, in this instance, Checkout brought forward advertising expenditure scheduled for somewhat later in the year. With reference to Figure 5, other retail sectors: generally 1977 data follow the average except for a slight difference around July 1977 and a slight decrease around October 1977. Advertising was above average around July 1977 which may have been due to:

- random advertising campaigns, quite independent;
- responses of firms with overlapping products/area markets with Tesco and other grocery based companies;
- responses to common market pressures.

It does not appear too unreasonable to believe that the Checkout campaign affected firms with overlapping product mixes but there is no evidence of a similar Checkout type advertising intensity in retail sectors, other than groceries. It is possible that Checkout accelerated some advertising and price campaigns in groceries, which were scheduled for later in 1977 or early 1978. There is, however, no way of escaping the fact that the Checkout period in the grocery sector was unique and, indeed, there is every reason to believe that the Tesco move was exceptional but not so exceptional in terms of across-the-board price strategies because clearly other companies had arrived first: the discounting chains and Key Markets. In the case of across-the-board price tactics, Tesco was a late developer.

From Table 5 we can see that non-food retailers suffered a slightly greater sales volume decline in 1977 than food retailers but this overall volume figure masks differences within the non-food area: for example, clothing and footwear retailers suffered a less severe decline than food retailers, whereas household goods retailers suffered a greater decline. Mixed retailers experienced a static sales volume in the period 1976–77. Note, however, that all sectors recovered sales volume growth in 1978 but not food retailers. Given these sales volume difficulties in the period 1977–78 it is perhaps surprising that the other retail sectors, outside the grocery-based groups, did not launch some type of advertising price campaign. That they did not is open to debate; we can speculate that it is due to the nature of the goods sold; one-stop shopping trips or not; brand loyalty or not; frequency of purchase; low–high turnover commodities; price–weight ratios, etc. Much of the difference may revolve around the importance of price projection in marketing strategies, and consumer price reactions – or can it be that the intensity of competition and market structures may be somewhat different than that associated with groceries, where the promotion of market baskets may be of overriding importance? As diversification continues, firms with an original grocery base will enter other markets taking with them a one-stop market basket philosophy. With it interdependence will slowly be realised.

All the points mentioned above are points for further research.

POST CHECKOUT

Once Operation Checkout was launched by Tesco, it was not immediately apparent by how much prices had been reduced across the board. As it turned out, prices were generally reduced by between 5 and 9 per cent on a wide range of goods. By dropping Green Shield stamps Tesco saved some £20 million; part of this financed the price reductions, part the advertising campaign and part was retained in reserves to buttress the expected short-term drop in profits as overall net profit margins were somewhat reduced.

We have examined previously the causes of Checkout, and we now know that the causes are more complex than was first thought at the time. The reactions to Checkout are also complex but there can be little doubt that interdependence, which may only have been weakly perceived prior to 1977, was realised after it. The development and encouragement of one-stop shopping, the consequent development of the projection of low overall prices combined with a static food market, made it inevitable that fierce competition would result among the major multiples for a larger-market share, and yet none of the large multiples, with the exception of Allied Suppliers, lost market share. In fact the *Financial Times* [1980] has stated that the price war fought by the major companies after Checkout was in fact not really directed at each other but at the smaller supermarket chains or independent grocers, who could not compete on prices. There is an apparent paradox here: commentators at the time talked of a price war *between* the major firms but at the same time considered that major firms *as a group* were fighting medium to small firms and the independents. The latter view generally emerges with hindsight, for as the grocery market settled down again after the Checkout operation, commentators realised how multiples, as a group, had continued to increase their share of the total market.

> By far and away the greatest influence upon retailing over the past two decades has been the capture of market share by the leading multiple and mail order companies. All else is embellishment and detail. [Hedderwick, Sterling, Grumbar & Co., 1980]

An article in the *Financial Times,* [1980] believed that the period between June 1977 and 1979 was a period of *Blitzkrieg* and that from 1979 onwards a 'war of attrition' was developing. This is an interesting view which deserves serious consideration. We have already stated that the intensification of price competition surrounding Checkout was a short-term manifestation which tends to obscure fundamental long-term changes. Certainly the *Financial Times* believed that during the 1960s and 1970s market growth of the large multiples was achieved especially at the expense of the independents; but in the 1980s, if market share growth was no longer available in this way, the multiples would have to concentrate on fighting each other. Given the developments in store technology and the superstore building programmes, much more research is needed of both short- and long-term competitive changes.

THE SUCCESS OF CHECKOUT

In May 1977 Tesco had 7.9 per cent of the grocery market; in July 1977 this had risen to 11.8 per cent. From 9 June to mid-July Tesco moved from second to largest grocery retailer; during this short time cash sales rose by 30 per cent. Table 6 shows, however, how net profit margins were reduced. By August 1977 the initial impact of Checkout decreased somewhat, and Tesco's market share fell slightly to 11.4 per cent. Other firms had, as has been seen, increased their advertising expenditures and in July 1977 International Stores launched its 'Plain and Simple' campaign. In late August Tesco seized the initiative again by extending Operation Checkout, which resulted in a continued increase in market share.

> The profits won't come immediately of course. In our business market share is the name of the game. If you lose share in a static market which food has been for the past 7 years, you've got big problems [Ian Maclaurin, Managing Director, Tesco, in *Financial Times,* 1977].

Just how successful Checkout was can be seen by examining Tesco's interim financial results for the 24 weeks ending 13 August 1977. Overall turnover (including VAT) increased 26.7 per cent but:

- sales for the 14 weeks to 4 June, just prior to Checkout, increased 14.4 per cent;
- sales for the 10 weeks to 13 August, post Checkout, increased 43.6 per cent.

Profits, however, increased by only one per cent in the same period. By Christmas 1977 Tesco sales were some 60 per cent higher than in the previous year.

SAINSBURY'S DISCOUNT '78 CAMPAIGN

Sainsbury's long awaited campaign, Discount '78, came on 10 January 1978. The causes of this are not as straightforward as commentators at the time believed. After a thorough search of newspapers at the time, and knowing what this study has revealed, it is possible to suggest a number of reasons.

(a) In reacting to a loss of market share, Sainsbury put more emphasis on selective pricing [Livesey, 1979: 55]. About 100 lines were cut from 10 to 15 per cent in price, whereas traditionally only a few goods had had prices cut for a limited time of two weeks. But it may be argued that Discount '78 was really a move in the direction of across-the-board pricing, similar to Key Market's campaign in 1976. The fact that the Discount operation has been reintroduced and extended each year up to and including the time of writing, reinforces that view. Sainsbury have been as anxious as any of the large groups to promote a low price image but backed by a quality image, at which they are particularly successful.

(b) Sainsbury had apparently been prevented from introducing its scheme earlier, in response to Checkout, because of a distribution dispute; was this valid or had the company adopted a cautious 'wait and see' policy?

(c) Had Sainsbury waited because it wished to retain its traditional policy of relatively stable prices? (During a time of high inflation it is doubtful whether this is valid.)

(d) *The Times* in 1978 argued that Sainsbury may have waited for the food inflation rate to slow down so that any price reductions made would be more apparent to the consumer.

(e) Perhaps Sainsbury did not feel pressured, to the same extent as competitors, by market circumstances.

Whatever the real reasons, or more likely, combination of reasons, Sainsbury was by the beginning of 1978 losing somewhat its share of the market. The following day after Discount '78, on 11 January, Tesco immediately revised prices in those stores directly in competition with Sainsbury. This is a clear indication of the recognition of rivalry, of interdependence. What is also clear is that from 1978 the picture, in terms of intensity of advertising expenditures and price strategies, became more complex. From 1978 the large multiples entered a period of increasing awareness of interdependence and rivalry not because any one of them was taking market share away from any of the other leading firms, but the threat was always there. The 'war of attrition' had begun. During 1978 Sainsbury slowly emerged with a substantial profits growth and, up to the time of writing, has proved rather more successful in terms of profitability than Tesco.

Whilst branded, packaged groceries continued to carry the brunt of price cuts, as part of the market basket competition, nevertheless Sainsbury continued to place great emphasis on fresh food and produce: meat, fruit, vegetables and dairy products. Tesco, in watching closely the success of Sainsbury, also began to place emphasis on fresh foods, as did International Stores with an experiment begun in 1980 of fresh and high quality stores called 'Country Market'. Emphasis on fresh food did not, however, stop diversification into non-food areas but falling consumer expenditure on clothing, textiles, electrical appliances and so on did produce a pause for thought.

1978, 1979 and early 1980 also saw the signs of casualties amongst the leading groups.

(1) In February 1980, International Stores sold 52 Pricerite shops to Fine Fare, and began dispensing with Green Shield trading stamps as early as March 1978.

(2) Key Markets introduced during 1979 various bingo schemes with prizes to revive sales and in May 1978 sold its discount food shops to Hillards.

(3) British Home Stores began closing food departments in its stores as early as April 1978; these closures continued into 1979.

(4) F.W. Woolworth also began closing food departments.

Even Asda introduced an extensive price cuts campaign in January 1980, with price cuts ranging from 5 to 20 per cent on both food and non-food products, designed more as a promotional exercise than as a real attempt to launch a major offensive. The biggest surprise of all came, however, in August 1979 when Marks and Spencer launched a major low-price campaign on a wide range of food and non-food items. Although increases in market shares were not, by and large, derived from within the group of leading multiples, nevertheless rivalry was well and truly recognised.

In examining advertising expenditures during 1978 and 1979, there are no logical explanations. One cannot be sure that a company, by increasing advertising expenditures, is responding to Sainsbury, Tesco, International Stores *et al.*, engaging in normal Easter or Christmas promotions or acting in an independent and random manner. All one can do is identify those groups who intensified advertising (a) earlier than 1977, and later than 1977, and (b) those groups which appear to have reverted in 1978 to pre-Checkout advertising levels.

(a) Groups whose intensive advertising started much earlier than in previous years (n.b. Sainsbury introduced Discount '78 on 10 January 1978): Budgen; Co-operatives; Lennons; Caters; Fine Fare; International; Mace; Tesco; VG; Hinton, Wm. Low (except for the latter two, all are in competition with Sainsbury in the south and south Midlands).

(b) Groups who reverted to 1976 advertising patterns: Asda; Bishop; Macmarkets; Safeway; Spar; Key Markets.

CONCLUSIONS

The events of the period 1976–80, and indeed to the present time, show a lively, competitive grocery market of considerable change, which is worthy of detailed study.

One can see quite extraordinary changes in grocery companies' advertising in 1977 which could not have been predicted, and which are substantially different from preceding and continuing years. In comparison with other retail sectors, Checkout produced identifiable, albeit complex, advertising and other competitive moves and counter moves, not all of which could be ascribed to prevailing general market conditions. It is possible that Checkout accelerated some advertising and price campaigns which were scheduled for later in 1977 or early 1978.

The reactions to Checkout are complex; the causes of Checkout itself are complex but there can be little doubt that interdependence, which may only have been weakly perceived prior to June 1977, was realised afterwards. It focused attention on long-range marketing planning and strategies in a fast changing technologically based world, of consumer mobility and increasing disposable incomes. When asked to give ideas about future trends, Matt McKenzie (Operations Director of Fine Fare's Superstores Division) wrote:

> There will be no economic miracles and therefore 'price' is likely to be as dominant a factor in five years' time as it is today. Thus, margins and costs will remain under severe pressure and only the ruthlessly efficient will prosper. [McKenzie, 1982: 18]

After 1978 the grocery picture became very complex, but there are sufficient indications to show the strength of rivalry. There is much to the argument that grocery multiples have entered a period of attrition, and modified to some extent the concept of a full price war; indeed the term 'price war' is too convenient a shorthand for what is occurring.

Some casualties in terms of closures and falling market shares can already be seen – Woolworth, Key Markets, International Stores, (although its Mainstop superstores look promising) the Co-operative societies and food departments in British Home Stores. Whilst Checkout initially may not have taken market share from other leading multiples, it will be interesting to see what the leading group of Sainsbury, Tesco and Asda will do in the remaining years of this decade.

As a postscript to this article, in 1982 Key Markets, owned by Fitch Lovell, was involved in a fierce takeover battle between Safeway and Linfood. Linfood won, and in the autumn of 1982 went on to purchase Fitch Lovell itself. In 1982/83 Sainsbury, the market leader, and the emerged winner of the competitive battles of 1977–82, showed a substantial 20 per cent rise in profits to £109 million on sales of £2.5 billion, with sales volume up 10 per cent. As competition has eased somewhat, pre-tax profit margins for Sainsbury have risen to 4.4 per cent, well ahead of Tesco at 2 per cent and Asda at 3.5 to 4 per cent. However, Tesco's market share has risen following its campaign to move more 'up market' which takes the group more into competition with Sainsbury; while Asda continues to make steady progress. Clearly Tesco, Sainsbury and Asda are pulling further away from the pack, and concentration continues to increase.

One recent feature since 1981 has been the introduction of unbranded generic or brand-free ranges, a no-frills presentation introduced by Carrefour in the mid-1970s and adopted by International Stores, Tesco, Fine Fare, Mace and Allied Suppliers. Whilst investment and modernisation programmes will continue, we shall continue to see an emphasis on price, a continued move towards fresh foods (with higher margins) and a slowing down of non-food diversification, which had gathered pace in the late 1970s.

A future article will examine price competition between grocery multiples at regional level, in the continuing examination of competition in grocery retailing. Much research needs to be done; what is especially important is to see in-depth long-run analyses rather than short-term studies of varying company strategies and tactics.

NOTES

The Consumers' Association magazine *Which?* has published grocery price surveys annually up to October 1979; surveys were not published in 1980 or 1981 but a restricted survey appeared in October 1982. The aim is to show, region by region, how the grocery groups compare on price, and indicate which groups could be cheapest for consumers. Full details of the surveys can be found in *Which?* (see references), but in brief, roughly 1,300 shops are visited throughout the UK, covering some 30 to 50 groups, including all major multiples and most regional multiples. In each shop the prices of the shopping basket items (which are carefully predetermined) are noted, producing four main samples: well-known brands, own brands (or cheapest alternatives), fresh fruit and vegetables, and fresh meat.

The number of items in the shopping baskets (19 in 1974 rising to 32 in 1979) has been carefully controlled. Items are those which a typical household of four persons might purchase in a given time period. From 1976 prices of items have been weighted to take account of how often people actually purchase them.

National data show how much the basket costs in each group on average for brands and own brands, and show how the different chains compare, averaged over the whole country. With reference to Figures 2 and 3, rather than produce detailed data, which is clearly impractical, a clear picture emerges by standardising the sample means of the *Which?* basket for each company (calculated from the *Which?* surveys as noted above) and considering the distribution of company means around the national mean in terms of standard deviations. This has the advantage of allowing comparisons between the years 1973 to 1979 without the distortions of inflation, etc., and in a readily understood manner. It also eliminates the tedious and unnecessary comparison of *Which?* company baskets in each year in each region. With reference to Figures 2 and 3 and Table 4, positive and negative deviations from μ can clearly be seen. The negative deviation shows a company sample mean less than the national mean.

In examining Figure 2, note:

1. Prior to 1976 Tesco prices were on average about equal to the national mean or just below it.

2. In 1976 Tesco became uncompetitive in comparison with Asda, Sainsbury and particularly Key Markets, who had introduced their price cuts campaign that year.

3. The considerable effect of Checkout in 1977 can be seen but this lead is eroded by 1979 by Asda. However, in 1979 Tesco prices were on average well below those of the other major companies.

TABLE 14

STANDARD DEVIATIONS FROM MEAN: REGIONAL DATA (WELL-KNOWN BRANDS)
FOR 5 LEADING MULTIPLES

	1974	1975	1976	1977	1978	1974	1975	1976	1977	1978
	London					Southeast				
Tesco	-0.4*	-0.92	0	-2.31	-1.68	-0.4*	-0.78	-0.25	-2.27	-1.6
Sainsbury	-0.93*	-1.1	-0.69	-1.11	-1.4	-0.93*	-0.89	-0.34	-1.05	-1.32
Fine Fare	-0.67*	-0.28	-0.2	-0.16	+0.09	-0.67*	-0.45	-0.25	+0.13	-0.31
Internationa	+0.53*	+0.09	+0.59	+0.32	na	+0.53*	0	+0.76	+0.49	-0.51
Key Markets	-0.93*	+1.1	-1.96	na	na	-0.93*	+1.12	-2.19	-1.22	-0.69
	Midlands					North				
Tesco	-0.35	-0.2	+0.12	-2.08† / -1.85	-1.42† / -1.42	-0.12	0	+0.54	—	—
Sainsbury	-0.17	-0.26	+0.06	-0.96† / -0.6	0.99† / -0.69			-1.84**	-1.16**	
Fine Fare	-0.35	+0.2	+0.12	+0.2† / -0.24	+0.15† / +0.5	-0.25	+0.19	+0.36	0**	+0.39**
International	+1.22	+0.26	+0.68	+0.4† / +0.3	-0.33† / -0.55		+0.9	—	—	—
Key Markets	+0.17	+0.72	-1.12	-0.79	-0.3		—	—	—	—

Key: *   London and SE only.
      †   Top figure in each pair is for West Midlands; bottom is for East Midlands.
      **   NW only.

See Notes for explanation.

4. Sainsbury virtually mirrors Tesco until 1977 although its prices are marginally cheaper prior to 1977 compared with Tesco. From 1977 Sainsbury prices are clearly competitive but somewhat higher than Tesco. However, the gap between the two is seen to narrow as Discount '78 and '79 took effect and Checkout began to lose momentum.

5. Key Markets clearly became very uncompetitive in 1975. From 1977 Key Markets has been more expensive than the three leaders (Tesco, Sainsbury and Asda) but noticeably cheaper than fine Fare and International Stores.

6. The unfortunate position of Fine Fare can also be seen: until 1975 it was marginally competitive but remained more expensive since 1976 compared to all companies except International Stores. In 1979 it came adrift from the leading group.

7. The uncompetitive position of International Stores can be seen for the years 1973 to 1978 but 1979 saw a considerable improvement following their 'Plain and Simple' campaign.

8. Asda is, except for 1977–78, cheapest overall.

Figure 3, own brands, shows broadly the same picture except for four important exceptions.

(a)   Sainsbury has sustained lower own brands prices over the period 1973–79 than many companies.

(b)   Asda, although not having many own brands, seems to have overtaken Tesco about 1978–79 in terms of cheaper prices of secondary brands.

(c)   The position of Key Markets has been consistently good over the period from 1974.

(d)   The own brands market is even more competitive than that of well-known brands, but own brands are on permanent price promotion.

Table 14, regional data, shows broadly the same trends as above, although Asda is not shown because it was not located in all the regions shown. Generally, prior to 1977 Sainsbury was more competitive (i.e., cheaper on average than Tesco); Tesco became cheaper as a result of Checkout but by 1978 Sainsbury was narrowing the gap. A fuller analysis of regional price competition will appear in a future article.

Major Developments 1977–79

1977

March	International gain control of F.J. Wallis
April	Tesco announce renegotiation of Green Shield stamps contract
May	Tesco drop Green Shield stamps in all stores; no details of proposed price cuts
	International interested in taking up about 100 Green Shield stamp franchises
June	Tesco launch Operation Checkout
	International offer double Green Shield stamps and series of 'money off' offers
	Unofficial industrial action at Sainsbury distribution depots
	Fine Fare: extensive advertising and promotions
July	International launch 'Plain and Simple' with three-month price freeze and price cuts
August	Tesco extend Checkout
	Fine Fare launch Elmos, medium-sized discount stores (two stores experiment)

| September | International extend price freeze to end of January 1978 |
| November | Tesco move advertising to new agency |

1978

January	Sainsbury launch 'Discount '78'; cutting prices by 10 to 15 per cent on 100 lines
	Tesco re-examine prices in stores directly competing with Sainsbury stores
	International consider dropping Green Shield stamps
February	Tesco purchase two Scan superstores from Debenhams, announce computer trial for Autumn, cut-price petrol war
	International hold prices of Plain and Simple range for six months plus other wide price cuts
March	Asda offers £20 million p.a. to develop shopping centres in partnership with local authorities
	International drop Green Shield stamps in 40 stores and 50 shops to be converted to Pricerite discounting
April	British Home Stores close 18 food departments out of 77 in stores
May	Key Markets pulling out of discount food stores selling KD Discount Stores to Hillards
June	International launch with Green Shield stamps 'Super Discount' campaign stamps redeemed for low price lines
	Tesco start 'Bake'n'Bite' experiments and change sales mix towards higher margin non-foods and fresh foods. Asda consider non-foods will give growth
July	Both Tesco and Sainsbury increase prices slightly to ease profit margins
August	International announce will drop Green Shield stamps from all but 100 stores
	Asda start take-over of Wades
	Marks & Spencer announce own credit card soon to be followed by Fine Fare and Tesco
September	International drop Green Shield stamps, aggressive price cutting with some brands being sold at cost
October	British Home Stores close food departments in all but six stores
	Sainsbury to operate department store with Bentalls
	International trial computer checkout at two stores over a year
November	Asda acquire Allied Retailers
December	Tesco take control of '3 Guys', Eire; offer in-shop concessions

1979

January	Sainsbury relaunch price campaign with 'Discount '79' but restrict scope
	Tesco launch own credit card
February	International announce credit card for food and non-food
	Key Markets launch 'Cash Bingo' with prizes
	Sainsbury experimenting with laser scanning at SavaCentre
March	Fine Fare launch 'Cash In' campaign: basic items price cuts
	Six British Home Stores food departments being closed
	Tesco reorganise distribution network
April	Tesco attempt DIY superstore planning permission
	Marks & Spencer extend credit card to more stores
May	International start 'Big I' credit card
	British Home Stores start small specialised stores experiment

June	Tesco absorb VAT on non-food lines and certain other items BAT acquiring MacMarkets (Unilever) Key Markets first with operational laser scanning and starts second 'Double Bingo' Fiat UK and Fine Fare plan car retail outlet at a store
July	Tesco purchasing Cartiers
August	Both Tesco and Sainsbury accelerate plans to computerise stores following Key Markets Marks & Spencer launch major new low-price campaign on wide range of food, clothing and furnishing: most unusual Asda reluctantly announce plans for customer credit card
September	Tesco start Autumn campaign with special coupons Marks & Spencer plan to extend credit card to all stores by Christmas Fine Fare laser testing at Hyde, Manchester store
October	Asda investigating laser scanning Tesco price cuts on clothes Sainsbury diversify into DIY with 'Grand Bazaar SA'
November	Key Markets open non-food 'House and Home' store
December	Tesco consider entering TV rentals Key Markets' third promotion: 'Christmas Bingo'

1980

January	Sainsbury announce 'Discount '80' Asda extensive price cuts campaign, cuts of 5 to 20 per cent International quietly drop Green Shield stamps from all stores
February	Fine Fare announce price cuts of over 100 lines, guaranteed until Easter; purchase 52 Pricerite stores from International Tesco responds to Sainsbury and Asda price cuts

REFERENCES

Akehurst, G.P. 1982, 'The Economics of Retailing – A Note', *Service Industries Review,* Vol.2, No.1

Akehurst, G.P., 1983, 'Concentration in Retail Distribution: Measurement and Significance', *Service Industries Journal,* Vol.3, No.2.

Bamfield, J.A.N., 1980, 'The Changing Face of British Retailing', *National Westminster Bank Quarterly Review,* May

Baumol, W.J., Quandt, R.E. and Shapiro, H.T., 1964, 'Oligopoly Theory and Retail Food Pricing', *Journal of Business,* Vol.37.

Consumers' Association, 1974, *Which?,* November.

Consumers' Association, 1975, *Which?,* October.

Consumers' Association, 1976, *Which?,* October.

Consumers' Association, 1977, *Which?,* November.

Consumers' Association, 1978, *Which?,* October.

Consumers' Association, 1979, *Which?,* October.

Consumers' Association, 1982, *Which?,* October.

Daily Mail, 1976, 31 July.

Economist Intelligence Unit (EIU), 1974, *Retail Business,* No.200, October; No.201, November; and No.202, December.

EIU, 1976, *Retail Business,* No.225, November.

EIU, 1977, *Retail Business,* No.232, May.

EIU, 1979, *Retail Business,* No.251, January.

EIU, 1980, *Retail Business,* No.271 September.

EIU, 1983, *Retail Business,* No.309, November.

Euromonitor, 1979, *Retail Trade International, 1977–78,* London: Euromonitor Publications.

European Economic Community (EEC), 1976 and 1977, *A Study of the Evolution of Concentration in the Food Distribution Industry for the United Kingdom,* Vol.1: *Industry Structure and Concentration* (1977), Vol.2: *Price Surveys* (1976), Brussels – Luxembourg: Commission of the European Communities.

Financial Times, 1977, 26 April and 29 September.

Financial Times, 1980, 'The Grocery Industry', 25 April.

Fulop, C., 1966, *Competition for Consumers,* London: Allen and Unwin.

Hay, D.A. and Morris, D.J., 1979, *Industrial Economics,* Oxford: Oxford University Press.

Hedderwick, Sterling, Grumbar & Co., 1980, *Multiple Explosion,* London: Hedderwick, Sterling, Grumbar & Co.

Holdren, B.R., 1960, *The Structure of a Retail Market and the Market Behaviour of Retail Units,* Englewood Cliffs, NJ: Prentice Hall.

Holton, R.H., 1957, 'Price Discrimination at Retail: the Supermarket Case', *Journal of Industrial Economics,* Vol.6.

Hood, J. and Yamey, B.S., 1951, 'Imperfect Competition in Retail Trades', *Economica,* Vol.8.

Jones, P.M., 1982, 'Hypermarkets and Superstores – Saturation or Future Growth?', *Retail and Distribution Management,* Vol.10, No.4, July/August.

Linda, R., 1976, *Methodology of Concentration Analysis Applied to the Study of Industries and Markets,* Brussels: Commission of the European Communities.

Livesey, F., 1979, *The Distribution Trades,* London: Heinemann.

McClelland, E.G., 1966, *Costs and Competition in Retailing,* London: Macmillan.

McKenzie, M., 1982, 'Fine Fare Superstores. Their Past and Future', *Retail and Distribution Management,* Vol.10, No.1, January/February.

Media Expenditure Analysis Ltd. (MEAL), 1969–80, various annual and quarterly Advertising Expenditure Reports.

Metcalf, D., 1968, 'Concentration in the Retail Grocery Industry in GB', *Farm Economist,* Vol.11.

Metcalf, D., and Greenhalgh, C., 1968, 'Price Behaviour in a Retail Grocery Sub-Market', *British Journal of Marketing,* Vol.1.

Monopolies and Mergers Commission, 1981, *Discounts to Retailers,* London: HMSO.

Naden, L.D. and Jackson, G.A., 1953, 'Prices as Indicative of Competition Among Retail Food Stores', *Journal of Farm Economics,* Vol.35.

The Nielsen Researcher, 1979, No.2.

This chapter first appeared in *The Service Industries Journal,* Vol.4, No.2 (1984).

9

The Outlet/Off-Price Shopping Centre as a Retailing Innovation

by

J. Dennis Lord

Beginning in the late 1970s there has been a major development in US retailing: the factory outlet/off-price shopping centre. The origins can be traced back to where manufacturers operated factory site stores for employees; later there was a change in location and customers, particularly in the grouping of outlet stores to form shopping centres. This clustering is very recent. This paper examines the reasons for growth, the types and size of centres, market segments served, the geography of centres and their future. Whether these outlet centres are creatures of recession and will fade as the US economy improves or whether this is a significant trend in retailing remains to be seen.

During the past half-century US retailing has witnessed several innovations in the kinds of retail businesses or configurations which are used to deliver goods to consumers (Figure 1). The modern supermarket can trace its origins to the 1930s. This retailing innovation was followed during the 1950-60 decade by the planned shopping centre whose importance on the American retailing landscape mushroomed during the succeeding decades [Lord, 1982]. The discount department store dates largely from the 1960s and has had a profound impact on retailing

FIGURE 1
RETAILING INNOVATIONS SINCE 1930

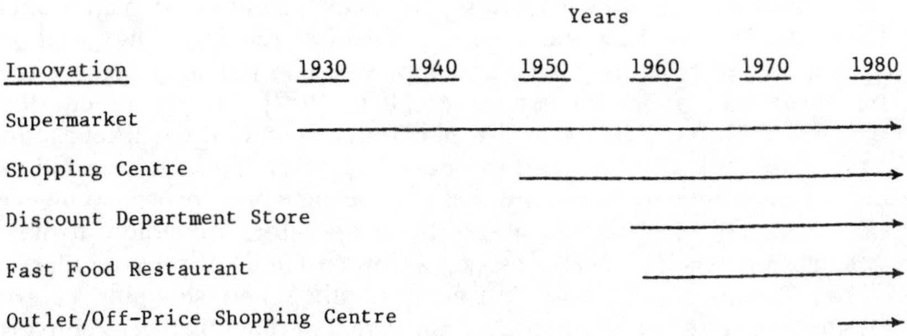

Innovation	Years					
	1930	1940	1950	1960	1970	1980
Supermarket	———————————————————————————→					
Shopping Centre			———————————————————→			
Discount Department Store				———————————————→		
Fast Food Restaurant				———————————————→		
Outlet/Off-Price Shopping Centre						———→

patterns, particularly within suburban settings. Somewhat later in time has been the rapid rise in franchise fast food restaurants typified by McDonald's, Kentucky Fried Chicken and others.

Beginning in the late 1970s, and continuing at a rapid pace into the 1980s, has been another major development in retailing: the factory outlet/off-price shopping centre. While the eventual impact of this new retailing form may not be as great as some of the earlier innovations, it certainly represents a significant new direction on the American retailing scene. The outlet/off-price centre functions much like other more conventional centres by providing a cluster of stores at one site, to provide the consumer with the opportunity to make multi-store visits and to comparison shop.

EVOLUTION OF OUTLET/OFF-PRICE RETAILING

Factory outlet stores and off-price retailing have undergone a significant evolution in recent years involving changes in location, merchandise mix, and consumer market orientation. Factory outlet and off-price retailing can trace their origin back in time to the situation where a manufacturer operated a store at the site of the factory as a service to its employees [National Mall Monitor, 1981]. Often these stores carried seconds or irregular merchandise. Later, the general public was allowed to buy goods and outlet stores began to appear at sites other than the factory location such as free standing sites, downtown locations, and in strip shopping centres. With this change in location and customers came the realisation that outlet stores could become a significant source of revenue for the manufacturer, not only in the sale of seconds but also close-out stock, over-produced items and goods similar to the merchandise sold in conventional stores. The next step in this evolution was to group several outlet stores together to form an outlet shopping centre. These outlet stores along with other off-price retailers increasingly carried quality name brand merchandise at discounts well below the price levels of conventional retailers. While outlet stores have existed for a considerable period of time, the clustering of outlet and off-price stores together to form a specialised shopping centre is very recent. In fact, a majority of the outlet/off-price centres currently in operation have opened since 1978.

A number of theories exist in regard to change in retail institutional structure. One of these theories, the 'wheel of retailing', may well be appropriate to describing the initial appearance as well as changes in the outlet/off-price shopping centre [McNair, 1957]. Simply stated, the wheel of retailing theory says that new retailers enter the market as low price, low cost and low margin operators. Over time, these retailers engage in trading up, in other words they become higher cost and higher price retailers. Such action makes these operators vulnerable to new competition which enters the market as low cost and low price retailers.

Two trends in the outlet/off-price retailing and shopping centre business suggest some evidence for the wheel of retailing theory. First is the improvement in the quality of merchandise, thus leading to fewer seconds and irregulars and more top quality goods. Second is the gradual upgrading of the physical plant of the shopping centre to bring it more in line with conventional centres. The entry into the off-price retailing field by several conventional retailers is evidence of an upgrading trend in the outlet/off-price business [*Off-Price News*, 1983: 8]. However, there seems to be a lack of consensus among developers and store operators as to how much upgrading should be done. One view is that the consumer expects something less than plush surroundings in order for the merchants to offer merchandise at a significant markdown from conventional prices. Thus, too much upgrading could raise questions in the consumer's mind regarding the real value of the outlet centre merchandise.

IMPETUS FOR GROWTH

The impetus for outlet and off-price retailing and the planned shopping centre environment has come from both the demand and supply side of the market. Certainly the recession beginning in the late 1970s and continuing into the early 1980s has been a significant boost. The current economic stress has caused consumers to be more price sensitive when shopping for name brand merchandise [Green, 1983:96]. As a result of this financial insecurity, the consumer has substituted price for selection and service while still retaining the same level on the quality dimension. Certainly price, quality and fashion are all important elements of the value equation in outlet/off-price retailing compared to the discount store environment, where price is the dominant element in the value equation.

The recession and high unemployment have also meant a slack demand for goods ordinarily sold by conventional retailing methods and a backlog of inventory by the manufacturers [Bivins, 1983: 26-28]. The outlet and off-price stores have provided a means for the manufacturer and the retailer to sell these goods. Also, evidence of the supply side impetus is to be seen in the numerous outlet/off-price centres which are conversions of conventional centres. Some shopping centre owners with older centres, which were in economic difficulty due either to a deteriorating market and/or new competitors, have attempted to recycle the centre as an outlet/off-price facility. One question which arises concerns how much of the impetus for factory outlet/off-price centres comes from a determination on the part of real estate owners or developers of a real market opportunity in contrast to a strategy simply to recycle unsuccessful real estate, in other words, a positive market opportunity strategy or a panic reactionary one. The later discussion of conversion and adaptive re-use projects will shed some light on this question.

TYPES OF OUTLET/OFF-PRICE CENTRES

The recent explosion of outlet/off-price centres has seen the emergence of three distinct types: (1) new construction centres, (2) conversion of existing conventional centres, and (3) the adaptive re-use of other facilities which had not been used previously as shopping centres. By the fall of 1982 there were a total of 129 outlet/off-price centres in the US: either open, under construction or in the planning stages [*The Outlet Center Manual and Directories*, 1982]. Some 43 per cent of these centres were new constructions, while 35 per cent were conversions of existing centres. An additional 22 per cent were adaptive re-use projects.

Various developers have debated the advantages and disadvantages of new construction versus conversion [Floyd, 1983: 65-66]. Arguments which favour conversion projects point to a number of factors: (1) shopping centre property may be available at a good price, (2) renovation can often be done cheaply, and (3) rental rates for converted centres can be increased over previous rates. Also, conversions allow developers with existing conventional centres to ease into and test this new retailing form, thus reducing time requirements and the risks of new construction projects. Quite notable in this regard are major developers such as Melvin Simon and Associates and the Rouse Company. Those developers who favour new construction indicate the following advantages: (1) lower energy costs, (2) less maintenance, (3) better security, (4) newer centres can be built fairly cheaply, and (5) locations can be controlled. The adaptive re-use facility has both advantages and disadvantages when compared with new construction and conversion. On the plus side are the low purchase price of these structures and the uniqueness of the facility which can create a different sort of shopping environment. On the negative side are problems with maintenance and building codes, and the odd shapes and sizes of the structures.

The size of outlet/off-price centres does not appear to differ by type. A typical centre, regardless of whether it is new construction, conversion, or adaptive re-use averages approximately 150,000 sq. feet of floor space. Most centres will range in size from 50,000 to 250,000 sq. feet. The largest new construction and conversion centres are of the order of 350,000 sq. feet. Adaptive re-use projects vary somewhat more in size.

The tenant mix of outlet/off-price centres include true factory outlets, off-price retail chains, conventional stores and off-price stores operated by conventional retail chains. Of the more than 10,000 outlet/off-price stores today, only about 10 per cent are true manufacturers' outlets. One advantage of the off-price retailer over the true factory outlet is the ability of the former to offer a greater assortment of goods. Today, only a small minority of the outlet/off-price stores are located in shopping centres.

The developers involved in the outlet/off-price centre industry vary from small, new developers who specialise in these types of centres to big conventional centre developers as exemplified by the Rouse Company. On several occasions, such as in New Jersey and Wisconsin, a new developer has constructed several centres with similar size and design characteristics. One problem for outlet/off-price chains which has arisen concerns the credibility of some of these developers who are new to the shopping centre industry.

MARKET SEGMENT FOR OUTLET/OFF-PRICE CENTRES

The market segment most important to the outlet/off-price industry is comprised of middle- and upper-income consumers who are fashion conscious and goods-acquiring orientated. The outlet customer is the person who can recognise that a $20 shirt is a bargain if it sells for $30 in a conventional retail store. The consumer who is looking for the $5 shirt is not in the outlet/off-price market segment. Instead, these types of customers will most likely find their needs met by discount variety and discount department stores. Because of this market orientation, the outlet/off-price trend is likely to have a much greater impact on conventional department stores than discount chains. It is interesting to note that some of the department stores who could be significantly affected by the outlet/off-price trend are now joining the game. One such example is Dayton-Hudson with its Plums' stores.

MARKET AREA CONFLICT

One of the significant questions for outlet/off-price stores, and thus shopping centres, regards the co-existence in a geographic market of outlet or off-price stores with conventional retailers who sell the same name brand products. There is fear on the part of the manufacturer of alienating conventional stores that have sold the manufacturer's products. Pressure may be exerted by these retailers on manufacturers not to sell their goods in outlet or other off-price stores in the same market. A concrete illustration of this conflict is provided by Outlet Square, an outlet/off-price centre in Charlotte, North Carolina. One of the principal tenants of the centre is Burlington Coat Factory, a national chain off-price retailer selling family apparel and accessories. In late 1982, this firm filed a lawsuit claiming that Belks, a south-eastern US department store chain with three stores in Charlotte, had pressured several manufacturers not to sell those brands to Burlington Coat Factory which were also carried by Belks. At the time of writing, a decision on this restraint of trade lawsuit is still pending.

Outlet and off-price stores and shopping centres have become sensitised to this potential problem and have employed a number of strategies to avoid conflicts. These strategies include the following: (1) no direct advertising by the outlet/off-price stores in the market, (2) no mention of the store's name on the centre's advertising – only institutional advertising, (3) selling only the less popular products of the manufacturer, (4) locating stores in areas where they would not compete directly with conventional retailers; and (5) using some name other than the manufacturer's for the outlet store. Many of these strategies are well illustrated by Factory Outlet Mall in Orlando [Fesperman, 1982: 5].

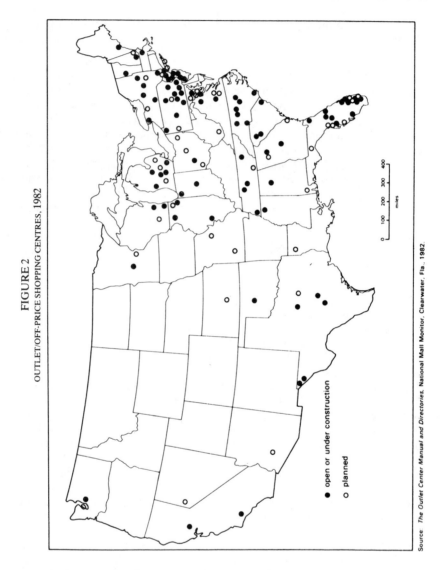

FIGURE 2
OUTLET/OFF-PRICE SHOPPING CENTRES, 1982

• open or under construction
○ planned

Source: *The Outlet Center Manual and Directories, National Mall Monitor, Clearwater, Fla., 1982.*

THE GEOGRAPHY OF OUTLET/OFF-PRICE CENTRES

By the fall of 1982 there were some 86 outlet/off-price centres either open or under construction with an additional 43 in the planning stages. Most of these existing centres are post-1978, although the oldest centre, located in Reading, Pennsylvania, dates from 1950. Growth has been so rapid recently that the list of centres changes almost weekly.

What is the American geography of the outlet/off-price centre? In order to answer this question, data were obtained from an industry source regarding the locations of all centres either open, under construction, or planned as of October 1982. The geographical pattern of centres is portrayed on Figure 2 with centres which were either open or under construction being distinguished from those in the planning stages. It is quite apparent from this map that the outlet/off-price centre to date is largely an eastern American phenomenon with the greatest densities occurring in the North-East, Florida and the Carolina Piedmont. Only a smattering of centres are located west of the Mississippi River. The leading states are Florida, New York and Pennsylvania with 19, 12, and 12 centres respectively. These three states account for one-third of all

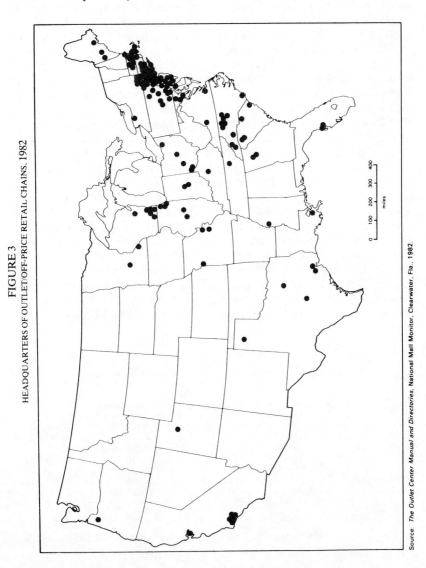

FIGURE 3

HEADQUARTERS OF OUTLET/OFF-PRICE RETAIL CHAINS. 1982

Source: *The Outlet Center Manual and Directories*, National Mall Monitor, Clearwater, Fla., 1982.

centres. The pattern of concentration is further revealed by the fact that thirteen states account for 76 per cent of all centres.

Why is there an eastern American concentration of these centres and a conspicuous absence from the west coast? The answer probably can be found in terms of the influence of the location of manufacturers and outlet/off-price chains, and logistical and operational costs in serving the west coast market [Serwer, 1983: 7]. Perhaps the east coast concentration and the west coast lag is best understood if one views the factory outlet/off-price stores and shopping centres as an outgrowth of manufacturing and not retailing. Many of the manufacturers, particularly in apparel, are located in the eastern United States. Figure 3 displays the locations of the headquarters of those firms with outlet or off-price store chains. The major concentration of these firms is in the North-East with much smaller concentrations in the southern Piedmont and Mid-West areas. Two-thirds of the chains shown on Figure 3 are located in the North-East, Middle Atlantic and South Atlantic regions. West coast locations for stores operated by these manufacturers present a number of difficulties, including problems in merchandise distribution, staffing and field supervision. Also it has been suggested that high real estate costs on the west coast may be an inhibitor in that outlet/off-price chains need low occupancy costs in order to maintain their low profit margins.

There are also some interesting regional differences in the relative importance of new construction, conversions and adaptive re-use outlet/off-price centres. Table 1 illustrates these differences for the four major census regions. The majority of centres in the North-East are conversions of existing centres (60.5 per cent) with an approximately equal proportion of new construction and adaptive re-use projects. In the South, the opposite pattern is indicated with over 60 per cent of the centres being new construction facilities. By comparison, the North-Central region is fairly evenly balanced among the three types of centres. The West has too few centres for any meaningful comparison.

TABLE 1

OUTLET/OFF-PRICE SHOPPING CENTRES BY REGION AND TYPE

Region	New Construction	*Type* Conversion	Adaptive Re-use	Totals
North-East	7 (18.4)	23 (60.5)	8 (21.1)	38 (29.5)
South	37 (61.7)	13 (21.7)	10 (16.6)	60 (46.5)
North Central	9 (34.6)	8 (30.8)	9 (34.6)	26 (20.1)
West	3 (60.0)	1 (20.0)	1 (20.0)	5 (3.9)
	–	–	–	–
Totals	56 (43.4)	45 (34.9)	28 (21.7)	129

*Figures in parentheses are percentages

Source: *The Outlet Center Manual and Directories,* Clearwater, Florida: National Mall Monitor, Inc., 1982.

Why are there these regional differences in types of centres? The answers are partly found in the contrasts in the economy and demographic trends. The greater importance of conversion projects in the North-East probably reflects the poorer state of the economy and the lack of population growth, which have in turn increased the incidence of problem shopping centres. On many occasions the owners have sought to bring life back to these sagging centres by recycling them as off-price facilities. In contrast, better economic conditions and faster population growth in the South have meant that there have been fewer conventional centres in trouble. Instead, the off-price centre developer has responded with new construction projects. Florida typifies this growing market. Fourteen of the nineteen centres in the state are new construction facilities. It has been suggested that future development in the West is likely to produce new and enclosed malls, because the industry has now obtained the expertise and ambition which are necessary for larger and more costly projects [Dunham, 1983: 26-38].

The adaptive re-use projects constitute a fairly constant proportion across the American regions, varying from 16.6 to 34.6 per cent of total. Almost half of these centres involve the re-use of former factory buildings. Former uses include textile mills, a spaghetti plant, a dental plant and an automobile parts factory. The second most frequent adaptive re-use project involves the conversion of either a department store or a discount store. Other interesting re-use centres include a truck terminal, train depot and a school.

THE FUTURE OF OUTLET/OFF-PRICE CENTRES

The impact of the outlet centre to date has been relatively small; for example, at the end of 1982 only 0.5 per cent of shopping centres and shopping centre square footage were accounted for by this form of retailing. There are two contrasting views as to the future of these centres [Floyd, 1983: 65-66]. One view is that the centre is a child of recession and will thus fade away when the economy improves. The opposing view sees them as a significant trend in retailing with a lasting impact. While it is difficult to forecast which of these situations will be correct, one can identify a number of issues which will influence the future of these centres.

The outlook for outlet centre industry will be affected by improvements in the economy and by the supply of merchandise available to off-price retailers. As the economy improves one can anticipate that some consumers will be less willing to make the trade-off between selection, service and price. One industry expert suggests that the major resistance to the growth of the industry will come from a limitation on the amount of goods available for sale at off-price, a sort of built-in delimiter. If the manufacturer begins to provide current seasonal merchandise, this would cause a blurring of the images between off-price and conventional retailing, particularly if department stores were to respond with lower prices [Green, 1983: 96].

We may also see some changes in the locations of outlet centres. One type of location which occurs a number of times is a centre near major tourist areas. Examples include Orlando, Myrtle Beach and Williamsburg. It has been suggested that these centres may have a limited future because when tourists have one of them in their own community, they will become less of a tourist draw [Dunham, 1983: 26-38]. We may see more boldness in centre locations, even to the extent of being adjacent to regional malls. This boldness may extend to off-price stores in general as they locate close to department stores, even to the extent of locating in regional malls.

A final limiter on the growth of outlet centres may be related to the fears of manufacturers of alienating conventional retailers. However, as noted earlier, outlet/off-price retailers can employ a number of strategies to minimise the potential conflict.

REFERENCES

Bivins, J., 1983, 'Retailing's Runaway Offspring: Off-Price', *Chain Store Age,* Executive edition, March.

Dunham, T., 1983, 'Outlet/Off-Price Malls: A New Deal of the Cards', *Shopping Center World,* Vol. 12, March.

Fesperman, D., 1982, 'The Lure of a Factory-Outlet Mall Brings in 5 Million Visitors a Year'. *The Miami Herald,* 9 August.

Floyd, M., 1983, 'Major Trend or Passing Fancy? Off-Price and Factory Outlet Centers', *National Mall Monitor,* Vol. 12, January-February.

Green, H. L., 1983, 'Retail Chains Entering Off-Price Field May Blur Lines of Existing Market', *Shopping Center World,* Vol. 12, March.

Lord, J. D., 1982, 'The Malling of the American Landscape', paper presented at the annual meeting of the South Eastern Division of the Association of American Geographers, 21 November.

McNair, M. P., 1957, 'Significant Trends and Developments in the Postwar Period', in Smith, A. B. (ed.), *Competitive Distribution in a Free High Level Economy and Its Implications for the University,* Pittsburgh, Pa: University of Pittsburgh Press.

National Mall Monitor, 1981, 'Factory Outlet Malls: There'll Be No Stopping These Things', Vol. 11, January-February.

Off-Price News, 1983, Dayton-Hudson Opens 'Plums' Prototypes Next Month', Vol. 1, 10 February.

The Outlet Center Manual and Directories, 1982, Clearwater, Florida: The National Mall Monitor.

Serwer, Jeremy, 1983, 'West Coast: Young and Largely Untapped', *The Off-Price News,* Vol. 2, February.

This chapter first appeared in *The Service Industries Journal*, Vol.4, No.1 (1984).

Spatial-Structural Relationships in Retail Corporate Growth: A Case-Study of Kwik Save Group P.L.C.

by

Leigh Sparks

Retail companies develop and expand by combining both structural attributes and spatial awareness. The spatial-structural development and growth of individual retail companies has been neglected in the growing retail literature. Through examining in detail the growth and development of retail companies, concentrating on both the spatial and structural dimensions of development and using the concepts and ideas emerging in cognate fields such as entrepreneurship, competitive strategy and innovation diffusion, it is postulated that a better understanding of the complexities of retail growth will be produced. A case-study of Kwik Save Group P.L.C. is used here to explore these concepts, to build a spatial-structural theory of retail change and to demonstrate the relevance and usefulness of detailed study of individual firms.

INTRODUCTION

'Every marketing strategy leaves a spatial imprint' [Jones and Simmons, 1987: 331].

Retail companies operate in both a business and a spatial environment. It has often been claimed that location is crucial to retailing, but it is equally true that the retail offering and operation has to fit both the marketing and the wider competitive environment. Retail businesses develop by considering both the spatial and the structural elements of the company and the environment. Retailers have to determine what and how they are going to retail, where outlets are to be located in respect of the market and the competition and how the retail operations are going to be organised. These questions and decisions are magnified when placed in the context of expanding a retail business. How do retail companies grow in terms of location and operations? Why are certain companies successful at certain times and places? Why do apparently very similar companies have widely differing results? How are the dispersed elements of a retail company organised and controlled? As McNee [1974] pointed out, there are a considerable number of structural and spatial questions to be asked about any multi-point organisational stystem. There are also spatial-structural questions to be asked.

The aims of this article are two-fold. The first aim is to suggest that a detailed approach to corporate development combining not only managerial and strategic decision-making but also spatial aspects of development can help in an understanding of the processes of the management of change and of retail company growth. This can be seen as a preliminary step towards the development of a spatial-structural understanding of retail change. It is founded on the belief that the structural and spatial elements of retail change need not operate in isolation and that business practice clearly suggests that they operate in harness. Within this approach there is a need to understand also how companies combine these spatial and structural attributes in order to develop and expand. The second aim is to demonstrate that conceptual and theoretical development in retailing requires a detailed understanding based on specific retail cases. Specifically, a case-study of Kwik Save Group P.L.C. is used. The choice of company here is designed to demonstrate how valuable lessons can be drawn from company-specific studies, and how theory or concept development is aided by such detailed work. The case-study demonstrates in particular how structural and spatial concerns are indivisible. This study of Kwik Save Group P.L.C. provides material for use both in managerial and geographical disciplines and also aids understanding of the process of managing change and in particular the change from entrepreneur to fully corporate status.

In order to meet these extensive and complex aims the article is structured into five sections. These provide a review of previous research, resumés of retail theory and retail development, a brief analysis of food retailing in Great Britain, the specific case-study of Kwik Save Group P.L.C. and a conclusion based on the lessons learnt from this analysis. The nature of the topic, the breadth of the aims and the integral case-study mean that this article is not a short one.

PREVIOUS RESEARCH

Retailing has come under close scrutiny in recent years from a variety of viewpoints and academic subjects and disciplines. As Dawson [1988: 1] states:

> the sociologists have undertaken studies of status and roles of ethnic retailers, political scientists have studied the influence of trade associations on public policy, operational researchers have

modelled supermarket checkout queues, economists, anthropologists, planners, historians, accountants, engineers, and even the meteorologists ... have research interests in retail activities.

It is, however, the subjects of geography and business studies (including management and marketing) in their widest senses that are perhaps at the forefront of retail analysis. As Dawson [1988] further points out, there is a considerable volume of academic literature on retailing available. This is demonstrated by the source material in Jefferys [1954], Scott [1970], Davies [1976], Beaujeu-Garnier and Delobez [1979], Dawson [1979], Dawson [1980], Guy [1980], Dawson [1982], Potter [1982], Davies [1984], Davies and Rogers [1985], Gayler [1985] and Johnson [1987a] in particular. Among the topics relevant to this analysis and case-study are theories of retailing [Stampfl and Hirschman, 1981], institutional change or theories of institutional change [Martenson, 1981; Brown, 1987a, 1987b, 1988b], analyses of retail forms [Dawson, 1983; Dawson and Lord, 1985], strategy in retailing [Knee and Walters, 1985; Johnson, 1987a, 1987b; Laulajainen, 1987; Walters, 1988], retail location [Davies and Rogers, 1984; Ghosh and McLafferty, 1987; Jones and Simmons, 1987; Berry, et al., 1988; Wrigley, 1988], planning for retailing [Davies, 1984; Gayler, 1984] and the internationalisation and globalisation of retailing [Kacker, 1985; Kaynak, 1988]. Specific review articles such as Brown [1988a] on the 'theory' of the wheel of retailing and McGoldrick [1987] on pricing or the bibliography produced by Kirby [1988] further emphasise the volume of retail research that is available. Academic journals both within and across academic disciplines and also the trade press demonstrate this diversity of work on retail topics.

It is relevant to consider how much of this material has in fact aided our understanding of retailing [Warnes and Daniels, 1980], especially at the level of corporate development. There is a surprising dearth of studies of the development and evolution of retail firms. This has been commented upon particularly by Savitt [1982, 1984] who has argued cogently for greater attention to be paid to the 'history' of retail development at both the firm and institutional levels. Savitt's attempt to introduce company-specific studies to aid theoretical development has itself attracted criticism [Hollander, 1986]. Such detailed company studies, however, could improve the understanding of retail change and development by linking the realities of practical business experience with the academic rigour of detailed study, and by combining relevant approaches and considerations across subjects and disciplines. As Savitt [1982: 22] has claimed, 'the theories of retail change are the antithesis of historical research because they are based on generalisation', and it follows that 'if retail change theories are going to become more valuable in structuring marketing strategy, more attention must be paid to ... specific retail firms' [Savitt, 1984: 53].

The lack of study of and research into the development of individual retail companies has been to the detriment of the concepts of retail theory and retail analysis as an academic discipline, and maintains an artificial barrier between academics and practitioners. Retail companies are mainly used as examples or small illustrations to reinforce a single point. There is much that is useful and illuminating in this method, but it is important that more detailed study is also attempted that provides a much fuller understanding of the processes involved in retail change and development. While it is understandable that much of the work in retailing is developed implicitly from an understanding and awareness of the processes of retail change, it is equally important that detailed work is used to provide a base for knowledge and to test existing understanding. Retail theory, for example, can suggest reasons and models for the introduction of food superstores in Great Britain. It is not able as yet, however, to say much about the spatial spread of the introduction nor of the companies involved.

In particular there would not appear to be any combination of spatial and structural elements in retail analysis. For example, there is a geographical strand to retail study that is concerned with form and changing form but excludes much consideration of the companies, entrepreneurs and managers driving the processes of change. This provides a spatial axis for understanding. There is also a managerial and business approach which is strong on the corporate and strategic dimensions, including markets and competition, to retailing. This provides a structural axis for understanding. This structural approach however generally ignores any spatial considerations of retailers at both the macro- and micro-(store) levels, while the spatial approach often ignores the structural realities of corporate life. Retail companies themselves clearly incorporate both spatial and structural approaches in their tactics and strategy and grow through a harnessing of both aspects. This combination is at the heart of the approach of Jones and Simmons [1987]. Similarly Laulajainen [1987: 1] comments that 'space matters in business ... space steers business activity', while Ghosh and McLafferty [1987: 1] broaden the influence of location strategy to be 'an integral and important part of corporate strategy'.

Of particular interest therefore is the possibility of combining a spatial approach, i.e. geography, with a structural approach, i.e. the managerial and operational focus of the business, management and marketing subjects. Such a spatial-structural approach has been suggested before [Dawson, 1984] although not in any detail. This approach has also been stated as the theoretical justification for a recent important textbook [Jones and Simmons, 1987] which has attempted to show the links between the geographical and the managerial perspectives at a variety of spatial scales. Such a spatial-structural approach, however, is not often easy to identify and carry through, and much work remains to be undertaken in combining these elements, particularly at the levels of retail theory and the retail company. A better understanding of the structural and spatial imperatives of retail companies would begin to provide the detailed work necessary to produce a spatial-structural theory of retail development. This is the overriding objective of this study.

The potential of such an approach has been partially recognised before. From the geographical background Kivell and Shaw [1980: 147] made a plea for 'more thought ... to be given to the measurement of locational change ... through examining the spatial dynamics of retail firms'. This plea has fallen largely on deaf ears. Jones [1981] responded by examining Asda, focusing on the spatial diffusion of an innovation (food superstores). The result, however, is really only a description of the spatial pattern of trading stores rather than an understanding. His study is one of pattern but not process. He followed this up by examining MFI in a similar vein [Jones, 1982]. Davies and Sparks [1986] took these to a logical conclusion by analysing the merged Asda–MFI, and in the same series Burt [1986] has reviewed the development of Carrefour. Bird and Witherick [1987] added immeasurably through their examination of Marks and Spencer but tellingly felt it necessary to justify in their introduction a geographical interest in corporate affairs. By examining the spatial strategies of a large number of retailers in Sweden and particularly the USA, mainly in historical terms but across many retail trades and organisation forms, Laulajainen [1987] appears to have attempted to incorporate spatial decision-making with structural and corporate realities. On closer examination, however, it is clear that these very short case-histories merely identify spatial outcomes of processes rather than place the spatial decision-making within the corporate context. Laulajainen [1987] is a start but no more. There is scope, however, to 'mine' these case-studies and investigate specific aspects of retail change and test specific hypotheses. In this way Laulajainen [1988a, 1988b] is moving towards developing a spatial-structural understanding of corporate growth.

Where Laulajainen [1987, 1988a, 1988b] is useful is in making a link with the earlier work of Watts [1974] and Schiller [1981]. Both these works, Watts on Boots' development in an historical context and Schiller on Mothercare, suggest that spatial development is the progress of an innovation within a hierarchy of urban centres or towns and cities. Laulajainen [1987] finds similar patterns for some retailers but not others, and concludes that while some companies follow similar growth paths and even locations there is no one spatial strategy for retail growth. It has to be remembered, however, that all this work tends to study spatial strategy independently to other strategies. This work also raises a number of questions about retail growth and diffusion as a function of a number of factors such as outlet size, retail type, distribution requirements and facilities, management policy, micro-location (street level) and other elements of location (urban-suburban). Doubt is also thrown on the validity of retail hierarchies identified by retail branch counts [e.g. Schiller and Jarvett, 1985].

Apart from these works, there has been silence on the geographical side in terms of any explicit spatial analysis of corporate development, although there is a respectable literature on spatial changes in retailing in terms of historical studies [e.g. Jones, 1979; Shaw, 1978; Shaw and Wild, 1979; Wild and Shaw, 1974, 1975], retail forms [e.g. Bennison and Davies, 1980; Davies and Sparks, 1989; Dawson, 1984; Jones, 1988; Knox, 1981] and individual locations [e.g. Brown, 1984; Davies, 1971; Giggs, 1972; Guy, 1976; Parker, 1962; Pocock, 1968; Whysall, 1974, 1989], which contain some structural elements but relatively little on individual retail companies.

On the managerial or business side the literature is perhaps more rich, but generally has been limited to being tied to one aspect of a company. For example, Akehurst [1984] examined Tesco's Operation Checkout, and Savitt [1984] used Comet to explore anew the wheel of retailing. Knee and Walters [1985] incorporated case studies of GB-Inno-BM, Habitat/Mothercare and Magasin du Nord to illustrate the diversity of strategic thinking in retailing, an approach also used in Walters [1988]. Green [1987] produced John Collier as an illustrative case-study of failure to adapt to change. Similarly Johnson [1987b] has developed a detailed strategic analysis of Foster Brothers. The rationale for this work is that Johnson (an ex-manager turned academic) felt strongly that academic theory ignores the practical realities of managers and decision-making. His method of bringing the two closer together was a detailed case-study of Foster Brothers. Some studies have taken an historical/geographical approach in a business context as for example Watts [1974] in his study of the spatial development of Boots or Osborne [1975] for the Greater Nottingham Co-operative Society. Other more general business accounts of retail companies and retail entrepreneurs can be found in Thil [1966], Havenhand [1970], Smethurst [1974], Ornstein [1976], Goldsmith and Clutterbuck [1984] and Kay [1985].

One exception to this single aspect brand of study is Mintzberg and Waters [1982] who tried to examine strategy in an entrepreneurial retail company. This article is important for two reasons. First, it clearly places spatial strategy within the context of the retail company and identifies spatial strategies, not always successful, over a period of 60 years, as one aspect of corporate strategy. Second, the article is important in the context of the company-specific study (Kwik Save) developed here. Mintzberg and Waters identify the 'split' between entrepreneurialism and planning as the two aspects in the growth of this retail company and focus on the transition from one to another. They conclude:

> the danger is that the planning mode forces out the entrepreneurial one; procedure tends to replace vision, so that strategy

making becomes more extrapolation than invention ... the success of the entrepreneurial mode evokes the forces ... that weaken it [Mintzberg and Waters, 1982: 498].

Within the management strand of research there is also the approach of company histories, either authorised versions by the company or journalistic accounts. In the main these tend to concentrate on personalities and within-company issues, and while interesting and occasionally illuminating they often give a summarised and 'squeaky-clean' picture. A list of many of these can be found in Goodall [1987]. A notable exception to this is the work on Allied Suppliers by Mathias [1967]. Such works also often ignore the spatial development and changing offering of the company at the expense of developing a broad-brush personality cult. Among others [Goodall, 1987] books have been produced on Empire Stores [Beaver, 1981], W.H. Smith [Wilson, 1985], Marks and Spencer [Rees, 1969; Tse, 1985], Currys [Lerner, 1984], Tesco [Corina, 1971], Sainsbury [Boswell, 1969] and the John Lewis Partnership [MacPherson, 1985]. There is also a vast body of literature of variable rigour and quality on co-operative development [Smethhurst, 1974]. American examples run from classics such as the study of Macy's [Hower, 1943] through to the recent tome on MacDonalds [Love, 1987]. A number of retail entrepreneur biographies can be found in Jeremy [1984–86], but these in the main, while interesting, are of historical figures and again concentrate on personality rather than practice.

Both the geographical and the managerial literature have considered the process of retail change. The concern of this article is to link the spatial and structural elements of development. The questions that need to be posed include the topics of how companies grow in both spatial and structural terms, how companies choose broad locations for outlets and why companies are structured and located how and where they are. In considering location decisions, the focus is not on the detailed site location choice decisions which are explicitly and well covered elsewhere [for example, Davies and Rogers, 1984; Ghosh and McLafferty, 1987; Wrigley, 1988] but on the general strategic patterns of spatial development. Such considerations need of necessity to be linked to the body of retail theory that has been developed and to wider theories of corporate change.

RETAIL THEORY AND RETAIL DEVELOPMENT

Retail theory contains a considerable number of elements, many of which have attracted enormous criticism over their specification and validity [Stampfl and Hirschman, 1980; 1981; Martenson, 1981; Rosenbloom and Schiffman, 1981; Savitt, 1982, 1984; Klein and Roth, 1987]. There is no need here to detail all the strands of retail theory that have been identified. The concentration instead can be on the most pervasive of those theories concerning retail change. Retail change theory has concentrated on the theories of organisational change as the comprehensive listing of the literature in Brown [1987a, 1987b] shows. Brown [1987b] has detailed the theories of retail institutional change under the broad heading of environmental, cyclical and conflict theories. He has broadly suggested that there needs to be an overlay of a spatial dimension to these theories [Brown, 1987c], again pointing to the need to combine structural and spatial issues.

The most well-known 'theory' is that of the wheel of retailing [Brown, 1988a; Savitt, 1988]. This states that new retail institutions begin with crude facilities, little prestige and a price- and margin-cutting reputation. As they progress, they acquire more expensive trappings and techniques and thus become vulnerable to the next low-cost competition. The problems with the wheel of retailing are debated more fully elsewhere [Brown, 1988a; Savitt, 1984, 1988; Klein and Roth, 1987]. It can be suggested that such simplistic notions are really only a basic description of a standard progression and that the wheel of retailing has its 'validity' in that it describes one aspect of the entrepreneurial process. Other retail theories [Stampfl and Hirschman, 1981] similarly describe elements of the entrepreneurial process without providing any understanding of the growth element of retail change. As Brown [1988b: 11] notes, '(these theories) do not *explain* ... change' (original emphasis). Having developed a new formula for retailing how, where and why does that formula or that company develop? Retail theory as it stands at present is wholly unable to answer such questions. Part of the difficulty may lie in trying to generalise theories without first undertaking the detailed and specific work from which understanding will be forthcoming. In addition it is clear that much of the theory development in retailing has failed to address the spatial and structural elements of retail change concentrating instead on the institutional forms themselves rather than seeing the institutional forms as one element only.

The growth of businesses has also been the focus of study in other subjects and disciplines. In particular industrial geography has developed a considerable body of theory ranging from neoclassical theory through behavioural location theory and the geography of enterprise to structuralist theories [Hayter and Watts, 1983; Lever, 1985; Chapman and Walker, 1987]. Much of the detailed work, however, appears not to be applicable to retail growth.

Retail growth strategists have demonstrated that there are a number of ways in which retail businesses can grow and develop [Ghosh and McLafferty, 1987; Jones and Simmons, 1987; Knee and Walters, 1985; Worztel, 1987; Miller 1981]. Figure 1 shows some of the avenues through which growth can be achieved. What is suggested by the figure is the link between spatial and structural elements of development. Implicit within the figure is the recognition that retail expansion could be by organic or by takeover mechanisms. In either case spatial-

FIGURE 1
RETAIL GROWTH STRATEGIES

		Existing Merchandise	New Merchandise
New outlets	New market areas	Increase market coverage	Geographical expansion and store diversification
	Existing market areas	Expand network of outlets	Store diversification
Existing outlets		Increase market share	Scrambled merchandising

Source: Reproduced from A. Ghosh and S.L. McLafferty, *Location Strategies for Retail and Service Firms* (Lexington, MA: Lexington Books, D.C. Heath & Co., 1987) by kind permission of the publishers. Copyright 1987 D.C. Heath & Co.

structural questions will be raised [Laulajainen, 1988a, 1988b]. Such growth strategy considerations are relevant for established retail firms as well as newly emergent ones. It is worthwhile, however, to begin with the entrepreneurial process in retailing. Retailing as an industry has relatively low entry barriers. Although it can be argued that entry barriers are now rising, this is a relatively recent phenomenon associated with the investment needed to operate large stores. Certainly, entry barriers in retailing are usually considered as significantly lower than for many other sectors of the economy. If an entrepreneur has an idea for a new retail format, then the entry barriers are such that it is likely that introduction will occur. The problems arise in controlling the business, becoming successful and in expanding from a small, independent business into a larger company. The process of moving from an entrepreneurial company to a managed one is often hazardous, and particular problems emerge when the goals of the entrepreneur and the business come into conflict [Churchill and Lewis, 1983; Mintzberg and Waters, 1982; Scott and Bruce, 1987]. Drucker [1985] has suggested that entrepreneurs in a new business venture require four elements to be successful:

i. the need to focus on the market and to identify and satisfy customers capitalising on unexpected opportunities;

ii. the requirement for financial foresight, especially planning for

cash-flow and capital needs and the control systems to support
these;
iii. the requirement for a top management team to be produced early
and ahead of needs, a requirement that leads to
iv. the need for the entrepreneur to define his own responsibilities
within the business.

For retailing, there is a requirement in particular to have a focus on
and to understand the market and satisfy customer needs. Developing mainly out of the work of Porter [1980; 1985], there have therefore
been a number of attempts to link the successful growth of retail
companies with the elements of competitive advantage (Miller, 1981;
Knee and Walters, 1985; Omura, 1986; Johnson, 1987a, 1987b;
Ghosh and McLafferty, 1987; Laulajainen, 1987 and Walters, 1988).
This concentration on retail strategy has in the main been concerned
with established companies rather than examining the development
and growth of companies from new business ventures and entrepreneurship through to established large businesses.

Porter [1980] argues that success in an industry is due to a sustainable
competitive advantage. This competitive advantage is of two basic
types: low-cost or differentiation. Porter [1980] also discusses a third
'strategy' – the focus strategy – which involves following one or other
strategy but focused on only a narrow market segment. Porter [1980]
argues that the low-cost strategy requires sustained capital investment
and access to capital, process engineering skills, intense supervision of
labour, products designed for ease of use and a low-cost distribution
system. Organisational requirements include tight cost control,
frequent detailed control reports, structured organisation and
responsibilities and incentives based on meeting strict targets. The
second strategy, differentiation, is where a firm seeks to be unique
along some dimension that is widely valued by buyers. The company
selects one or more attributes that buyers perceive as important and
uniquely positions itself to meet these needs. This strategy requires
strong marketing, product engineering, creative flair, basic research,
corporate reputation for quality, long tradition in the industry and
strong co-operation from channels. In organisational terms strong co-
ordination, incentives based on status and subjective criteria and social
amenities are required. Porter [1980, 1985] views these two strategies
as being very different, but recently they have been seen as acting in
association and together providing the firms 'value platform', or
competitive advantage [Karnani, 1984; Ghosh and McLafferty, 1987].
Certainly cost leadership and the implications this has for operational
style and retail offering can produce a highly differentiated retail unit
and company.

These concepts of Porter [1980, 1985] have been applied in analysing
the retail industry. Knee and Walters [1985] examine how companies
can make themselves different by following product-market strengths

or productivity advantages. Similar themes are pursued in Walters [1988] and Johnson [1987a]. Porter [1985] has extended the concepts of strategies for competitive advantage further by introducing the concept of the value chain for a company. The value chain stems from the realisation that competitive advantage can only be understood by examining the many discrete activities a firm undertakes, as each of these activities contributes to cost and can form a basis for differentiation. The value chain is thus composed of primary activities such as logistics, operations, marketing and sales, and service combined with the support activities of firm infrastructure, human resources management, technology development and procurement. This concept has again been used by other authors [e.g. McGee, 1987] to understand competitive advantage and to underpin detailed study of aspects of retail strategy [Ghosh and McLafferty, 1987]. Johnson and Scholes [1988: 92] provide a brief example of value chain analysis applied to Kwik Save.

There are therefore two strands or elements raised here. First is the role of decision-makers and entrepreneurs in developing new retail concepts and formats, making these profitable and successful and expanding from an owner-operated shop to full company or corporate status. The second interlinked element is the strategy adopted by entrepreneurs and companies in developing retail businesses and gaining and holding a competitive advantage. Competitive strategy can be understood as deriving from a consumer base and being dependent on the configuration of markets, operations and the product and service offered. Expansion of a company has therefore to be founded on a competitive advantage, but with spatial components to expansion and structural considerations both within the firm (organisational) and outside the firm (competition). It is the combination of these that decides the performance level of the company.

Once a company is firmly settled as a successful retailer, the problems of expansion remain. Expansion of large and successful companies requires a knowledge of the market, spatial awareness and structural organisation. Expansion in only one sphere (existing business in an existing area) may be much less risky than expansion in several spheres (new products in an overseas market). Decisions have also to be made about the mode of expansion which is generally seen as being either organic or through acquisitions and take-overs, although of course these modes can be combined to a greater or lesser extent. All these decisions about expansion have both a spatial and a structural component [Dreesmann, 1980; McGee, 1987; Kacker, 1985; Knee and Walters, 1985].

It can be suggested that there are deficiencies in retail theory particularly in the consideration of the growth and success of companies. One way forward is to examine spatial and structural elements separately before trying to combine them in an overall analysis. A number of ideas about spatial development have been produced. The most relevant would seem to be the theories of innovation diffusion. Studies of innovation diffusion have generated a considerable literature in a variety of fields [Rogers, 1983; Brown, 1981]. Some of this work has concerned retail institutions or formats [e.g. Cohen, 1972; Sheppard, 1976; Dawson, 1981]. Most of this work is not applicable to company-specific studies, but the body of work reported particularly in Brown et. al., [1981], Brown [1981], and Meyer and Brown [1979], relating to diffusion agency establishment is especially useful. Brown et. al., [1981] sought to explain the links between innovation diffusion and entrepreneurial activity in a spatial context. By laying particular emphasis on the role of innovators and diffusion agencies a model of innovation diffusion based on four major criteria was developed. These criteria as shown in Figure 2 are the availability of capital, the sales potential of the innovation, the logistics requirements and the elasticity of profitability with reference to urban size. The combinations of these criteria predict the relative importance of neighbourhood (local) or hierarchy diffusion processes. The analysis is supported by a retail case showing classical neighbourhood diffusion. This retail case is also examined in Brown [1981] and Meyer and Brown [1979].

This model provides a link to the work of Watts [1974], Jones [1981, 1982] and Schiller [1981]. For Boots, for example, the criteria would be a significant logistics effect, a significant elasticity of agency profitability and initially a low capital availability, within an innovation whose sales potential was related to the number of persons in an urban area. The model suggestion of hierarchical diffusion constrained by a neighbourhood effect accords well with the findings of Watts [1974]. Similar assessments could be made of the companies detailed in Jones [1981, 1982], Schiller [1982] or even Laulajainen [1987]. Such an assessment is beginning to be made by Laulajainen [1988a], although he has reservations about the use of this model alone.

The innovation diffusion theory thus provides a useful interpretation of spatial development. It does not, however, cover the structural development of companies. For analysis of models and theories of business growth recourse has to be made to managerial texts. There are a number of recent attempts to link strategy and retailing [Knee and Walters, 1985; Johnson 1987a, 1987b, Walters, 1988]. In the main, beyond emphasising the importance of the market (a structural factor) these do not provide any real help. An exception perhaps is where Knee and Walters [1985] point to the importance of the strategy-structure links and in particular the problems companies can have in mastering the transition from entrepreneur to corporate status [Knee and Walters, 1985: 112]. In the same vein, Mintzberg and Waters [1982] show how spatial growth and organisational structure change through time as a business develops. They too, emphasise the problems of entrepreneurial resistance to 'letting go' or to structural change.

These concerns have been brought together by Churchill and Lewis [1983] who first review the literature on business growth and in

FIGURE 2
EXPECTED PATTERNS OF DIFFUSION

	Characteristics of the Innovation			
Characteristics of the Firm	Market or Sales Potential Related to the Number of Persons in an Urban Area		Market or Sales Potential Not Related to the Number of Persons in an Urban Area	
	Logistics Effect			
	Significant	Minimal	Significant	Minimal
	Elasticity of Agency Profitability			
	Sig / Min	Sig / Min	Sig / Min	Sig / Min
Low Capital Availability	Hierarchy Effect Constrained by a Neighborhood Effect / Neighborhood Effect	Hierarchy Effect Slightly Constrained by a Neighborhood Effect / Slight Neighborhood Effect	Neighborhood Effect with Random Element / Neighborhood Effect	Random Element Slightly Constrained by a Neighborhood Effect / Slight Neighborhood Effect
High Capital Availability	Hierarchy Effect Constrained by a Neighborhood Effect / Neighborhood Effect with Slight Hierarchy Effect	Hierarchy Effect / Slight Neighborhood and Hierarchy Effects	Neighborhood Effect with Random Element / Neighborhood Effect	Random Element / Slight Neighborhood Effect with Random Element

Source: Brown, *et al.*, 1981: 77. Reproduced with permission.

particular the models of business development. From this review a five-stage model of business growth was developed. Each of these stages has implications for management style, organisational structure, the extent of formal systems, the strategy followed and the relationship between the business and the owner. These are detailed in Figure 3. Churchill and Lewis [1983] go further and identify a number of critical factors in the success or failure of a company as it moves through these five stages. For the company these are the financial position, personnel resources, system resources and general business resources or position in the market. For the entrepreneur the factors are the entrepreneur's goals, organisational abilities, willingness to delegate and strategic awareness. In particular they argue that these factors vary in importance in each stage of the business development and that critical points can emerge, as for example when the entrepreneur's goals become inconsistent with the company's goals. These characteristics accord well with those put forward by Drucker [1985].

FIGURE 3

THE CHARACTERISTICS OF SMALL BUSINESS DEVELOPMENT

	Stage I Existence	Stage II Survival	Stage III-D Success- Disengagement	Stage III-G Success- Growth	Stage IV Take-off	Stage V Resource Maturity
Management Style and Organisation	Direct Supervision	Supervised Supervision	Functional	Functional	Divisional	Line and Staff
Extent of Formal Systems	Minimal to Nonexistent	Minimal	Basic	Developing	Maturing	Extensive
Major Strategy	Existence	Survival	Maintaining Profitable Status Quo	Get Resources for Growth	Growth	Return on Investment
Business and Owner Relationship	Core 50:50	Core 10:90	Sharing 50:50	Sharing 60:40	Sharing 75:25	Periphery 90:10

Source: Adapted from Churchill and Lewis, 1983: 38.

The model put forward by Churchill and Lewis has clear attractions in its linking of structural changes with business development. Where it is at its weakest is in terms of strategy where a major strategy is stated (see Figure 3) but the more detailed strategies that the company uses are not presented. This omission would seem to be reduced if the ideas of Brown *et al.* [1981] are wedded to those of Churchill and Lewis [1983]. This occurs particularly in terms of the development of a spatial strategy developing with the stages of growth and the more common business strategy. Thus in Figure 3, in addition to the major strategy identified there should be other elements of business strategy including a spatial growth strategy. It has also to be noted that different spatial patterns and strategies may be exhibited by different parts of one company and that many of the arguments presented here in terms of a retail company may apply to retail formats or concepts within a company.

The suggestion is that the beginnings of a spatial-structural theory of retail development can be found by linking the spatial models of innovation diffusion to the corporate models of business development. Underpinning this combination is the strategy and market opportunity of the entrepreneur and the notions of sustainable competitive advantage. For example, it can be assumed that a new retail formula has been developed and that it will successfully enter the market. The growth of that company will depend on the characteristics of the new formula (affects spatial development) and the entrepreneurial drive (affects structural change). The actual characteristics of the formula and thus competitive advantage it is assumed will be provided by the entrepreneur's ability to examine the market and to spot opportunities. The nature of the innovation is itself therefore an element of structural and spatial decision-making and development.

These concepts are examined by analysing the growth of one food retailer in Great Britain: Kwik Save. A brief general review of food retailing trends in Great Britain is first necessary in order to provide the background and context to this company-specific study.

FOOD RETAILING IN GREAT BRITAIN

Food and grocery retailing in Great Britain has developed into a very competitive market in the last 30 or so years. The sector has changed considerably over this period. One of the major trends has been a growing concentration in the sector [Akehurst, 1983]. This has been associated with the increasing power of multiple retailers and a decline in the strength of co-operatives and independents [Davies, Gilligan and Sutton, 1985]. Table 1 provides overall figures for the period since 1961 and a clear growth in domination of firms with over 50 units can be found. The process of concentration has gone further in grocery retailing with the multiple retailers' share of the grocery market increasing from 42 per cent to 70 per cent between 1970 and 1985 [Beaumont, 1987].

The rise of the multiple retailers [Baden-Fuller, 1984] through economies of scale and replication has produced only a handful of retail companies who dominate many of the regional food and grocery markets [Davies, Gilligan and Sutton, 1984, 1985]. Companies such as Tesco, Sainsbury, Asda, Gateway (Dee) and Safeway (Argyll) are dominant, although the total strength of the co-operative movement must not be under-estimated. Behind these first rank multiples are regionally based companies such as Wm Low and Wm Morrisons and the limited range discounter Kwik Save. Table 2 provides details of market share for packaged groceries in Great Britain. The figures show the dominance of the leading multiples, but also the importance of the co-operative movement. Scotland has been used here as an illustration

TABLE 1

GENERAL COMPARISON OF RETAILING IN GREAT BRITAIN

All Retailing			1961	1971	1981	1991 (estimate)
Number of Businesses						
Total '000			394	351	240	216
With Single Store '000			356	327	210	180
With Over 10 Stores			1900	1270	1200	900
50 Stores			430	330	300	280
Number of Establishments						
Total '000			540	480	356	310
In Businesses With Over	10	Stores	96	79	73	64
	50	Stores	66	60	55	54
Percent of Sales						
In Businesses With Over	10	Stores	40	44	51	66
	50	Stores	31	36	46	58
Percent of Capital Expenditure						
In Businesses With Over	10	Stores	63	73	70	73
	50	Stores	31	36	45	54

NB: Precise comparisons for 1961 and 1971 with later years are not possible but an attempt has been made to make the data as comparable as possible.

Primary Sources: Business Monitors, Retail Inquiry 1991 figures based on estimates of trends.
Sources: Dawson and Broadbridge, 1988: 18.

of how a regional market can differ from the national market. This shows how national figures mask regional differences and local dominance. As a further example Davies, Gilligan and Sutton [1984] quote Audits of Great Britain (AGB) figures which give Kwik Save a national market share of packaged groceries in 1982 of 5.4 per cent; this hides a 23.2 per cent market share in Lancashire and a zero share in Scotland. There is clearly a regional locational strategy at work here.

Kwik Save are the focus of study here. Kwik Save were one of the pioneers of the limited range discount format in food retailing in the UK. This format basically involves high volume sales of a limited range of goods at discounted prices in a low cost retail environment. The aim is to offer convenience to consumers. At the same time as Kwik Save was emerging, a number of other discount food retailers, including Asda, Wm Morrisons, Grandways, Pricerite and KD Discount, were beginning to develop chains of stores. Some of these were limited-range food-discount store operators in their own right whereas others were main-line multiples offering a range of price cuts or emerging

TABLE 2

MARKET SHARES FOR PACKAGED GROCERIES*
SCOTLAND AND GREAT BRITAIN COMPARED 1985

	Scotland	Great Britain
Total Value of Sales £mn	740	7600
% Breakdown By Outlet		
Multiples	72.5	76.1
of which		
Tesco (excl Hillards)	8.7	13.7
Asda	8.2	8.9
Argyll (inc Safeway)	22.5	8.8
Dee (inc Fine Fare)	9.5	12.8
Sainsbury	–	17.2
Wm Low	12.1	1.2
Kwik Save	–	5.8
Other Multiples	1.5	7.7
Co-ops	15.2	13.8
Symbol Independents	5.6	4.5
Other Independents	6.7	5.6
TOTAL	100.0	100.0

* Packaged groceries include food in cans and packets including frozen food (except ice cream), dairy foods, yoghurt, detergents, household cleansers.
Note: While the data refer to 1985, the figures for Argyll and Dee Corporation have been recalculated to include their subsequent takeovers. This has not been possible in the case of Tesco.
Source: Dawson, Shaw and Harris, 1987.

retailers developing early forms of the superstore concept [Thorpe, 1972]. There was thus a developing divergence into limited-range discounters and superstores. Most of these discount operations existed, however, either as one format of a larger company or as independent retailers. In many cases, these companies were unable to maintain their position and ceased trading. This left Kwik Save in the late 1970s as the pre-eminent limited-range food-discount operator.

Since the late 1970s there have been four major operators (Figure 4). Kwik Save are the largest, followed by Lo-Cost (a part of the Safeway [Argyll] Group). Victor Value were once part of Tesco, but were purchased by Bejam in 1986. In 1989 Iceland Frozen Foods took over Bejam and sold the Victor Value chain to Kwik Save, thus reinforcing their position (see later). The other competitor was Shopper's Paradise which was part of Fine Fare [Allan, 1980], but has now been dismantled by Gateway (Dee). Figure 4 shows for these four companies the

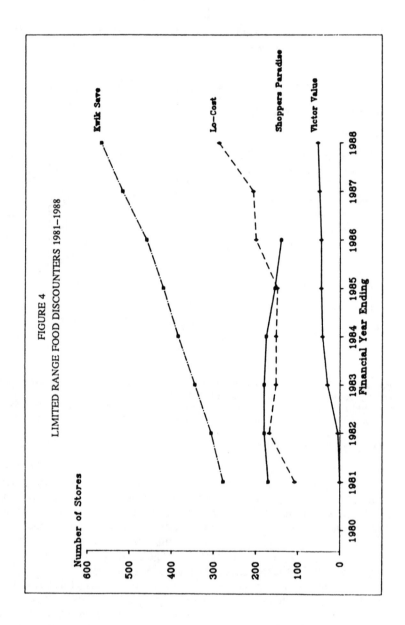

FIGURE 4
LIMITED RANGE FOOD DISCOUNTERS 1981–1988

changes in store numbers since 1981. Figures before this date and financial figures are very difficult to obtain because of mergers and take-overs and the subsidiary nature of all the companies other than Kwik Save. What is clear from the figure is, with the exception of Kwik Save, the lack of sustained growth by these companies and trading fascias. The rise in Lo-Cost numbers is to a great extent a function of its role as a depository for those stores which did not fit the other trading names in the Safeway (Argyll) group, such as Presto and now Safeway. There would seem to be a lack of concerted management attention to the opportunities with the format. This may be due both to the presence of 'better' opportunities elsewhere in retailing and the difficulty in successfully running such an operation. This exception is Kwik Save which is the leading retailer in the field of food discounters.

Similar success stories in limited-range food discounting are found elsewhere in the world (Lord *et al.*, 1988), including the USA and Australia [Tieck, 1985]. Within Europe the pre-eminent operator of this retail format is the German company, Aldi. It should be emphasised, however, that despite its apparent simplicity it is not an easy retail format in which to succeed.

A review of changes in food retailing over the last 20 years suggests that a number of common themes can be identified.

1. There has been a massive rise in the average size of stores, associated particularly with the growth of the food superstore [Dawson, 1984], although the same trend is found in non-food retailing [Gibbs, 1987]. The average sales floorspace of new food stores for many multiples is now over 30,000 sq ft. For example, in 1988 the average sales area of Tesco and Sainsbury store openings was 34,250 and 30,650 sq ft respectively. This increase in unit size in food retailing has been associated with a ruthless pruning of small shops in established companies. For example Tesco have reduced their number of stores from 790 in 1972 to 337 in 1987, but in the process have extended sales floorspace from 3.7m sq ft to 7.0m sq ft, increasing average store size from 4,700 sq ft sales area in 1972 to 20,000 sq ft in 1987. Sainsbury have increased their proportion of stores over 20,000 sq ft sales area from 10 per cent in 1977 to 44.5 per cent in 1988. The average sales area of an Asda superstore in 1988 is 39,000 sq ft.

2. There has been a move towards out-of-town or off-centre locations [Dawson, 1988; Gayler, 1984; Kivell and Shaw, 1980]. This again is linked to the superstore [Davies and Sparks, 1989; Rowley, 1985] and the requirement for ample car parking to meet customers' needs. Food retailing by mainline food multiples has been withdrawn from the majority of UK high streets [Dawson, 1988].

3. There has been a steady increase in the percentage of own-brand food products [Davies, Gilligan and Sutton, 1986; McGoldrick, 1984; Morris, 1979]. Sainsbury always had a high level of such products but Tesco, and the forerunners of Safeway (Argyll) and Gateway moved

heavily into own-brands in the 1970s. More recently Asda has decided to develop its own brands, as a method of improving its margins and competitive position.

4. Sufficient finance has been provided to enable expansion to occur. Most retailers, and especially the food multiples, carry a high level of debt on their balance sheets and often trade out of leaseholds. This is common among the dominant food retailers. Obtaining access to this finance and the sums needed for development when one superstore can cost upwards of £15 million and an average figure of £7–8 million is seen, is difficult, and in general only successful and established retailers can compete in this market.

5. The physical distribution systems of the major food retailers have undergone massive changes, particularly in the last five years. This process of change is still not complete. In particular, physical distribution systems have been increasingly centralised with a high level of sub-contracting. This process was started by Sainsbury [Quarmby, 1989] and Kwik Save but the other major food retailers such as Asda, Tesco [Sparks, 1986], Safeway (Argyll) and Gateway (Dee) all moved in the same way in the 1980s [McKinnon, 1985, 1989; Sparks, 1988].

6. Major food retailers have become increasingly reliant on service and added value to sell to customers, rather than through a strict reliance on price competition. Prices are generally competitive, but it is the quality, the value, the environment [Larkham, 1988] and the service provided that have become important. The concept of customer service and customer care are now crucial to most food retailers. This is seen in staff development and training, but also in product development and the addition of previously 'exotic' lines. This is the result, it is argued, of changing customer preferences and requirements.

These trends are found not only in the main-line food multiples but also in the regional multiples such as Wm Low and Wm Morrisons and, before their takeover, Hillards and Lennons. The emphasis may be less on service and more on price, although all these companies have extended the service they offer in recent years. The remaining trends are all present, however. The implication of these trends has been that companies have taken decisions to concentrate on large food superstores or supermarkets (a structural decision) particularly in off-centre locations (a spatial decision). This has polarised much food retailing along both a structural axis (size of shop, range of goods) and a spatial axis (off-centre, neighbourhood stores). The exception perhaps is that of Kwik Save, a company which has been successful in British food retailing by going against many of the trends and occupying a niche left open by these general corporate strategies. Kwik Save claim that they offer the 'antidote' to superstore shopping [Kwik Save Annual Report, 1987: p.9], through their 'no-nonsense food stores' [Kwik Save Annual Report, 1988]. The specific case-study below will explain how this success has been achieved and draw lessons from the growth and practice of Britain's foremost limited-range discount food retailer. These lessons will concentrate on the spatial-structural dimensions of retail change.

KWIK SAVE GROUP P.L.C.

As will become clear, the history of Kwik Save is best described in two main phases, Gubay and post-Gubay. This is the format followed here. A brief section on the future is also presented. A fuller study of the retailing operations of Albert Gubay across the world can be found in Lord *et al.* [1988].

Entrepreneurial Flair and Hiatus, 1959–73

On 11 May 1959 a private company was registered that eventually became the largest and most successful limited range discount food retailer in Great Britain. The company, Value Foods Ltd, had as its founder a Welsh entrepreneur named Albert Gubay. Albert Gubay was born in 1928 in Rhyl, North Wales, the son of an Irish mother and a Middle East Jewish emigrant father from Baghdad. After national service, Gubay returned to Rhyl and began a business career involving a variety of activities including selling non-sugar sweets during confectionary rationing. His main companies were Norwales Confections Ltd and Norwales Development Ltd. The confectionery business began to have difficulties in the late 1950s as rationing ended, and Gubay moved into retailing via market stalls and then a rented grocery shop in Rhyl. Value Foods Ltd represented a further step down a retail path.

Value Foods Ltd was based in Prestatyn in North Wales and opened its first traditional-style grocery shop in Rhyl in July 1959. By 1962 further shops were open in Chester and Wrexham. A disagreement between Gubay and his partners saw the rented stores at Rhyl and Wrexham remain with Gubay and the Chester store being briefly retained by his partners before being sold on. The first supermarket operated by the company opened in Prestatyn in 1962 and was claimed to be the first drive-in supermarket in the United Kingdom. Supermarkets then became the main business of the company. These supermarkets, trading as Value Foods, were approximately 2,000 sq ft, a standard size for new self-service supermarkets being developed at this time, although the Prestatyn store was somewhat larger at 7,000 sq ft. These stores therefore were mainly nothing exceptional in size or turnover, although there was a reliance on the provision of car parking and the (then) dubious activities of late night opening and price-cutting below the manufacturers recommended resale price [Fulop, 1964].

The real starting point for Value Foods Ltd, however, came after a trip by Albert Gubay, Ken Nicholson (another Value Foods director) and Ian Howe to the United States in late 1964/early 1965. In the USA they learnt about 'baby shark' retailing, the selling at very low prices but high volume of a limited range of nationally branded goods, from small 'stripped-down' stores, particularly in the drugstore market. Enthused by the possibilities Gubay translated the idea, together with some operating ideas gained from Aldi food stores in West Germany, into a 2,000 sq ft food supermarket trading as Kwik Save Discount at Colwyn Bay. So successful was this unit that the remaining stores were converted to the format and the company moved over totally to limited range food discount retailing. With growth coming in the next five years from new stores in converted garages, cinemas, showrooms and churches the company moved steadily forward. Growth was aided by the abolition of resale price maintenance in the mid-1960s, which helped retail entrepreneurs develop their skills in buying and selling. The size of store also increased towards an average of 7,000 sq ft. By 1967 there were 13 discount stores trading as Kwik Save, based particularly in North Wales and Cheshire (Figure 5). This is clearly a neighbourhood expansion strategy based on maximising local market share. Table 3 provides details of the product groups that each of these stores carried and shows the concentration on groceries, household/ soaps/cleaners, toiletries, sweets, bakery and textiles. It is likely that the butchery and fruit and vegetable sections in some stores represent the beginnings of the use of concessions in the stores to retail certain goods [Singer and Friedlander, 1970].

The company's conversion into a public company in November 1970 was preceded by a name change in July 1970 from Value Foods Ltd to

TABLE 3

PRODUCT RANGE IN KWIK SAVE DISCOUNT STORES 1967

Store / Product Group	Abergele	Rhyl	Denbigh	Colwyn Bay	Llandudno	Mold	Connahs Quay	Prestatyn	Wrexham	Chester	Ellesmere Port	New Ferry	Wallasey
Groceries	*	*	*	*	*	*	*		*	*	*	*	*
Butchery		*			*					*		*	*
Fruit & Veg		*								*		*	*
Soaps/Household	*	*	*	*	*	*	*		*	*	*	*	*
Toiletries	*	*	*	*	*	*	*		*	*	*	*	*
Sweets	*	*	*	*	*	*	*	NA	*	*	*	*	*
Bakery	*	*	*	*	*	*	*		*	*	*	*	*
Hardware													
Frozen													
Off Licence													
Delicatessen													*
Textiles	*	*	*		*	*	*		*	*	*	*	*

* Product Group present in store.

NA – Information on Prestatyn store not available.

Source: Self-Service and Supermarket, 1968, *Annual Survey and Directory*, London.

FIGURE 5

THE LOCATION OF KWIK-SAVE DISCOUNT STORES, 1967

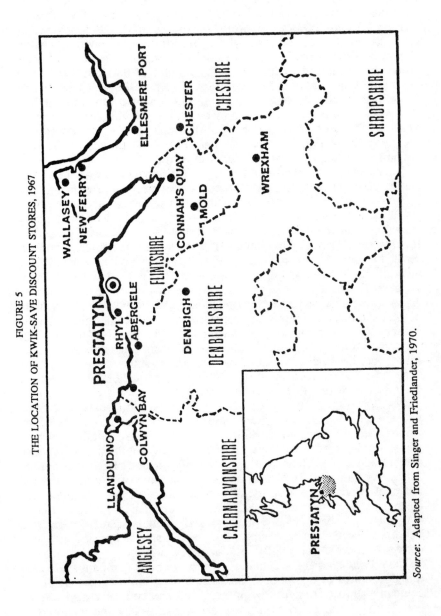

Source: Adapted from Singer and Friedlander, 1970.

Kwik Save Discount Group Ltd [Stock Exchange Yearbook 1986/7]. Gubay's earlier companies of Norwales Developments Ltd and Norwales Confections Ltd which had operated with Value Foods Ltd as a group for some years were formally acquired in May 1970. Norwales Confections Ltd was used as a wholesaler for the retail operation while Norwales Developments Ltd was used to build, correct and repair properties to be used by the group. At the time of flotation Kwik Save Discount Group Ltd had 24 stores based in North Wales, Cheshire and Shropshire (Figure 6). The 24 outlets in the chain at this time totalled 115,000 sq ft of selling space and made profits of £643,000 on turnover of £11m. Albert Gubay and his family retained effective control of the company at flotation with 45 per cent of the shares, while Ken Nicholson owned a further 15 per cent of the shares.

The basic idea behind the Kwik Save retail operation was classically simple. The company believed that customers could be attracted and their needs satisfied by offering basic goods at very competitive prices [Watkin and Joseph, 1976]. This pricing stance was particularly appealing to low-income consumers. It is difficult to obtain price data for this early period, but figures from a variety of sources [Thorpe, 1972; Livesey, 1979], including 'Which' surveys of the early 1970s, mention Kwik Save as being cheap, while since 1977 when 'Which' included Kwik Save in their surveys for the first time, the company has always been at or very near the top (cheapest). Thorpe [1972] in a study of prices in discount stores and superstores found Kwik Save to be the cheapest. This is shown in Table 4 which provides details of a number of surveys of prices in discount stores. More recent price data from other sources confirm that Kwik Save remains amongst the cheapest retailers (Table 5). The competitive pricing policies were enabled by a number of inter-connected factors. The first element was the 'stripped-to-basics' approach of the stores. Fixtures, fittings and fascias were basic with the goods sold from manufacturers' cardboard boxes placed on wooden shelving designed, built and fitted in-house. Stock was held above the shelves allowing easy re-stocking and minimising warehouse and storage space. There was nothing sophisticated or fancy about the stores. As Tanburn [1974: 51] notes, 'Kwik Save offer a very limited range of products ... and literally dump them in opened outers for customers to help themselves. The grocery area ... looks like a warehouse or shed'. Many of these early outlets were in converted buildings. Even at an early stage, however, it was recognised that such conversions were not wholly satisfactory.

The second element was that of control with the company dedicated to tight control of operations. Computers were an integral part of the company almost from the beginning, and the company also moved early into central distribution, a process enabled by the technology. Both centralised distribution and extensive computerisation were innovations in food retailing at this time. In particular the company introduced a sophisticated computer-based stock control system, again

FIGURE 6
THE LOCATION OF KWIK SAVE DISCOUNT STORES, 1970

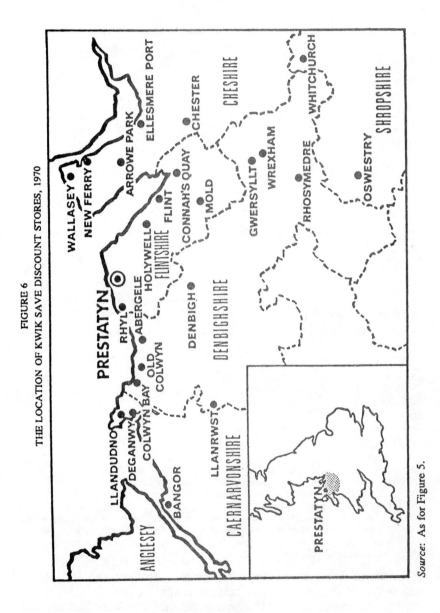

Source: As for Figure 5.

TABLE 4

SHOPPING BASKETS COMPARISONS* – PERCENTAGE SAVING OVER

	FT	CA/TBN	Which	TV Audit			NW Survey
				Groceries	Groceries & Soaps	Median	
A Cheapest Multiple							
Kwik Save	7.3	1.2	10.2	5.1	4.2	8	7.4
Whelan	7.3	5.2	7.1	3.1	2.4	4	
Asda	7.0	2.4	8.8	6.1	2.7	6	6.3
Discount Foods	6.4	3.8	9.6	5.1	3.3	8	
Brierleys	6.3	6.4	7.1	3.1	0.7	1	
Morrison	5.3	0	6.9	1.5	-0.4	3	
Cee-N-Cee	4.6	2.8	4.1	4.8	1.0	3	
Moneysave	3.2	-0.8	5.4	-0.9	-1.8	2	4.1
U-Save	2.1	-1.2	4.2	-1.0	-1.9	1	
B Average of Multiples							
Kwik Save	8.4	4.6	13.1	7.0	7.0	10	
Whelan	8.4	8.5	9.5	5.0	5.2	6	
Asda	8.2	5.8	11.5	8.0	5.5	8	
Discount Foods	7.6	6.7	12.4	7.0	5.9	10	
Brierleys	7.4	9.6	9.5	5.0	3.3	3	
Morrison	6.5	3.5	9.3	3.5	2.4	5	
Cee-N-Cee	5.8	6.2	6.2	6.7	3.9	6	
Moneysave	4.4	2.7	7.6	1.2	0.9	4	
U-Save	3.2	1.5	6.2	3.1	0.8	3	
C Recommended Prices							
Kwik Save	18.9	19.1	19.4	17.8	17.8		
Whelan	18.9	22.3	16.4	16.0	16.4		
Asda	18.7	20.1	18.1	18.6	16.6		
Discount Foods	18.2	20.9	18.6	17.8	17.0		
Brierleys	18.1	23.3	16.4	16.0	14.8		
Morrison	17.2	18.1	16.2	14.6	13.9		
Cee-N-Cee	16.6	20.4	13.6	17.5	15.1		
Moneysave	15.3	17.5	14.8	12.6	12.7		
U-Save	14.3	26.5	13.6	14.2·	12.6		
Cheapest Multiple	12.5	18.1	9.6	13.3	14.1		

* FT   = *Financial Times* basket
CA/TBN   = Consumer's Association/*Times* Business News
Which   = Pricing Survey – *Which* November 1971
NW Survey = Distribution Research Ltd
Note: Median column was calculated not on the overall price of the basket but by taking the median value of lines in the basket, with lines expressed relative to recommended price.
Source: Thorpe, 1972: 12.

developed in-house which enabled stock levels to be kept to a minimum and orders and deliveries to be computer processed. Centralised buying and particularly centralised distribution produced further cost savings through better deals, less pilferage, lower stock levels and better use of stock space. Materials handling revolved around layers on

TABLE 5

PRICE SURVEYS OF MAJOR FOOD RETAILERS

(a) Top Brand Price Basket		(b) Own-Label Price Basket	
1.	Kwik Save	£5.74	1.	Kwik Save[1]	£8.40
2.	Asda	£5.90	2.	Asda	£8.78
3.	Gateway	£5.91	3.	Presto	£8.91
	Wm Low	£5.91	4.	Morrisons	£8.97
5.	Hillards	£5.92	5.	Co-op	£9.00
	Presto	£5.92		Gateway	£9.00
	Tesco	£5.92	7.	Sainsbury	£9.07
8.	Morrisons	£5.94	8.	Wm Low	£9.12
	Sainsbury	£5.94	9.	Tesco	£9.14
10.	Co-op	£5.97	10.	Hillards	£9.23
	Waitrose	£5.97	11.	Safeway	£9.35
12.	Safeway	£6.04	12.	Waitrose	£9.38
13.	M & S	£6.10	13.	M & S	£11.73
Average		£5.94			£9.24
Kwik Save cheaper than average by (%)		3.4%			9.1%[2]

Notes:
1. For Kwik Save the cheapest brand in each product group was chosen as an own-label
   equivalent.
2. 7.0 per cent if M & S is excluded from the calculations.
Source: Manchester Business School, 1987a, *UK Grocery Retailing*.

pallets and where possible pallets were sent untouched direct to the store from the warehouse and merchandised by the pallet-load on to the shop floor. Goods were picked on pallets according to the store layout which was approximately standard across all stores. The result was an efficient and cost-effective operation. Control of costs produced low overheads, low operating costs, low staffing costs including management and a dedication to low levels of shrinkage [Singer and Friedlander, 1970]. Kwik Save also operated its own fleet of vehicles, garage facilities, joinery and waste-paper baling station, further reducing costs. By controlling centrally as much of the business as possible and by standardising operating procedures across the outlets, Gubay de-skilled the store management task. This allowed the recruitment of store managers from a variety of previous occupations and reduced costs while improving performance.

The third element was that of buying muscle combined with a reliance on manufacturer branded goods. In spite of being small, the company had considerable buying muscle through the very rapid stockturn and large volume on a small number of items. This was linked to a decision not to use own-brand or generic products but to buy aggressively from manufacturers and pass on the savings to the customers. Only a very limited range of packaged goods (c.450 lines), all manufacturer brands but mainly second-line national brands, was sold. Stocking policy for goods was dependent on the price deal to be obtained. If this was not good enough then the line was not stocked. Cheapness was the driving motivation. There were no tailored promotions or special offers in the stores, and manufacturers' representatives were not permitted to merchandise. The strategy of 'loss leaders' was not often pursued but rather prices were discounted across the entire range, with all goods being sold very cheaply [Singer and Friedlander, 1970; Thorpe, 1972] at a price equivalent or better than other companies 'specials'. The idea was, as Gubay stated, 'not to sell cheap groceries but to sell groceries cheaply'. The limited range approach allowed the removal of item pricing, replacing it with shelf-edge pricing or hand-written price cards pinned to a wooden rail running above the stock. This system required the checkout operators to memorise the prices, through the use of a limited number of pricing points. Staff costs were kept low and the trolley-to-trolley checkout operation allowed rapid flow through the check-out. As Watkin and Joseph [1976] show in comparing two discount stores in Wales, Kwik Save employed fewer people than smaller stores run by competitors. Indeed, nationally the Kwik Save operation has for many years had the highest sales per employee figures for food retailing companies. The limited range was also important for efficient distribution, merchandising, buying and computerisation.

The final element was that of risk reduction through the use of concessions in the store to cover the goods that Kwik Save itself did not want to and could not handle, that is, the non-packaged sectors such as fresh meat, fruit, vegetables and bread. This approach reduced the risk by allowing Kwik Save to concentrate on the procedures it did best, but also provided the company with a range of products in the store and, as importantly, with rental income. In 1970 this income comprised 10 per cent of pre-tax profits. The rental paid to Kwik Save by a concession was based on the turnover of the Kwik Save unit, which was an unusual practice. In the main the concessions were run by independent traders or small companies. However, there was a notable experiment at the Rochdale Shopping Centre, which Albert Gubay, chairman of Kwik Save, termed Britain's first Discount Shopping Centre. At this 72,500 sq ft (gross) centre, Kwik Save took 16,000 sq ft, letting the remainder to non-food concessions. Of this 16,000 sq ft, 3,000 sq ft was beyond the checkouts and 2,500 sq ft was in a loading bay. Greengrocery and butchery were counter service concessions within the Kwik Save unit [Thorpe and McGoldrick, 1974]. The non-food concessions in the centre included Kettering Tyres, Allied Carpets [Davies and Sparks, 1986], Newhome Status (later Status Discount) [Livesey, 1979; Davies and Sparks, 1986] and Comet Discount Electrical [Savitt, 1984] all of which became major companies in their own right. Status took space in several Kwik Save developments [Tanburn, 1974], as Kwik Save and Albert Gubay began to act as a property developer.

It is important to realise that Kwik Save introduced discount food retailing as an innovation in Great Britain, although discounting itself was being practised by several food retailers. The difference for Kwik Save and other northern-based discounters was that they offered price cuts on far more products than established retailers and did not use selective price cuts, loss leaders or trading stamps [Thorpe, 1972]. At a time of high inflation this was to give them a clear advantage over other food retailers which were changing and were forced to change prices regularly [Livesey, 1979]. Several companies became 'leaders' of the discount operation, although as noted before a polarisation was emerging between superstores on the one hand and discount stores on the other. What seems clear is the northern base of discounters [Fulop, 1964; Thorpe, 1972] perhaps because of the relative lack of modern food outlets in the north of England, the greater requirement for urban renewal and the working-class, lower-paid orientation.

By 1970, Kwik Save had emerged as a limited range discount operation while Asda and Wm Morrison were moving towards super-stores. Other limited range discounters in the north of England at this time included Discount Foods and Cee-n-Cee. As can be seen in Figure 7 there was a degree of spatial separation of these chains which enabled them to co-exist. The main areas of conflict were in Leeds between Asda and Wm Morrison and Liverpool/Cheshire between Kwik Save and Discount Foods. To some extent, therefore, the initial development years were not ones of conflict. It must be remembered, however, that at this time these companies were very minor parts of the national British food retailing scene [Akehurst, 1983, 1984; Thorpe, 1972; Davies and Sparks, 1986; Livesey, 1979], although their neighbourhood expansion strategies aimed at local market share and penetration gave them a high local profile. Such a pattern of spatial separation and the relative lack of conflict between companies has been seen as important in the progress of innovations [Dawson, 1984] both in Great Britain and Continental Europe. A similar pattern has been identified in Sweden by Laulajainen and Gadde [1986], a process described by them as a 'locational avoidance' strategy.

At the time of flotation, therefore, Kwik Save though small had a proven formula that apparently suited the needs of consumers in North Wales, Merseyside and Lancashire. The problem was to translate that success into a retail company for the 1970s and 1980s. Much of this success in the 1960s can be attributed to the chairman, Albert Gubay. His retailing know-how had started and driven the company, overcome problems of operation, as shown in the data for 1961–71 in Figures 8, 9 and 10, and the flotation was as much a statement of the Stock Exchange's confidence in 'the controversial Welshman' Gubay as in Kwik Save which at this time was still only a very small retail company.

FIGURE 7

THE LOCATION OF NORTHERN DISCOUNT STORES AND SUPERSTORES, 1971

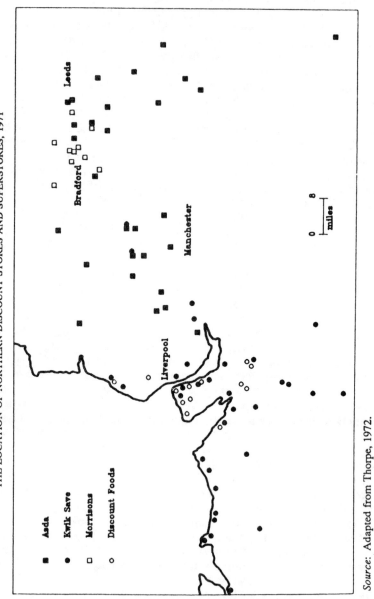

Source: Adapted from Thorpe, 1972.

FIGURE 8
KWIK SAVE GROUP P.L.C. – NET MARGIN

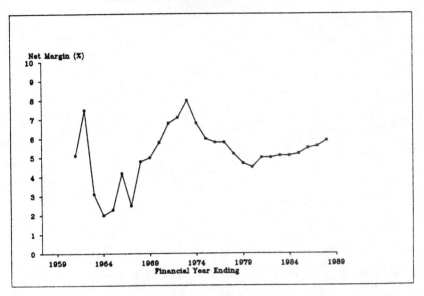

FIGURE 9
KWIK SAVE GROUP P.L.C. – PRE-TAX PROFITS

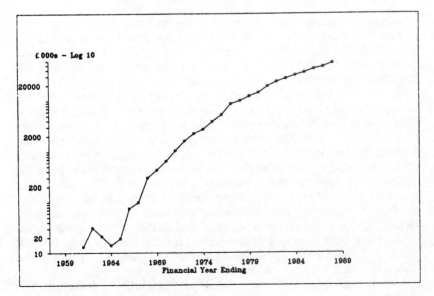

FIGURE 10

KWIK SAVE GROUP P.L.C. – RENTAL INCOME AS A PERCENTAGE OF
PRE-TAX PROFITS

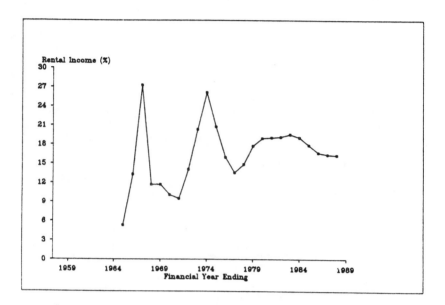

Albert Gubay was a very high-profile and controversial director,
perhaps too individual, forthright and independent to be 'shackled' by
institutional investors. He very much wanted to be his own boss. At the
same time he wanted to turn his paper profits into capital and also felt
alienated and penalised by the tax structure. At the time of flotation,
control of Kwik Save rested firmly in Albert Gubay's hands with his
family retaining c.45 per cent of the shares. In April/May 1972 the
Gubay family sold c.27 per cent of the total Kwik Save shares worth
c.£7.4 million, although Albert Gubay remained as a director and
declared his intention to retain the remaining shares (c.15 per cent) as a
permanent holding. In December 1972, Gubay stepped aside from the
chairmanship and became a non-executive director. This move was
symptomatic of Gubay distancing himself from the business. The
bombshell, however, struck later in the same month and in early
January 1973 when it became clear that Gubay's remaining share-
holding had been disposed of and he had left the country to go to New
Zealand [Moir, 1973]. These moves apparently came as a shock to the
company and their financial advisers.

It is difficult now to convey the impact of Gubay's departure. His
high-profile, controversial and successful style had made Kwik Save

well-known and indelibly associated with his name. Gubay's walk-out caused personal difficulties for him in that his departure and share dealings were investigated by the Department of Trade and Industry under the Companies Act and he also had to fight a long legal battle over his tax bill. The Department of Trade and Industry report [1974] found Albert Gubay to be in default of the Companies Act and found his explanations 'not acceptable'. The report however continued that Gubay's explanations 'involve a question of interpretation ... which does not fall within our functions as inspectors' [Department of Trade and Industry, 1974: 10]. Gubay's tax case eventually reached the House of Lords in 1984 where he won his case that his gift of his shares to his wife, who was by then an Isle of Man resident, meant that he had to pay almost no tax on the share deals (Lord et. al., 1988). The effect of both the tax judgement and the inspectors' report was that Albert Gubay succeeded in obtaining his profit from the founding of Kwik Save and also in avoiding the majority of British tax on his gains. His position as the 'bête noire' of British food retailing was confirmed. Since leaving Britain, Albert Gubay has founded, run and sold discount food retail chains (3 Guys) in New Zealand, Ireland and the USA. He is now resident in the Isle of Man where he owns and runs a major bank, the Celtic Bank Limited, and a large private property company, Montrose Holdings Limited, which are investors in retail property [Lord et al., 1988].

For the Kwik Save Discount Group the immediate problem in 1973 was that the company was seen as synonomous with Gubay and few institutions or shareholders believed that there was life after the founder. Gubay's 'walk-out' forced Kwik Save to manage a crisis of confidence if not operations where control was really invested in the system. It took several years for the company to convince the City that Kwik Save could survive and, more importantly, prosper. Gubay's departure also came at the time of the peak per cent profit margin (Figure 8) and its subsequent decline reinforced the City's suspicions. In the longer term Kwik Save had to convince investors and the public that their brand of retailing could be developed beyond the North Wales/Cheshire area, and that the company could manage this expansion. The strategic management of growth was therefore also a management of spatial expansion.

The Maturing of Kwik Save, 1973 to date

The company that Gubay left behind had to convince the City of its value and its operating performance. Figure 8 presents the net profit margin of Kwik Save. The net margin in the figure is an over-statement of operating efficiency in that it includes the income derived from concessions, which could be a considerable component of the profit figure. For example, in 1970 this revenue comprised 10 per cent of the pre-tax profits, a figure which had risen to 26 per cent by 1974 (Figure 10). What Figures 8 and 9 show is an inconsistent performance in the early stages of development, but increasing margins and profit during the entrepreneurial phase of the 1960s. This inconsistency in the early 1960s is shown by the fluctuating net margin and the underlying profit figures which fell from £31,000 in 1962 to £14,000 in 1964. Immediately after flotation and Gubay's departure, the net margin was driven lower as Kwik Save came under pressure both within the company and through the more difficult and government restricted trading conditions of the 1970s. In one sense the 1970s were beneficial to Kwik Save's brand of discount retailing as consumers were more price-conscious, but on the other hand inflation and product shortage as well as government controls made trading difficult. Food price inflation was above 10 per cent per annum for the majority of the period 1972–82, being particularly high in 1974–77 when annual food inflation reached 25 per cent (Figure 11). Price-consciousness among customers rose considerably at this time, especially among the lower-paid.

These initial years after the hiatus also saw the income from concessions contribute a very high share of pre-tax profits, emphasising the trading difficulties. By the 1980s, however, as Figures 8, 9 and 10 show, consistent growth rather than fluctuation is the pattern with net margin and rental income as a percentage of pre-tax profits remaining at relatively stable levels. It has to be noted that during the 1970s and early 1980s the margin produced by Kwik Save was ahead of most, if not all food retailers [Akehurst, 1984; Manchester Business School, 1987a;

FIGURE 11

YEAR ON YEAR CHANGE IN RETAIL PRICE INDEX (FOOD) 1961–1988

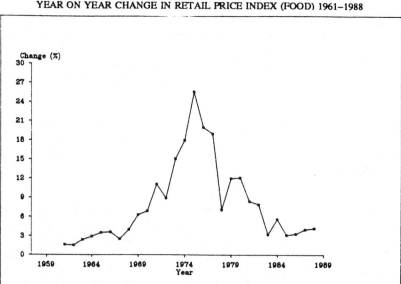

Institute of Grocery Distribution, 1987]. This can be seen in Table 6, which emphasises this aspect of Kwik Save's performance.

TABLE 6

NET MARGINS OF MAJOR UK FOOD RETAILERS 1970–88

	1970	1971	1972	1973	1974	1975	1976	1977	1978	1979
Sainsbury	2.9	3.1	4.0	4.0	4.0	3.6	3.2	4.4	3.5	3.2
Asda	3.8	4.1	4.1	5.1	4.7	4.6	4.8	5.6	4.8	5.2
Kwik Save	5.8	6.8	7.1	8.0	6.8	5.9	5.7	5.7	5.0	4.7
Morrisons	4.6	4.3	4.2	4.8	4.9	4.1	3.5	3.1	3.8	3.1
Wm Low			4.8	5.1	4.1	3.4	3.1	3.7	2.4	3.2
Tesco	5.3	5.4	5.5	6.1	5.8	4.7	4.1	4.3	3.0	3.1
Hillards	1.2	1.6	2.6	4.2	3.5	2.2	2.3	3.7	3.2	2.4
Argyll										
Allied Suppliers	2.1	2.4	2.4	3.0	3.2	2.3	1.4	2.4	1.8	1.3
Safeway	2.9	3.0	3.4	3.3	2.2	2.2	2.3	3.2	3.5	3.8
Hintons	3.9	3.7	3.8	3.3	3.4	3.0	2.0	2.7	2.9	1.1
Dee Corporation										
Fine Fare	3.3	1.5	2.1	2.2	2.6	1.0	2.8	2.8	1.5	1.8
Lennons	2.9	3.6	4.1	4.3	4.2	3.3	2.8	3.0	2.6	2.5
International	2.6	2.5	3.5	3.6	1.5	0.4	-0.02	1.1	-1.6	-0.4

TABLE 6 (cont.)

NET MARGINS OF MAJOR UK FOOD RETAILERS 1970–88

	1980	1981	1982	1983	1984	1985	1986	1987	1988
Sainsbury	3.9	4.3	4.5	4.6	5.1	5.2	5.6	6.4	6.4
Asda	5.0	4.3	4.6	5.1	6.0	6.2	6.6	7.1	6.9
Kwik Save	4.7	5.0	5.0	5.1	5.2	5.2	5.5	5.6	5.9
Morrisons	3.4	3.5	3.8	4.0	3.7	3.5	4.3	5.0	5.3
Wm Low	2.4	1.7	2.8	3.0	3.3	3.0	3.1	3.3	4.4
Tesco	2.4	2.0	2.1	2.7	2.8	3.0	3.9	4.9	5.6
Hillards	3.2	1.4	2.8	3.0	3.1	3.2	3.2		
Argyll	2.9	2.0	2.1	1.9	2.8	3.2	3.5	4.0	4.1
Allied Suppliers	1.5	1.3							
Safeway	3.1	3.5	3.0	4.2	4.1	3.9	4.4		
Hintons	1.4	2.5	2.8	1.5					
Dee Corporation	1.1	0.9	1.2	1.9	2.0	2.6	2.9	4.0	3.6
Fine Fare	2.1	2.0	2.3	2.1	2.1	2.2			
Lennons	2.3	2.4	1.6	0.6	1.3				
International	-0.3	-0.4	0.8	1.7					

Sources: 1970–79 Akehurst, 1984.
1979–88 Manchester Business School, 1988; Institute of Grocery Distribution, 1987, and previous editions.
1979–88 Annual Reports of Companies
Note: There are considerable difficulties in reconciling these various sources and this table should be seen as indicative of broad trends only.

The growth of Kwik Save is clearly demonstrated by Figures 12 and 13 which show the number of stores and the sales floorspace respectively. Figure 12 shows that the number of stores grew steadily in the early 1970s and then with increasing pace. In the late 1980s for example Kwik Save have been opening on average almost one store per week. This expansion has been mainly organic in nature. The exceptions are a 1978 take-over of the 49 unit-strong Cee-n-Cee supermarket chain, the 1986 acquisition of Tates which brought twelve food shops, fourteen wine shops and six convenience stores, the 1987 purchase of 23 Dee Corporation units, and in 1989 the purchase from Iceland Frozen Foods of the 53-strong Victor Value chain. Iceland Frozen Foods had acquired Victor Value as an unwanted part of their Belgian takeover. This latter purchase removed a minor rival from the market place, gave Kwik Save valuable presence in a particular regional market and, it is rumoured, stopped, temporarily at least, Aldi the German discount chain from entering the British market. From Figures 12 and 13 it can be argued that the takeover of Cee-n-Cee supermarkets, while reasonable in spatial terms (see below), actually slowed growth for the following few years and reduced Kwik Save's expansion. Certainly Kwik Save took their time in assimilating the Cee-n-Cee chain and learnt valuable lessons.

The changeover in the company is marked. From its entrepreneurial beginnings, Kwik Save had grown to have a turnover of £15.0 million and net profits before tax of £1.02 million in 1971. It retailed from

FIGURE 12
KWIK SAVE GROUP P.L.C. – NUMBER OF KWIK SAVE STORES

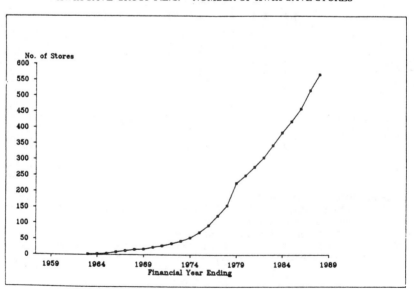

only 24 outlets with a sales floorspace of 115,000 sq ft. There were approximately 450 employees. By 1988 Kwik Save Group had a turnover of £974.1m, made profits of £55.2m, retailed from almost 575 locations, with 3.25m sq ft of floorspace and over 8,400 FTE employees. The management of change from the entrepreneurial beginnings, through the hiatus of Gubay's goodbye to the present mature retail chain had been safely and profitably achieved. It is important to consider how this process was managed. This can be undertaken in three ways: first, through a brief overview of the general food industry in the 1970s and 1980s; secondly, through examining Kwik Save's spatial expansion, and thirdly, through a review of Kwik Save's business operation.

Akehurst [1984] has examined food retailing in the 1970s in particular and has pointed to the difficulties many retailers were facing. Such problems led to the abandonment of trading stamps and the introduction of Operation Checkout by Tesco in 1977 which as Bamfield [1980: 41] states:

> marks a change in retail techniques, particularly promotional methods, rather than being a temporary phenomenon after which retail prices might return to normal ... the response to a change in consumer buying habits as reflected in the rapid growth of low cost discounters.

FIGURE 13

KWIK SAVE GROUP P.L.C. – SALES FLOORSPACE (000 sqft)

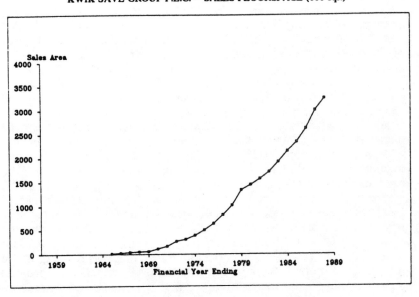

The success of discounters such as Asda with superstores and Kwik Save with discount stores brought conflict to food retailing. Their success produced imitators from established food retailers such as Tesco with superstores and Shoppers Paradise [Allan, 1980] and Key Discount with discount stores. Expansion of Asda and Kwik Save brought conflict through spatial expansion of trading areas and traditional selective price cutters began to stand still in market share terms [Akehurst, 1983, 1984]. Across the board discount pricing while attractive to consumers also provided business efficiencies which in turn enabled expansion. The market share discounters gained was at the expense of independents and co-operatives rather than the big multiple groups. Previously, however, this gain would have gone to companies like Tesco and Sainsbury. Hence the need for Tesco and Sainsbury to respond through a price-war based on across the board discounting. The success of Kwik Save at this time is well marked by the adoption of its pricing stance by major companies in the late 1970s and its style of operation in the 1970s and 1980s.

Imitation is claimed to be the sincerest form of flattery, and Kwik Save was imitated by many operators. Some were limited-range discounters from the 1960s. Most of these did not expand as fast as, or manage their expansion as well as, Kwik Save and were taken over or failed; for example, Discount Foods Ltd became one of the bases for Oriel Foods and thus Argyll (Safeway). A review of the discount operators listed by Thorpe [1972] and shown in Table 4 shows that only three of the nine companies remain in operation, and two of these operate superstores. Other imitators were set up as trading arms of major retailers. This does not mean that imitation brought success as the demise of KD Discount (Key Markets), Pricerite (International), Shoppers Paradise (Fine Fare) and Victor Value (Tesco then Bejam then Iceland Frozen Foods then Kwik Save!) among others show. All of these operations have been sold or closed down. Limited-range discount operations are difficult to run profitably and successfully and the success of Kwik Save is impressive.

The expansion of the Kwik Save Discount Group can also be viewed in spatial terms. In 1967, when the discount store format had been fully accepted by the company, as has been seen (Figure 5) there were 13 branches trading as Kwik Save Discount, mainly in North Wales, but with some expansion into Cheshire. By 1971 the company had 24 units trading in North Wales, Cheshire and Shropshire (Figure 6) with the headquarters and distribution depot remaining at Prestatyn. In 1973, a new depot was added to the Group at Ashton-in-Makerfield in Lancashire. The purchase of this depot was explicitly designed to allow for easier distribution to existing stores in Lancashire and to proposed new stores in both Yorkshire and the Midlands. The sites for these stores had been purchased in 1973 to allow for phased opening in the following 18 months. This period was important for the company as they now had to make their system work via a multiple depot situation.

Future expansion if the systems worked at the second depot would be easier. This expansion was also aided by the further extension of the motorway network. It is often forgotten that at this period physical distribution could not rely on good infrastructure and spatial expansion was often geared to infrastructure investment. This infrastructure investment can be public (e.g., motorways) or private (e.g., distribution warehouses). The spatial pattern of stores in 1974 is given in Figure 14. The beginnings of the move away, enabled by this investment, from the 'heartland' of Prestatyn, North Wales can be clearly discerned.

By 1975, the Annual Report stated that 'in order to maintain planned expansion into the Midlands, we are constructing a new distribution warehouse at Tipton, Staffs'. A clear strategy of careful, planned spatial expansion was in place. Being a very centralised distribution-driven company, Kwik Save used the locations of their distribution depots, and the motorway expansion programme, to open up the targeted areas for growth. Structural investment was taking place to allow planned spatial development. Thus the development at Tipton produced expansion plans for the Midlands, the South-West and South Wales which began to see stores opening wider afield in 1976–77. The position at 1977 shows clearly this drive southwards and into South Wales (Figure 15), continuing the spatial transformation of the company. At the same time Figure 15 shows the extent to which Kwik Save's strategy encompassed the 'in-filling' of existing trading areas with newer and more stores. Thus developments occurred as well in North Wales and Lancashire.

It was the opportunity to 'in-fill' existing target areas that attracted Kwik Save to Cee-n-Cee supermarkets in 1978. The purchase of this 49 unit chain gave further representation in Lancashire, Cheshire, and the Potteries. While the grasping of this opportunity is perfectly understandable it can be argued that the purchase disrupted Kwik Save's progress (see above). Certainly it took a considerable period to incorporate the chain fully into operations. Further evidence of this disruption is seen on the distribution side of the business. In 1977 plans were announced for a new warehouse at Swindon to serve expansion in the South-West, South and South-East. However, Cee-n-Cee also had a depot, although in Kwik Save's main area, at Winsford. The takeover of the Winsford depot led to the Swindon warehouse being sold in 1979. Kwik Save's fifth depot then opened in Newport in late 1979, clearly linked to major expansion into South Wales.

A similar pattern for development has also occurred in the 1980s. Minor changes to the distribution warehouse network in the early 1980s preceded the opening of a new warehouse at Sherburn in Elmet in North Yorkshire. This was clearly aimed at providing for expansion in the North-East of England. Such expansion is demonstrated in Figure 16 which shows the position in 1985. The locations can be clearly contrasted with the locations in the entrepreneurial phase and demonstrate the advance Kwik Save has made towards being a national

FIGURE 14
KWIK SAVE GROUP P.L.C. LOCATION OF STORES 1974

chain. Again, the figure shows the pressure Kwik Save maintains to 'in-fill' existing areas. Since 1985 expansion has continued with openings for example of stores in Southampton, Bournemouth, Carlisle and Newcastle. Opportunities to 'in-fill' existing areas of activities continue to be taken, the most notable being the purchase of 23 former Dee Corporation units in the Midlands to provide better sites and extend representation in the area.

However, the major change since 1985 has been the developments in the London and South-East area. This has included opening stores in Ilford and Tottenham, for example, and the purchase of a small number of Woolworth stores for conversion. These stores were fore-runners of a scheduled onslaught on the London market which will

FIGURE 15
KWIK SAVE GROUP P.L.C. LOCATION OF STORES 1977

probably have to be supported by further distribution centre developments. The location of stores in 1987 is given in Figure 17 which clearly
shows the further spatial expansion since 1985, and the emerging
presence in London and the South-East region. Since 1987 expansion,
particularly into this region, has continued. This has been substantially
advanced by the purchase of Victor Value which has most of its outlets
in the South-East. This is an example of spatial expansion strategy
aided by acquisition.

The company has also expanded from the 'traditional' food supermarket. Since 1984 a freezer centre chain (Arctic) has been operating,
often adjacent to existing Kwik Save units. The introduction of scanning
technology has now allowed these freezer centres to become part of the

FIGURE 16
KWIK SAVE GROUP P.L.C. LOCATION OF STORES 1985

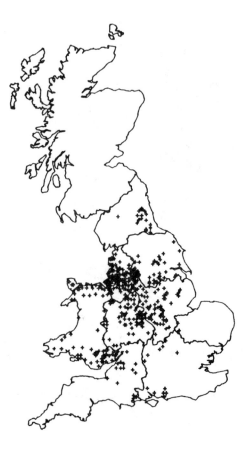

Kwik Save operation at any location, and conversions are under way to phase out Arctic Freezer Centres as separate trading identities. In addition, by 1988 there were also 23 Late Shopper convenience stores which were part of the Tates chain. This convenience chain is set for expansion, and a new distribution centre opened in Grimsby in the first half of 1987. The previous reliance on outside concessions has been reduced particularly through a subsidiary company, Colemans Meat (purchased in 1980). Coleman's retains the 'local touch' by operating almost 900 franchises for meat and delicatessen, fruit and vegetables and bakery products in many Kwik Save stores. In addition there are in-house Best of Cellars drinks units (off-licence sales) found in the larger Kwik Save developments, with 190 operating by the end of 1988. The

FIGURE 17
KWIK SAVE GROUP P.L.C. LOCATION OF STORES 1987

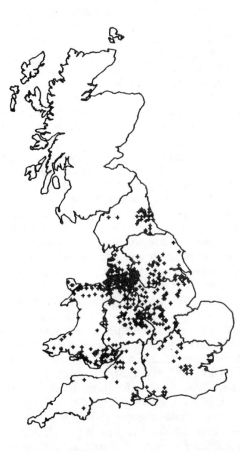

pattern of spatial development is therefore a strategically planned systematic one, concentrating on the core business and expanding in new areas and in-filling existing strongholds.

The transition from an entrepreneurial-led small company to a signficant corporate retailer has also meant changes in structural elements of the business as well as spatial expansion. However at a broad level the company has remained faithful to Gubay's original principles. This may be partly owing to the long-term presence on the board of several directors who started out with Gubay in the early 1960s or 1970s. For example, Ian Howe, the present chairman and chief executive, joined Gubay in 1963 and had responsibility for computerisation. In two particular aspects Kwik Save have remained faithful to the original principles. First, Kwik Save still operates out of small units. The average selling space of a Kwik Save supermarket is only 5,700 sq ft. This is against the trend in food retailing which is for polarisation into very large units such as superstores and very small specialist stores [Dawson, 1985]. The average Tesco store in 1988, for example, was nearer 21,800 sq ft sales area, with new store openings approaching 35,000 sq ft sales area. Kwik Save occupies a middle size range which most other companies ignore. Secondly, the company maintains its reliance on manufacturer branded goods and avoids the widespread trend towards own brands. This has ensured that Kwik Save is welcomed by manufacturers and the brands now sold are generally top manufacturer brands rather than the earlier reliance on secondary names. These brands are sold at very competitive prices (Table 5). As the Annual Report of 1985 states, the trading policy is one 'of offering the lowest possible prices on our range of top branded names'. By remaining faithful to these two principles, Kwik Save has isolated itself from two major trends in UK food retailing.

There is one other way in which Kwik Save has gone against the trends in UK food retailing: that is in its locational policy. Kwik Save is reliant on convenient locations which are often relatively central. This is against the general trend to segregate food shopping away from high streets into suburban superstores. The approach of Kwik Save is to take the shops to the customer, allowing Kwik Save to run several shops in a town where other retailers have been withdrawing to the edge-of-town or closing their presence completely. This also reflects the smaller catchment area and greater walk-in trade generated by Kwik Save compared with other food multiples. The site location strategy can be illustrated through a number of cases. Guy [1987] has shown how Kwik Save had three of the 42 multiple and co-operative grocery stores in Cardiff in 1982. By 1986 they operated four of the 30 such grocery stores trading. Their additional store was in fact a purchase from Argyll. In the same way, Lillywhite [1987] has shown how Kwik Save's representation grew from 16 out of 225 supermarkets in the West Midlands in 1977 to 31 out of 200 supermarkets by 1986. This is a change from 7 per cent of the supermarkets with 6.7 per cent of the sales floorspace in 1977 to 15.5 per cent of the outlets and 9.6 per cent of the floorspace in 1986. With the 1987 purchase of Dee Corporation outlets in the Midlands it is likely that these figures have risen even further. This ability to trade successfully from other retailers' former outlets has also been demonstrated by Rees [1987] in Swansea where a Kwik Save and an Arctic Freezer Centre trade out of part of a former Tesco unit in Morriston.

The approach is well summed-up by Ian Howe, the Chairman, in the Annual Reports of 1984 and 1986:

> There is an increasing polarisation in the trade between retailers concentrating on major developments and relying on large

catchment areas, and others, like ourselves, who see the opportunity to fill the vacuum that is created by the shrinking number of outlets to offer the best in price and convenience to urban, suburban and rural customers. The flexibility of approach allowed by our trading methods will ensure our continued growth in a highly competitive market [Annual Report, 1984: 4].

The growth of superstores, and the resultant decline in first generation supermarkets, is tending to reduce the number of shopping alternatives available to customers. The ability of our Group to trade profitably in stores of a wide range of sizes and locations will give us increasing opportunities to exploit this situation [Annual Report, 1986: 5].

The polarisation of retailing and the move to out-of-town locations are seen as providing opportunities for Kwik Save to expand its operations and to fill a gap or niche in the market place. This again emphasises the spatial element to retail change, this time at a different spatial level.

In a number of other ways, however, the company has moved away from the principles of Albert Gubay and instead has followed developments in the market. First, the stores now have considerably more lines that in the past, often over 1,000 compared with the previous 450. This extension to the number of lines has caused problems with checkout operators' abilities to memorise the prices. This is particularly acute in areas where it is difficult to ensure staff quality and reliability. The new stores therefore operate with a laser scanning system which allows price look-up and obviates the need for price memorisiation. The freezer centres had EPOS as an integral part of its operations. Perhaps a more notable change however is the extension to service and design that has occurred in the 1980s. While it is not true to say that Kwik Save has moved completely up-market in its positioning, it certainly has 'traded-up' in response to consumer changes. There is a world of difference between the interiors of the original Gubay stores and the current Kwik Save offering, despite the company's scathing comment that 'we do not wish to indulge in the "designer" look which characterises the stores of many of our competitors' [Kwik Save Annual Report, 1988: 7].

The consumer emphasis on quality and value and the new consumer perceptions which have steadily broadened have seen most firms in food retailing examine quality and value. The most notable change in Tesco's drive up-market [Akehurst, 1984], but other chains, including Kwik Save, have moved in the same direction. For Kwik Save this has meant new design, decor and layout and refurbishment of stores and staff attitudes. While prices are still keen, the emphasis is less on discount, a fact recognised by a change in name in January 1986 to Kwik Save Group P.L.C. (from Kwik Save Discount Group P.L.C.) and the disappearance of 'Discount' from all store fascias. While Kwik Save now promote themselves as 'no nonsense food stores', the comparison between the early Gubay-style Kwik Save and the modern stores shows just how far in design, style, decor and operating and merchandising practices Kwik Save have in fact moved.

There have also had to be changes in the management and operational structure of the company. In operational terms the company remains very centralised with most of the operations organised, controlled and carried out at head office. For example, computerisation is currently centralised in location although decentralised in format of machines. The company has now, however, expanded into divisions, hence the need for a group structure. The three divisions are Coleman Meat Company Ltd, Tates Ltd and Kwik Save Stores Ltd (which covers Kwik Save Stores, Arctic Freezer Centres and Best of Cellars). The group structure at August 1987 is shown in Table 7.

One of the interesting aspects of the table is the presence on the board of a number of directors who began with Albert Gubay. In particular, Ian Howe has spent over 25 years in the company. When Gubay left, Ian Hill became chairman with joint managing directors of Ian Howe and Michael Weeks. Weeks was in charge of all aspects of the business up to the opening of stores while Howe had responsibility for general administration. Other directors each had an area of responsibility; Mills for distribution, Edwards for sales and transport and Postlethwaite for buying [Manchester Business School, 1987b]. This young management team effectively managed the expansion of Kwik Save until 1983, since which ill-health and retirement have left Howe as chairman and chief executive and Postlethwaite as managing director. The links back to Gubay in terms of management are marked.

The final realisation that Kwik Save had moved from its entrepreneurial stage through to full corporate status came in 1987. Despite periodic rumours of possible takeovers, particularly during the two or three years after Gubay's departure, Kwik Save remained independent until mid-1987 when Dairy Farm International Ltd, a Hong Kong company mainly owned by Jardine Matheson, and operators of retail chains in Hong Kong (Wellcome and 7–11) and Australia (Franklins) took, against the Kwik Save Board's wishes, a 25 per cent stake in the company. There is a standstill agreement in operation which precluded a full bid being made until after April 1989. Kwik Save's future is therefore less clear, although a foreign bid may be preferable to a UK one if it allows a devolved management approach and freedom of action in the UK. One effect of the agreement is to place members of Dairy Farm on the Kwik Save Group board and indeed Graeme Seabrook of Dairy Farm took over in 1988 as managing director, replacing Postlethwaite.

The Future

In the long term discount stores are likely to disappear. However the disappearance may not be quick and will conceivably be an evolution into a store with a wider but less deep range

TABLE 7

GROUP STRUCTURE

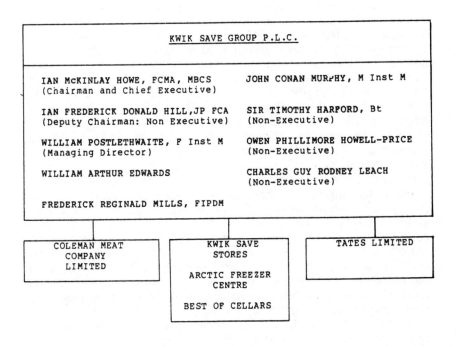

KWIK SAVE GROUP P.L.C.

IAN McKINLAY HOWE, FCMA, MBCS (Chairman and Chief Executive)	JOHN CONAN MURPHY, M Inst M
IAN FREDERICK DONALD HILL, JP FCA (Deputy Chairman: Non Executive)	SIR TIMOTHY HARFORD, Bt (Non-Executive)
WILLIAM POSTLETHWAITE, F Inst M (Managing Director)	OWEN PHILLIMORE HOWELL-PRICE (Non-Executive)
WILLIAM ARTHUR EDWARDS	CHARLES GUY RODNEY LEACH (Non-Executive)
FREDERICK REGINALD MILLS, FIPDM	

COLEMAN MEAT COMPANY LIMITED	KWIK SAVE STORES ARCTIC FREEZER CENTRE BEST OF CELLARS	TATES LIMITED

Source: Kwik Save Group P.L.C. Annual Report (1987).

of merchandise, an increase in service, and a declining price differential [Ornstein, 1976: 58].

The future of Kwik Save is therefore a little uncertain at the moment, depending to a considerable extent on the progress or otherwise of any bid, whether from Dairy Farm or any other third party. In trading terms, however, the future is somewhat clearer. Expansion into new geographical areas away from the company's base continues and will be the main feature of the coming years.

The targeting of London and the South-East is potentially a high-risk strategy, but the rewards could be enormous. Sites in London are expensive and traditionally Kwik Save has purchased freeholds and avoided debt on the balance sheets [Thorpe, 1974]. There is also uncertainty whether the affluent south will take to Kwik Save's 'cheap and cheerful' form of retailing, although international evidence with in particular Aldi suggests that middle-class urban dwellers can be attracted in such locations. Certainly there is likely to be a cost-conscious, brand-oriented, convenience-style consumer segment in London. If this segment can be tapped then the rewards will be considerable.

In the other areas of expansion – the north-west and the south-east – the search for stores continues while in-fill stores or relocations are always sought by Kwik Save, whose advertisements for sites can often list well over 350 towns in which sites are required. There would seem to be scope for continued expansion. In addition experience is being gained with the Late Shopper convenience stores which are being expanded. The implication for the Group is that a portfolio of operations and trading experience is being developed which will be useful in future adaptations to circumstances. The spatial expansion of Kwik Save has, as has been demonstrated, progressed in a systematic and controlled fashion. Developments in distribution to service the extending number of stores can again be expected. The one area of Great Britain into which Kwik Save has not ventured is Scotland. In some respects this is surprising, as Scotland would appear to have no real limited-range discount competitors to Kwik Save, while seemingly having a considerable pool of likely customers, especially in the urban areas of Glasgow, Edinburgh and the Central Belt. To be really considered as a national chain, Kwik Save will have to overcome its reluctance to enter the Scottish market. Perhaps the Central Belt can expect to be the location for a distribution depot. One explanation for the reticence might be the considerable costs that would have to be incurred in distribution until a critical mass of stores developed. In other areas this has been less of a problem, but the distances involved to Scotland could cause difficulties. What is clear is the interlinking of spatial and structural elements of business developments.

If Ornstein, as quoted above, is correct, then the signs of decline in Kwik Save can already be discerned. The title 'discount' has been dropped from the fascia, the service level has increased, the range has widened, although importantly the price *differential* appears not to have decreased markedly. To that extent the true discount store is in decline and being replaced by a price leader. Such changes have been necessary as price has become less important overall to consumers and the potential Kwik Save market has shrunk. Dangers for Kwik Save in the future, therefore, are either that their market will continue to shrink despite 'trading-up' or that a new cost leader could emerge to challenge Kwik Save, taking their market share. Kwik Save's cost leadership position may be based on past performance not present systems and controls. Certainly it appears that Seabrook's role in Kwik Save is to galvanise the company, encourage new talent and to improve performance at all levels whilst maintaining the traditional strengths [Lester, 1989]. At present the emergence of a new UK-based low-cost leader seems unlikely, and Kwik Save appear to be in a reasonable position. An international danger might be Aldi which are rumoured to want to enter the British market. Aldi run stores which are strikingly similar to the Gubay-style Kwik Save operation, and these could pose a threat to the new generation Kwik Save. The key will be Kwik Save's ability to keep on top of the business as before and to be successful in the London and south-east markets. The true limited range discount store may be a thing of the past but for Kwik Save it has been translated into the convenient and competitive food outlet with all the connotations both convenience and competition have to offer.

THE IMPORTANCE OF KWIK SAVE

Kwik Save Group P.L.C. are important for a number of reasons. First, they illustrate very clearly the transition from entrepreneur to corporation. In the initial stages, the concept was developed and put into practice by an entrepreneurial founder and a relatively young management team. This entrepreneurship and drive took the company from its small beginnings to being quoted on the Stock Exchange. It was at this stage that difficulties arose. Such difficulties and problems are not uncommon as companies try to bridge the gap between entrepreneurial roots and a corporate future [Churchill and Lewis, 1983; Mintzberg and Waters, 1982]. In this case the entrepreneur clearly felt the desire to return to the practice of entrepreneurship [Lord et al., 1988] rather than take Kwik Save forward. Kwik Save, however, retained many of the managerial staff who began with the company thus providing the continuity that is often deemed necessary in making this transition [Drucker, 1985]. Mintzberg and Waters' [1982] entrepreneurial vision was being replaced by corporate planning. The company therefore accords to the progression outlined by Churchill and Lewis [1983] and shown in Figure 3, although timings of discrete stages are difficult to ascertain. The transition was thus managed, not without a degree of difficulty, confusion or crisis management, but nevertheless successfully.

An important element in managing this transition and its aftermath is that the company have kept their 'eye on the ball' and were not tempted to expand into new operational areas until corporate success had been achieved. Kwik Save still see the general trends in food retailing as providing them with opportunities rather than threats. These opportunities are both structural (the polarisation of retailing) and spatial (the possibilities in the South-East and perhaps Scotland, and at the local level in terms of convenience). This is not to say that where general trends can be harnessed to the corporate good then they are ignored. Indeed, Kwik Save has changed and moved away from its original conception in line with changing consumer requirements and retail practice, and the company would see themselves as a convenient and competitive chain rather than a discounter *per se*. The focus, however, for a long time was solely on the core business.

The company managed change successfully for other reasons as well. Foremost among these was a clear view of the way forward and in particular a strategic and systematically planned approach to store location and numerical and geographical expansion. Having centralised distribution at an early stage, ahead of most of the other food retailers, and having adopted computers and technology to enable tight control of the business, Kwik Save were well aware of the importance of physical distribution. The planned development and spatial expansion was thus dependent on good distribution and this became a key element of the planning. Centralisation and computerisation provided, together with detailed business control and aggressive buying, the basis for competitive advantage.

The model proposed by Brown *et al.* [1981] predicts for Kwik Save an initial neighbourhood and expansion pattern (Figure 2). The combination of sales potential (arguably related), logistics effects (significant), elasticity of agency profitability (minimal) and capital availability (initially low) produce a predicted neighbourhood effect. Figure 18, which is based on the earlier location maps of Kwik Save stores, shows this to be the case. As capital availability increases, the model prediction is for a neighbourhood effect with a slight hierarchy effect. It can be suggested that this is found to an extent, with some leapfrogging over markets with later in-filling. The hierarchy effect is very slight, however, as the location maps and Figure 18 suggest.

Secondly, Kwik Save stores are important because of their distinctiveness. In food retailing in the UK, they no longer have any real competitors in their sector of the market with the possible exception of Lo-Cost. With Safeway concentrating on their extension of the Safeway name to Argyll stores the future for Kwik Save seems positive. The polarisation of retailing has left a gap to be exploited and Kwik Save are doing just that. Spatially, there are clear potential markets for the company. Any company that succeeds by going against the trends must be worthy of study even if it is only as a counterpoint to received wisdom.

This distinctiveness of Kwik Save is found in several ways. At a macro-level, the company is one of a number of North Wales based retail companies that have expanded towards becoming national chains. Another example from the same area are Iceland Frozen Foods, which with the growth of freezer sections in Kwik Save may increasingly come into conflict with Kwik Save. This provincial base does mean, however, that Kwik Save are only now trying to break into the south-east of the country where there is a large market, but the entry costs and competition are high. A similar problem has confronted other provincial-based food chains, most notably Asda [Jones, 1981; Davies and Sparks, 1986]. At a micro-level, the company are exploiting their indentified market niche by operating out of relatively small stores in convenient locations. The concept of convenience has several different facets, but the Kwik Save version stresses an ability to attract walk-in trade and shoppers travelling to 'traditional' locations. Kwik Save stores are thus found in High Streets, suburban sites, purpose-

FIGURE 18
KWIK SAVE GROUP P.L.C. MARKET AREA EXPANSION 1967–87

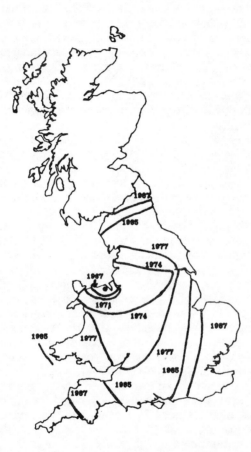

built precincts, near housing or close to workplaces and car parks. The emphasis is on bringing the stores to the public rather than relying on consumers travelling out to them. This goes against much of the superstore ethos and suggests an attempt to exploit a different consumer base or different consumer trips. This locational approach allows Kwik Save to operate in locations where other food retailers would not and also to place more stores in a given area than other retailers given their catchment areas. This is providing Kwik Save with a high profile, which is reinforced with a considerable spend on regional advertising.

This locational approach is important because it represents one of the few successful attempts to fill the void that superstores are claimed to leave. One of the often-quoted worries about the polarisation and decentralisation of retailing, and especially food retailing, is that of providing facilities for those consumers unable to travel to superstores [Bowlby, 1985]. It has been argued that these consumers are forced to rely on declining shop numbers and lower quality in traditional locations. The prices in such shops, it is suggested, are often higher than in superstores, thus further penalising the disadvantaged consumers. If Kwik Save are able to use these locations then they can ease the position considerably for these disadvantaged groups. While never matching the product range of superstores, the price advantage of Kwik Save remains considerable. They offer a cheap and convenient food shopping facility.

Kwik Save began from a very simple idea: that a company can be developed and be successful by selling manufacturer branded goods to consumers at the lowest possible price. While this is an attractively simple idea, in practice discount food retailing is far from easy. The casualties on the way have been considerable, both in this country and, for example, in the USA. Kwik Save, however, have grown and prospered by taking the basic idea and developing a series of strategies around it. These strategies are in turn held in place by rigorous managerial control. The strategies adopted by Kwik Save are based on the tenets of low-price, manufacturer branded goods, limited range, convenient locations, centralised distribution, and planned spatial expansion. Most of these strategies are aimed at exploiting a structural and spatial niche in the market. While other companies have similary seen the niche, few, if any, have been able to exploit it successfully. The management techniques provided a competitive advantage [Porter, 1980] that made Kwik Save the cost leader, and this, together with entrepreneurial drive, took the company forward.

The success of Kwik Save has been driven by commitment to make the strategies work and in particular by detailed control of the business. Discount food retailers need low costs and high turnover. The cost side is controlled by cutting shrinkage costs, through for example centralised distribution in which Kwik Save lead the way for many retailers; by cutting labour costs at all levels of the company, through for example de-skilling mangement, rapid checkout operation and a flexible labour force; by reducing overheads such as store furnishings and facilities; and through good buying deals with manufacturers enabled by bulk purchase. The effect has been a net margin higher than most other food retailers obtained from an industry low gross margin, that has been sustained for a number of years and sales per employee figures that are equally well-regarded.

Kwik Save may be considered to meet Drucker's [1980] four key elements for entrepreneurial success:

i.   Kwik Save clearly had a focus on the market, although in very general terms and believed totally that if they were the cheapest then they would be successful.

ii. Kwik Save demonstrate sound financial management with control systems to monitor cash flows in place from early days.

iii. The Kwik Save management team were set up early by the founder. The effect was that when Albert Gubay left, the management and the systems were in place.

iv. Gubay as founder clearly demonstrated his responsibility in the business, and began to withdraw when no longer needed, although his full reasons for withdrawing are clearly more complex than this.

Kwik Save are also a good example of Porter's [1980, 1985] cost leadership strategy. The initial idea was to be a cost leader and the business systems introduced produced the cost control and savings that allowed cost leadership. Kwik Save had access to capital as they grew and provided continued investment for expansion, standardised and simplified operational procedures, supervised and controlled labour rigorously, produced a low-cost and efficient distribution system and redesigned the basic in-store system for retailing. In organisational terms there was tight cost control, detailed reporting, a structured organisation and management incentives based on targets. All these attributes are those Porter [1980] describes as being needed for a cost leadership strategy. Having this cost leadership Kwik Save appealed to lower-income consumers and those wanting leading brand names. Service, which can add cost, has not been part of the offer until recently.

CONCLUSIONS

What has to be recognised from the case-study is the spatial-structural dimensions to the retail development of Kwik Save. Any analysis and understanding of the process of retail change as for example through an examination of corporate change has to include a spatial dimension. This case-study of Kwik Save stresses the spatial element to retailer decision-making. This spatial element, however, operates at a variety of scales as it interacts with wider strategic decisions. The study of retailing, it is argued, must consider the structural and spatial realities of retail life in order to understand more fully the retail fabric and retail decisions. This has not been fully appreciated in many of the studies previously undertaken.

The case-study of Kwik Save has been used here to indicate both the importance of spatial and structural considerations and their inter-relationships when analysing retail change and also to stress the need for company-specific studies to illuminate retail analysis and theory. The previous work on retail change and retail theory can be seen to address only weakly the structures, problems and events portrayed by the selected company. The wheel of retailing or the other retail 'theories' can be seen as nothing more than basic descriptions of retail practice – they offer no real understanding and explanation.

On the other hand however, the issues raised by the case-study are far more applicable to the concepts of business growth and competitive advantage that are beginning to be developed [Porter, 1980; 1985; Churchill and Lewis, 1983; Drucker, 1985]. At the same time it is clear that extensions to these concepts are required if a general theory of corporate retail development is to emerge. One of the ways in which this work has to be extended is in terms of spatial strategy. One suggested model is that Brown *et al.* [1981] and indeed using the framework developed by these authors, the predicted developmental spatial strategy for Kwik Save was the neighbourhood spatial diffusion pattern that was followed. Work remains to be done, however, on exploring the links between these two conceptual strands and models [Laulajainen 1988a]. In particular there is a need now for far more detailed and extensive analysis of corporate growth patterns, initially at the individual company level, focusing on the spatial-structural interactions and underpinned by the detailed review of competitive advantage and business growth. It is only through the production of a body of detailed corporate development knowledge that understanding and explanation in the form of a retail theory of spatial-structural development can be produced. Much remains to be attempted.

The author acknowledges with thanks the comments on earlier drafts of this work by Professor John Dawson and Dr Keri Davies, which helped immeasurably in clarifying issues and raising more questions. He would also like to thank Mr Graeme Seabrook, managing director of Kwik Save Group P.L.C. for his comments on a draft of this paper. All errors and omissions are of course those of the author alone.

SOURCES

Capel Cure Myers (1985), 'A cool move for Kwik Save', *Retail*, Vol.3, No.1.
Estates Gazette, The Property Times, June 1987.
Financial Times, 28 June 1985, 4 June 1987 (specials on the Isle of Man); 19 June 1987.
The Grocer, 6 January 1973; 25 September 1976; 24 April 1982; 26 June 1982; 16 October 1982; 4 February 1989.
Investor's Chronicle, 27 November 1970; 24 August 1984.
Kwik Save Group P.L.C., *Annual Reports*, 1971–88.
Management Today, August 1982; April 1986.
Manchester Business School, 1987a, *UK Grocery Retailing*.
Manchester Business School, 1987b, *Kwik Save Group PLC*, Teaching case prepared originally by Derek Channon and updated by Patrick Quarcoo and Rob Lees.
Manchester Business School, 1988, *Retail Reference Book 1988*, Manchester.
Singer and Friedlander Ltd, 1970, *Offer for Sale: Kwik Save Discount Group Ltd.*
Stock Exchange Official Yearbook 1986–87, London: Stock Exchange Press.
Sunday Times, 23 May 1976; 18 October 1981.
Supermarketing, 18 October 1985; 2 September 1988.
The Standard, 30 July 1982; 13 August 1984; March 1985.
The Times, 30 November 1970; 2 January 1973; 28 April 1973; 3 May 1973; 20 December 1974; 10 July 1981; 7 February 1984.

REFERENCES

Akehurst, G., 1983, 'Concentration in Retail Distribution: Measurement and Significance', *Service Industries Journal*, Vol.3, No.2.

Akehurst, G., 1984, 'Checkout: the Analysis of Oligopolistic Behaviour in the UK Grocery Retail Market', *Service Industries Journal*, Vol.4, No.2.

Allan, J., 1980, 'The Changing Retail Pattern', *Retail and Distribution Management*, Vol.8 No.4.

Baden-Fuller, C.W.F., 1984 'Rising Concentration in the UK Grocery Trade 1970–82', in K. Tucker (ed.), *Firms and Markets*, London: Croom Helm.

Bamfield, J.A.N., 1980, 'The Changing Face of British Retailing', *National Westminster Bank Quarterly Review*, May.

Beaujeu-Garnier, J. and A. Delobez, 1979, *Geography of Marketing*, London: Longman.

Beaumont, J., 1987, 'Trends in Food Retailing', in E. McFadyen (ed.), *The Changing Face of British Retailing*, London: Newman Books.

Beaver, P., 1981, *A Pedlar's Legacy: the Origins and History of Empire Stores*, London: H. Melland.

Bennison, D.J. and R.L. Davies, 1980, 'The Impact of Town Centre Shopping Schemes in Britain', *Progress in Planning*, Vol.14.

Berry, B.J.L. *et al.*, 1988, *Market Centres and Retail Location*, Englewood Cliffs: Prentice Hall.

Bird, J.H. and M.E. Witherick, 1986, 'Marks and Spencer: The Geography of an Image', *Geography*, Vol.71, No.4.

Boswell, J. (ed.), 1986, *JS 100: The Story of Sainsbury's*, London: Sainsbury.

Bowlby, S., 1985, 'Shoppers' Needs: Don't Forget the Old and Carless', *Town and Country Planning*, Vol.54, No.7.

Brown, L.A., 1981, *Innovation Diffusion: A New Perspective*, London: Methuen.

Brown, L.A., M.A. Brown and C.S. Craig, 1981, 'Innovation Diffusion and Entrepreneurial Activity in a Spatial Context', in J.N. Sheth (ed.), *Research in Marketing*, Vol.4, Jai Press.

Brown, S., 1984, 'Retail Location and Retail Change in Belfast City Centre', unpublished PhD thesis, Queen's University of Belfast.

Brown, S., 1987a, 'Institutional Change in Retailing: a review and synthesis', *European Journal of Marketing*, Vol.21, No.6.

Brown, S., 1987b, 'Institutional Change in Retailing: a geographical interpretation', *Progress in Human Geography*, Vol.11, No.2.

Brown, S., 1987c, 'An Alternative Paradigm for Retail Planning', *The Planner*, Vol.73, No.12.

Brown, S., 1988a, 'The Wheel of the Wheel of Retailing', *International Journal of Retailing*, Vol.3, No.1.

Brown, S., 1988b, 'Retail Change: Cycles and Strategy', *Quarterly Review of Marketing*, Vol.13, No.3.

Burt, S.L., 1986, 'The Carrefour Group – The First Twenty-five Years', *International Journal of Retailing*, Vol.1, No.3.

Chapman, K. and D. Walker, 1987, *Industrial Location: Principles and Policies*, Oxford: Blackwell.

Churchill, N.C. and V.L. Lewis, 1983, 'The Five Stages of Small Business Growth', *Harvard Business Review*, Vol.61, No.3.

Cohen, Y.S., 1972, 'Diffusion of an Innovation in an Urban System', The University of Chicago, Department of Geography, Research Paper 140.

Corina, M., 1971 *Pile It High, Sell It Cheap*, London: Weidenfeld & Nicolson.

Davies, B.K. and L. Sparks, 1986, 'ASDA-MFI: the superstore and the flat-pack', *International Journal of Retailing*, Vol.1, No.1.

Davies, B.K. and L. Sparks, 1989, 'Superstore Retailing in Great Britain 1960–1986: Results from a New Database', *Transactions of the Institute of British Geographers*, Vol.14, No.1.

Davies, B.K., C. Gilligan and C. Sutton, 1984, 'The Changing Nature of the Grocery Retail Sector in Great Britain: A Preliminary Investigation', *Sheffield City Polytechnic, Discussion Paper*, 18.

Davies, B.K., C. Gilligan and C. Sutton, 1985, 'Structural Changes in Grocery Retailing: The Implications for Competition', *International Journal of Physical Distribution and Materials Management*, Vol.15, No.2.

Davies, B.K., C. Gilligan and C. Sutton, 1986, 'The Development of Own Label Product Strategies in Grocery and DIY Retailing in the UK', *International Journal of Retailing*, Vol.1, No.1.

Davies, R.L., 1971, 'The Urban Retailing System of Coventry', Department of Geography, University of Newcastle, Seminar Paper 15.

Davies, R.L., 1976, *Marketing Geography*, Corbridge: RPA.

Davies, R.L., 1984, *Retail and Commercial Planning*, London: Croom Helm.

Davies, R.L. and D.S. Rogers, 1984, *Store Location and Store Assessment Research*, Chichester: Wiley.

Dawson, J.A., 1979, *The Marketing Environment*, London: Croom Helm.

Dawson, J.A., 1980, *Retail Geography*, London: Croom Helm.

Dawson, J.A., 1981, 'Innovation Adoption in Food Retailing – The Example of Self-Service Methods', *Service Industries Review*, Vol.1, No.2.

Dawson, J.A., 1982, *Commercial Distribution in Europe*, London: Croom Helm.

Dawson, J.A., 1983, *Shopping Centre Development*, London: Longman.

Dawson, J.A., 1984, 'Structural-Spatial Relationships in the Spread of Hypermarket Retailing', in E. Kaynak and R. Savitt (eds.), *Comparative Marketing Systems*, New York: Praeger.

Dawson, J.A., 1985, 'Structural Change in European Retailing: The Polarisation of Operating Scale', in E. Kaynak (ed.), *Global Perspectives in Marketing*, New York: Praeger.

Dawson, J.A., 1988, 'Future for the High Street', *The Geographical Journal*, Vol.154, No.1.

Dawson, J.A. and A.M. Broadbridge, 1988, *Retailing In Scotland In 2005*, University of Stirling: Institute for Retail Studies.

Dawson, J.A. and J.D. Lord (eds.), 1985, *Shopping Centre Development: Policies and Prospects*, London: Croom Helm.

Dawson, J.A., S.A. Shaw and D.G. Harris, 1987, *The Impact of Changes in Retailing and Wholesaling on Scottish Manufacturers*, 2 volumes, Institute for Retail Studies, University of Stirling.

Department of Trade and Industry, 1974, *Kwik Save Discount Group Limited*, London: HMSO.

Dreesmann, A.C.R., 1980, 'Economic, Social and Cultural Aspects of International Retailing', in M.P. Kacker, 1985, *Transatlantic Trends in Retailing*, Connecticut: Quorom.

Drucker, P.F., 1985, *Innovation and Entrepreneurship*, London: Heinemann.

Fulop, C., 1964, *Competition for Consumers*, London: André Deutsch.

Gayler, H.S., 1984, *Retail Innovation in Britain*, Norwich: Geo Books.

Ghosh, A. and S.L. McLafferty, 1987, *Location Strategies for Retail and Service Firms*, Lexington: Lexington Books.

Gibbs, A., 1987, 'Retail Innovation and Retail Planning', *Progress In Planning*, Vol.27.

Giggs, J.A., 1972, 'Retail Change and Suburbanisation in the Nottingham Metropolitan Community', *Geographica Polonica*, Vol.24.

Goldsmith, W. and G. Clutterbuck, 1984, *The Winning Streak*, London: Weidenfeld & Nicolson.

Goodall, F., 1987, *A Bibliography of British Business Histories*, Farnborough: Gower.

Green, S., 1987, 'From Riches to Rags: the John Collier Story', in G. Johnson (ed.), *Business Strategy and Retailing*, Chichester: Wiley.

Guy, C.M., 1986, 'The Location of Shops in the Reading Area', Department of Geography, University of Reading, Geographical Paper 34.

Guy, C.M., 1980, *Retail Location and Retail Planning in Britain*, Farnborough: Gower.

Guy, C.M., 1987, 'Accessibility to Multiple-Owned Grocery Shops in Cardiff: A Description and Evaluation of Recent Changes', *Planning Practice and Research*, Vol.2.

Havenhand, G., 1970, *Nation of Shopkeepers*, London: Eyre & Spottiswoode.

Hayter, R. and D. Watts., 1983, 'The Geography of Enterprise: A Reappraisal', *Progress in Human Geography*, Vol.7, No.2.

Hollander, S.C., 1986, 'If Small is Beautiful, is a Very Small Sample even Prettier?', *European Journal of Marketing*, Vol.20, No.2.

Hower, R.M., 1943, *History of Macy's of New York: 1858–1919*, Cambridge, MA: Harvard University Press.

Institute of Grocery Distribution, 1987, *Food Retailing Review 1987*, Watford.

Jeffreys, J.B., 1954, *Retail Trading in Britain 1850–1950*, Cambridge: Cambridge University Press.

Jeremy, D.J., 1984–86, *Dictionary of Business Biography*, 5 volumes plus supplement, London: Butterworth.

Johnson, G. (ed.), 1987a, *Business Strategy and Retailing*, Chichester: Wiley.

Johnson, G., 1987b, *Strategic Change and the Management Process*, Oxford: Blackwell.

Johnson, G. and K. Scholes, 1988, *Exploring Corporate Strategy*, 2nd edition, Hemel Hempstead: Prentice Hall.

Jones, K. and J. Simmons, 1987, *Location, Location, Location*, Toronto: Methuen.

Jones, P., 1981, 'Retail Innovation and Diffusion – The Spread of Asda Stores', *Area*, Vol.13, No.3.

Jones, P., 1982, 'The Locational Policies and Geographical Expansion of Multiple Retail Companies: A Case Study of MFI', *Geoforum*, Vol.13, No.1.

Jones, P., 1988, 'The Geographical Development of Convenience Stores in Britain', *Geography*, Vol. 73, No.2.

Jones, R., 1979, 'Consumers' Co-operation in Victorian Edinburgh: The Evolution Pattern', *Transactions of the Institute of British Geographers*, Vol.4, No.2.

Kacker, M.P., 1985, *Transatlantic Trends in Retailing – Takeovers and Flow of Know-how*, London: Quorom.

Karnani, A., 1984, 'Generic Competitive Strategies – An Analytical Approach', *Strategic Management Journal*, Vol.5.

Kay, W., 1987, *Battle for the High Street*, London: Piatkus.

Kaynak, E. (ed.), 1988, *Transnational Retailing*, Berlin: W. de Gruyter.

Kirby, D.A., 1988, *Shopping in the Eighties*, London: British Library.

Kivell, P. and G. Shaw, 1980, 'The Study of Retail Location', in J.A. Dawson (ed.), *Retail Geography*, London: Croom Helm.

Knee, D. and D. Walters, 1985, *Strategy in Retailing*, Oxford: Philip Allan.

Knox, P.L., 1981, 'Retail Geography and Social Well-Being: A Note on the Changing Distribution of Pharmacies in Scotland', *Geoforum*, Vol.12, No.3.

Larkham, P.J., 1988, 'The Style of Superstores', *International Journal of Retailing*, Vol.3, No.1.

Laulajainen, R., 1987, *Spatial Strategies in Retailing*, Dordrecht: D. Reidel.

Laulajainen, R., 1988a, 'Chain Store Expansion in National Space', *Geografiska Annaler*, Vol.70 B, No.2.

Laulajainen, R., 1988b, 'The Spatial Dimension of an Acquisition', *Economic Geography*, Vol.64, No.2.

Laulajainen, R. and Gadde L-E, 1986, 'Locational Avoidance: A Case Study of Three Swedish Retail Chains', *Regional Studies*, Vol.20, No.2.

Lerner, H., 1984, *Currys: The First 100 Years*, Cambridge: Woodhead-Faulkner.

Lester, T., 1989, 'Kwik Save's Chain Reaction', *Management Today*, March.

Lever, W.F., 1985, 'Theory and Methodology in Industrial Geography', in M. Pacione (ed.), *Progress in Industrial Geography*, London: Croom Helm.

Lillywhite, J., 1987, 'Equity Considerations in the Location of Retail Food Outlets', paper presented at Planning Practice and Research Conference, Cardiff, January.

Livesey, F., 1979, *The Distributive Trades*, London: Heinemann.

Lord, J.D., W. Moran, A.J. Parker and L. Sparks, 1988, 'Retailing on Three Continents: The Discount Food Store Operations of Albert Gubay', *International Journal of Retailing*, Vol.3, No.3.

Love, J.F., 1987, *McDonalds: Behind the Arches*, London: Bantam Press.

McGoldrick, P.J., 1984, 'Grocery Generics – An Extension of the Private Label Concept', *European Journal of Marketing*, Vol.18, No.3.

McGoldrick, P.J., 1987, 'A Multi-Dimensional Framework for Retail Pricing', *International Journal of Retailing*, Vol.2, No.2.

McGee, J., 1987, 'Retailer Strategies in the UK', in G. Johnson (ed.), *Business Strategy and Retailing*, Chichester: Wiley.

McKinnon, A.C., 1985, 'The Distribution Systems of Supermarket Chains', *Service Industries Journal*, Vol.5, No.2.

McKinnon, A.C., 1989, *Physical Distribution Systems*, London: Routledge.

McNee, R.B., 1974, 'A Systems Approach of Understanding the Geographic Behaviour of Organisations, Especially Large Corporations', in F.E.I. Hamilton (ed.), *Spatial Perspectives on Industrial Organisation and Decision-Making*, Chichester: Wiley.

MacPherson, H. (ed.), 1985, *John Speden Lewis*, London: JLP.

Manchester Business School, 1987a, *UK Grocery Retailing*, Manchester.

Manchester Business School, 1987b, *Kwik Save Group P.L.C.*, teaching case prepared originally by Derek Channon and updated by Patrick Quarcoo and Rob Lees.

Manchester Business School, 1988, *Retail Reference Book 1988*, Manchester.

Martenson, R., 1981, *Innovations in Multi-National Retailing: Ikea on the Swedish, Swiss, Austrian and German Furniture Markets*, University of Gothenburg: Gothenburg.

Mathias, P., 1967, *Retailing Revolution*, London: Longman.

Meyer, J.W. and L.A. Brown, 1979, 'Diffusion Agency Establishment: The Case of Friendly Ice Cream and Public Sector Diffusion Processes', *Socio Economic Planning Sciences*, Vol.13.

Miller, R., 1981, 'Strategic Pathways to Growth in Retailing', *Journal of Business Strategy*, Vol.1.

Mintzberg, H. and J.A. Waters, 1982, 'Tracking Strategy in an Entrepreneurial Firm', *Academy of Management Journal*, Vol.25, No.3.

Moir, C., 1973, 'Second Innings for Albert Gubay', *Retail and Distribution Management*, Vol.1, No.4.

Morris, D., 1979, 'The Strategy of Own Brands', *European Journal of Marketing*, Vol.13, No.2.

Omura, G.S., 1986, 'Developing Retail Strategy', *International Journal of Retailing*, Vol.1, No.3.

Ornstein, E., 1976, *The Retailers*, London: ABP.

Osborne, R.H., 1975, 'A Note on the Geographical Evolution of the Greater Nottingham Co-operative Society', *East Midlands Geographer*, Vol.7.

Parker, H.R., 1962, 'Suburban Shopping Facilities in Liverpool', *Town Planning Review*, Vol.33.

Pocock, D.C.D., 1968, 'Shopping Patterns in Dundee: Some Observations', *Scottish Geographical Magazine*, Vol.84.

Porter, M.E., 1980, *Competitive Strategy*, New York: Free Press.

Porter, M.E., 1985, *Competitive Advantage*, New York: Free Press.

Potter, R.B., 1982, *The Urban Retailing System*, Aldershot: Gower.

Quarmby, D.A., 1989, 'Developments in the Retail Market and their Effect on Freight Distribution', *Journal of Transport Economics and Policy*, Vol.23, No.1.

Rees, G., 1969, *St Michael: A History of Marks and Spencers*. London: Weidenfeld & Nicolson.

Rees, J., 1987, 'Social Polarisation in Shopping Patterns: An Example From Swansea', paper presented at Planning Practice and Research Conference, Cardiff, January.

Rogers, E.M., 1983, *Diffusion of Innovations*, 3rd edition, New York: Free Press.

Rosenbloom, B. and L.G. Schiffman, 1981, 'Retailing Theory: Perspectives and

Approaches', in R.W. Stampfl and E.C. Hirschman (eds.), *Theory in Retailing: traditional and non-traditional sources*, Chicago: AMA.

Rowley, G., 1984, 'Data Bases and their Integration for Retail Geography: A British Example', *Transactions of the Institute of British Geographers*, Vol.9, No.4.

Savitt, R., 1982, 'A Historical Approach to Comparative Retailing', *Management Decision*, Vol.20, No.4.

Savitt, R., 1984, 'The Wheel of Retailing and Retail Product Management', *European Journal of Marketing*, Vol.18, No.6/7.

Savitt, R., 1988, 'Comment on The Wheel of the Wheel of Retailing', *International Journal of Retailing*, Vol.3, No.1.

Schiller, R., 1981, 'A Model of Retail Branch Distribution', *Regional Studies*, Vol.15.

Schiller, R. and A. Jarrett, 1985, 'A Ranking of Shopping Centres using Multiple Branch Numbers', *Land Development Studies*, Vol.2.

Scott, M. and R. Bruce, 1987, 'Five Strategies of Growth in Small Business', *Long Range Planning*, Vol.20, No.3.

Scott, P., 1970, *Geography and Retailing*, London: Hutchinson.

Shaw, G., 1978, *Processes and Patterns in the Geography of Retail Change with Special Reference to Kingston-upon-Hull, 1880–1950*, Hull: University of Hull Press.

Shaw, G. and M.T. Wild, 1979, 'Retail Patterns in the Victorian City', *Transactions of the Institute of British Geographers*, Vol.4.

Shepherd, E.S., 1976, 'On the Diffusion of Shopping Centre Construction in Canada', *Candian Geographer*, Vol.20.

Smethurst, J.B., 1974, *A Bibliography of Co-operative Societies' Histories*, Manchester: Co-operative Union.

Sparks, L., 1985, 'The Changing Structure of Distribution in Retail Companies', *Transactions of the Institute of British Geographers*, Vol.11, No.2.

Sparks, L., 1988, 'Change in UK Retail Distribution', *Focus on Physical Distribution and Logistics Management*, Vol.7, No.4.

Stampfl, R.W. and E.C. Hirschman (eds.), 1980, *Competitive Structure in Retail Markets: The Development Store Perspective*, Chicago: AMA.

Stampfl, R.W. and E.C. Hirschman (eds.), 1981, *Theory in Retailing: Traditional and Non-Traditional Sources*, Chicago: AMA.

Tanburn, J., 1974, *Retailing and the Competitive Challenge*, London: Lintas.

Thil, E., 1966, *Les Inventeurs du Commerce Moderne*, Paris: Arthaud.

Thorpe, D., 1972, 'Food Prices: A Study of Some Northern Discount and Superstores', *Retail Outlets Research Unit Report No. 5*.

Thorpe, D., 1974, 'Locating Retail Outlets', in D. Thorpe (ed.), *Research into Retailing and Distribution*, London: Saxon House.

Thorpe, D. and P. McGoldrick, 1974, 'Superstores, Discounters and a Covered Centre', *Retail Outlets Research Unit Research Report Number 11*.

Tieck, N., 1985, 'The Franklin Story – A Unique History of a Discount Retailer in Australia', in J. Gattorna (ed.), *Strategic Retail Management*, Bradford: MCB University Press.

Tse, K.K., 1985, *Marks and Spencer*, Oxford: Pergamon.

Walters, D., 1988, *Strategic Retailing Management*, Hemel Hempstead: Prentice-Hall.

Warnes, A.M. and P.W. Daniels, 1980, 'Urban Retail Distributions: An Appraisal of the Empirical Foundations of Retail Geography', *Geoforum*, Vol.11.

Watkin, D.G. and Joseph M.E., 1976, 'The Day of the Discounter', *Retail and Distribution Management*, Vol.4, No.4.

Watts, H.D., 1974, 'The Market Area of a Firm', in L. Collins and D. Walker (eds.), *Locational Dynamics of Manufacturing Industry*, Chichester: Wiley.

Whysall, P., 1974, 'The Changing Pattern of Retail Structure of Greater Nottingham, 1912–1971', unpublished PhD Thesis, University of Nottingham.

Whysall, P., 1989, 'Commercial Change in a Central Area: A Case Study', *International Journal of Retailing*, Vol.4, No.1.

Wild, M.T. and G. Shaw, 1974, 'Location Behaviour of Urban Retailing during the

Nineteenth Century: The Example of Kingston-upon-Hull', *The Transactions of the Institute of British Geographers*, Vol.61.

Wild, M.T. and G. Shaw, 1975, 'Population Distribution and Retail Provision: The Case of the Halifax-Calder Area during the Second Half of the Nineteenth Century', *Journal of Historical Geography*, Vol.1.

Wilson, C., 1985, *First with the News: The History of W.H. Smith 1792–1972*, London: Jonathan Cape.

Wortzel, L.A., 1987, 'Retailing Strategies for Today's Mature Marketplace', *Journal of Business Strategy*, Vol.7, No.4.

Wrigley, N. (ed.), 1988, *Store Choice, Store Location and Market Analysis*, London: Routledge & Kegan Paul.

This chapter first appeared in *The Service Industries Journal*, Vol.10, No.1 (1990).

Further Reading

Akehurst, G.P., 1982, 'The Economics of Retailing – a Note', *Service Industries Review*, Vol.2, No.2.

Andrews, P.W.S., 1964, *On Competition in Economic Theory*, London: Macmillan.

Bamfield, J.A.N., 1980, 'The Changing Face of British Retailing', *National Westminster Bank Quarterly Review*, May.

Baumol, W.J., R.E. Quandt and H.T. Shapiro, 1964, 'Oligopoly Theory and Retail Food Pricing', *Journal of Business*, Vol.37.

Brown, S., 1988a, 'The Wheel of Retailing', *International Journal of Retailing*, Vol.3, No.1.

Brown, S., 1988b, 'Retail Change: Cycles and Strategy', *Quarterly Review of Marketing*, Vol.13, No.3.

Burt, S.L., 1991, 'Trends in the Internationalization of Grocery retailing: The European Experience', *International Review of Retail Distribution and Consumer Research*, Vol.1, No.4.

Davies, K., C. Gilligan and C. Sutton, 1984, 'The Changing Structure of British Grocery Retailing', *The Quarterly Review of Marketing*, Autumn.

Davies, R.L., 1984, *Retail and Commercial Planning*, London: Croom Helm.

Dawson, J.A., 1979, *The Marketing Environment*, London: Croom Helm.

Dawson, J.A., 1982, *Commercial Distribution in Europe*, London: Croom Helm.

Dawson, J.A., 1984, 'Structural-Spatial Relationships in the Spread of Hypermarket Retailing', in E. Kaynak and R. Savitt (eds.), *Comparative Marketing Systems*, New York: Praeger.

Doyle, P. and D. Cook, 1979, 'Marketing Strategies, Financial Structure and Innovation in UK Retailing', *Management Decision*, Vol.17, No.2.

Edvardsson, B., L. Edvinsson and H. Nystrom, 1992, 'Internationalisation in Service Companies', *Service Industries Journal*, Vol.13, No.1.

Fernie, J., 1995, 'The Coming of the Fourth Wave: New Forms of Retail Out-of-town Development', *International Journal of Retail and Distribution Management*, Vol.23, No.1.

Fulop, C., 1966, *Competition for Consumers*, London: Allen and Unwin.

Hall, M., 1949, *Distributive Trading*, London: Hutchinson's University Library.

Helms, M.M., P.J. Haynes and S.D. Cappel, 1992, 'Competitive Strategies and Business Performance within the Retailing Industry', *International Journal of Retail and Distribution Management*, Vol.20, No.5.

Hogarth-Scott, R.A. and S.P. Rice, 1994, 'The New Food Discounters: Are

They a Threat to the Major Multiples?', *International Journal of Retail and Distribution Management*, Vol.22, No.1.

Holdren, B.R., 1965, 'Competition in Food Retailing', *Journal of Farm Economics*, Vol.47.

Hollander, S.C., 1960, 'Competition and Evolution in Retailing', *Stores*, Vol.42.

Hood, J. and B.S. Yamey, 1951, 'Imperfect Competition in Retail Trades', *Economica*, Vol.18.

Jeffrys, J.B., 1950, *Distribution of Consumer Goods*, London: Cambridge University Press.

Jefferys, J.B., 1954, *Retail Trading in Britain 1850–1950*, London: Cambridge University Press.

Johnson, G. (ed.), 1987a, *Business Strategy and Retailing*, Chichester: Wiley.

Johnson, G., 1987b, *Strategic Change and the Management Process*, Oxford: Blackwell.

Kacker, M.P., 1985, *Transatlantic Trends in Retailing – Takeovers and Flow of Know-how*, London: Quorum.

Kaynak, E. (ed.), 1988, *Transnational Retailing*, Berlin: W. De Gruyter.

Kirby, D.A., 1982, 'Retailing in the Age of the Chip', *Service Industries Review*, Vol.2, No.1.

Knee, D. and D. Walters, 1985, *Strategy in Retailing*, Oxford: Philip Allan.

Lewis, W.A., 1945, 'Competition in Retail Trade', *Economica*, Vol.12.

McClelland, W.G., 1966, *Costs and Competition in Retailing*, London: Macmillan.

McKinnon, A.C., 1989, *Physical Distribution Systems*, London: Routledge.

McNair, M.P., 1931, 'Trends in Large-scale Retailing', *Harvard Business Review*, Vol.10.

Metcalf, D. and C. Greenhalgh, 1968, 'Price Behaviour in a Retail Grocery Sub-market', *British Journal of Marketing*, Vol.1.

Moore, E.J., 1991, Grocery Distribution in the UK: Recent Changes and Future Prospects', *International Journal of Retail and Distribution Management*, Vol.19, No.7.

Porter, M.E., 1980, *Competitive Strategy*, New York: Free Press.

Porter, M.E., 1985, *Competitive Advantage*, New York: Free Press.

Rees, G., 1969, *St. Michael: A History of Marks and Spencer*, London: Weidenfeld and Nicolson.

Robinson, T.M. and C.M. Clarke-Hill, 1990, 'Directional Growth by European Retailers', *International Journal of Retail and Distribution Management*, Vol.18, No.5.

Segal, M.N. and R.W. Giacobbe, 1994, 'Market Segmentation and Competitive Analysis for Supermarket Retailing', *International Journal of Retail and Distribution Management*, Vol.22, No.1.

Thomas, A.B., 1978, 'The British Business Elite: The Case of the Retail Sector', *Sociological Review*, Vol.26, No.2.

Tucker, K.A., 1978, *Concentration and Costs in Retailing*, Farnborough: Saxon House.

Ward, T.S., 1973, *The Distribution of Consumer Goods*, London: Cambridge University Press.

Wrigley, N., (ed.), 1988, *Store Choice, Store Location and Market Analysis*, London: Routledge and Kegan Paul.

Notes on Contributors

Gary Akehurst is at Portsmouth University Business School, Department of Business and Management, Locksway Road, Southsea, Hants PO3 8JF, UK.

Nicholas Alexander is at the School of Commerce and International Business, University of Ulster, Coleraine, Northern Ireland, BT52 1SA.

Stephen Brown is at the School of Commerce and International Business, University of Ulster, Coleraine, Northern Ireland, BT52 1SA.

John Dawson is in the Department of Business Studies, University of Edinburgh, William Robertson Building, 50 George Square, Edinburgh EH8 9JY, UK.

J. Dennis Lord is at the University of North Carolina, Charlotte, North Carolina, USA.

Alan McKinnon is at the the Business School, Heriot-Watt University, PO Box 807, Riccarton, Edinburgh, EH14 4AT, UK.

Toshio Sato is at the College of Commerce, Nihon University, Japan.

Leigh Sparks is at the Institute for Retail Studies, and School of Management, University of Stirling, Stirling, FK9 4LA, UK.

Alan Thomas is at Manchester Business School, University of Manchester, Booth Street West, Manchester, M15 6PB, UK.